THE
SUN
IS STILL
RISING

THE
SUN
IS STILL
RISING

POLITICS HAS FAILED
BUT AMERICA WILL NOT

SCOTT W. RASMUSSEN

Library of Congress Control Number: Pending

978-0-9989604-2-5 - Paperback
978-0-9989604-3-2 - ePub

Published in the United States by
Sutherland Institute
15 W. South Temple, Suite 200
Salt Lake City, UT 84101

Book cover design by Sherwin Soy
Interior book design by Francine Eden Platt • Eden Graphics, Inc.

Manufactured in the United States of America

10 9 8 7 6 5 4 3 2 1

This book is dedicated to my "extra" mom, June MacDade.
Thank you, Momma Mac, for the love you shared,
the memories you created, and the lessons you taught.

CONTENTS

FOREWORD

"I N NO COUNTRY IN THE WORLD has the principle of association been more successfully used or applied to a greater multitude of objects than in America." So wrote Alexis de Tocqueville nearly two centuries ago. The physical committees and clubs in the pub which Tocqueville so lovingly surveyed are often missing from our towns today. Thus our municipalities, counties, and states no longer provide the check on despots they once did.

But as Scott Rasmussen shows, powerful communities still exist in the United States. And, as in the time of Tocqueville, these American communities can provide a robust alternative to a dysfunctional Washington, D.C. The only difference is that these are new kinds of communities, some virtual rather than physical, and many spread out across the country.

To understand how this is so, consider our national problem. Face up to it—says Rasmussen, a seasoned and respected political analyst—our American political system is broken. Citizens look to the federal government for everything, from prescription drug subsidies to nursery school. Washington responds by always offering more, notwithstanding the great debts it thereby loads on coming generations. Yet it can't possibly fulfill everyone's expectations, as we see by D.C.'s perpetually low approval ratings.

Still, two forces may obviate Washington's folly. The first is technology. The old vision was that technology would centralize American power and reduce individual freedom: Think of the 1960s punch cards at the Social Security Administration, with one all-powerful IBM mainframe controlling all information and depriving individuals of privacy. Instead, the opposite happened: Computers liberated Americans to work individually. Communities sprang up through technology, and these new communities surpassed their predecessors in intensity and benefit. Though the 19th-century sewing circle of housewives honored the talented craftswomen in their village, no one can say that Etsy does not do more for those talented in the crafts. After all, Etsy, the online craft marketplace, places a spotlight on talent visible around the world. Capital has never been more democratized.

The second cause for optimism is a group of Americans: millennials. These young people have a reputation as selfish and ignorant. Journalists, for example, criticize millennials for their lack of interest in the political process. But as Rasmussen notes, the journalists have it backwards. This new generation recognizes something: that "we live in a world where culture leads and politics lag behind." They rightfully look to the private sector and NGOs to make their mark, rather than flocking to government work for its security.

The combination of technology and youthful initiative changes more than politics. It also changes our economy. For half a century Americans believed that our country would run out of energy, becoming ever more dependent on the autocrats of the Middle East. And for years government efforts—stimuli approved by Congress or the Federal Reserve—were believed to be the only way out of the financial crisis that began so violently in 2008. But the recovery in the end was driven by an unexpected source: a technological innovation in the energy field. Because of fracking and other energy advances, America's economy is growing. Because of innovation, America has also become an energy exporter, rather than an importer. A combination of innovation, technology, communities and youthful energy and intuition has confounded a world of memos and predictions.

Nor is this energy miracle the only such miracle. As Rasmussen, a keen student of history, notes, a century ago the frustrated federal government spent years trying to develop an airplane, dedicating the largest appropriation in U.S. military history at the time to the project. But it fell to two private innovators, the Wright brothers of Dayton, Ohio, to manage the feat.

Tocqueville does much to illuminate such phenomena. So does the Scotsman philosopher Adam Ferguson, who wrote of spontaneous, rather than planned, order in society. Order and progress, Ferguson noted, was the "result of human action, but not the execution of any human design." Later thinkers, most especially Ludwig von Mises and Friedrich Hayek, made "spontaneous order" the central emphasis of their explanation for economic growth. The best government organization can't stand up to the local time-and-place knowledge of individuals in community.

The Sun is Still Rising draws on distinguished philosophy. But author Rasmussen also highlights the legitimacy of optimism today. As disconcerting as politics has seemed recently, politics does not determine our future. Our future rests in the hands of individuals of great talent, many as yet unknown to us. As Rasmussen shows us, we can count on those unknowns to surprise us into further progress. If we turn our eyes from D.C. for a moment, we might even be able to join them.

AMITY SHLAES is author of four *New York Times* best sellers: *The Forgotten Man*, *The Forgotten Man/Graphic*, *Coolidge*, and *The Greedy Hand*. She serves as chairman of the board of the Calvin Coolidge Presidential Foundation and is a presidential scholar at The King's College.

PUBLISHER'S NOTE

S UTHERLAND INSTITUTE believes that the strength of America is housed not in Washington, D.C., but in each and every heroic citizen who cares for their family, starts a small business, works the night shift, volunteers at a local charity or otherwise contributes to their community. Scott Rasmussen has captured the essence of America in this important work. Sutherland Institute is honored to publish it.

The mission of Sutherland Institute is to nurture each generation's "New Birth of Freedom." This book demonstrates that all of us have the ability and opportunity to sustain and renew the principles and virtues upon which our freedom is predicated.

It has been said that ideas go booming through the world like cannons, thoughts are mightier than armies, and principles have achieved more victories than horsemen or chariots. Inspiring ideas, transformational thoughts, and powerful principles await you within these pages.

SUTHERLAND INSTITUTE
SALT LAKE CITY, UTAH

INTRODUCTION

LOOKING BACK NOW, the creation and subsequent success of the U.S. Constitution seems inevitable.

However, that was far from the case during the long hot summer of 1787. Just over a decade earlier, 13 British colonies declared their independence and sought to govern themselves. Defeating the British had made that declaration a reality, but the war's aftermath created a severe economic crisis. Governing a country was different than winning a war, and many doubted the young nation could survive.

Those attending the Constitutional Convention in Philadelphia also faced doubts about whether they could find agreement on the momentous questions before them. The ultimately successful outcome was so stunning that both George Washington and James Madison called it the "miracle at Philadelphia."

As the last of 39 delegates were signing the historic document, Benjamin Franklin eloquently captured the hopes and fears of all involved. The respected elder statesman looked toward a carving of the sun on George Washington's chair and commented on the difficulty distinguishing between a rising and a setting sun. Franklin confessed that he had often "looked at that sun behind the President without being able to tell whether it was rising or setting. But now at length I have the happiness to know it is a rising and not a setting sun."

Since the day that Franklin uttered those words, there have been numerous times when large segments of the population worried anew that the sun might be setting on America's future. We are living through one of those times now. Our toxic and dysfunctional political system is alarming even to an optimist like me.

On the other hand, the tools of today's tech industry have created the most powerful force for change in our nation's history. While few recognize it yet, this redistribution of power means that middle-class and lower-income Americans are on the verge of being empowered as never-before.

The tools are great, but it is the American people who must use them. Fortunately, Americans still love working together in community to create a better world. And our younger generations are leading the way with enthusiasm and idealism. Put it all together and every day we are getting closer to living out our nation's founding ideals of freedom, equality, and self-governance.

These are reasons to be optimistic and thankful we live in a land where the culture leads and politics lags behind. Sooner or later, our political system will catch up with where the country is going and ratify what the public has already decided.

That's the way it has always worked in America—even in Ben Franklin's time.

The great system of checks and balances put into words during the summer of 1787 was the product of the American culture, just like the Declaration of Independence that preceded it. The Declaration gave voice to America's founding ideals and the Constitution created a governing structure broadly consistent with those ideals. That's the reason it worked.

Twenty-first-century America is a far different place than the America of Ben Franklin's time. Our challenges are different, but they are not any more difficult to overcome. As we seek to solve today's challenges, we draw upon the same strength that has always sustained our nation—a deep and abiding cultural belief in the founding ideals of freedom, equality, and self-governance.

As long as the American people remain committed to those ideals, the sun will continue to rise in America.

SCOTT RASMUSSEN

CHAPTER 1

LOSING FAITH IN OUR POLITICAL SYSTEM

Like most Americans, I believe our nation's political system is badly broken.

Unlike most Americans, however, I have spent more than two decades up close experiencing and observing the reality of national politics. What I have seen convinces me that the corruption and self-serving behavior is even worse than the critics imagine. The system we have today is rigged at every level to benefit political insiders and their friends.

The corruption I see is not merely among those we normally think of as politicians or bureaucrats; it has infected large segments of what is considered the private sector as well. Far too many large corporations now focus on making money by seeking favors from government rather than by serving customers.

Sadly, I have come to recognize that this is not something that can be fixed or reformed. Instead, we are rapidly approaching a time when our political system will completely break down and need to be rebuilt from the bottom up.

Despite this, or perhaps because of it, I am optimistic about America's future.

I believe that our nation's best days are still to come. I am confident that our children and grandchildren will have much better lives than we have enjoyed. They will get to see and do many wondrous things beyond our current ability to imagine. Most importantly, they will help our nation draw ever closer to becoming a land filled with opportunity, liberty, and justice for all.

Despite my belief that the political system is broken beyond repair, I fully expect our nation to successfully address many critical issues in the coming years. We will see great progress in health care, vast improvement in education, a major reduction in poverty, a renewed commitment to individual freedom, improved race relations, and more. In fact, we'll even see the big banks cut down to size, something that should have happened after the bailout debacle in 2008.

When I share these views—optimism about the nation combined with pessimism about politics and government—I get a wide variety of skeptical reactions. Some are simply dismissive and tell me that if their favorite candidate or party doesn't win the next election, the nation is doomed. I heard this a lot—from both sides—during Election 2016.

Others miss the point and ask how we can fix our failing political system. When I tell them we can't, they are discouraged. When I say we don't have to or that there are more important things to worry about, they are doubtful.

Upon hearing about my optimism, a few want to believe that I'm right but can't really imagine how it's possible.

I understand these reactions because younger versions of me have held them all. I was once an innocent idealist who believed that the process worked and was fair to all. Sure, politics was sometimes rough around the edges, and sometimes we took the wrong turns, but things eventually moved in the right direction. At least that's what I thought.

I loved my country and its founding ideals—that the people were in charge, that all of us are created equal, and that everyone had the chance to pursue their own dreams. I knew that we had never fully lived up to these ideals, but I still wanted to believe that elected politicians would listen to the people and respond.

That's why I got involved in the term limits movement and other efforts to try and make our government work a little better. It's why I became a pollster, to give voice to the voiceless and to lift up public attitudes that were being ignored. It seemed important in those days to help the political class understand what people were really thinking. That was before I learned that they really don't care what the rest of us think.

Recognizing that truth was painful. The problem wasn't—as I used to believe—that well-intentioned elected politicians had lost touch with the voters; it was much worse. Too many of our elected politicians now believe their own agendas are more important than the voters they are supposed to represent.

As you might suspect, grasping this unpleasant reality did not instantly inspire my optimism about our nation's future. Quite the contrary, in fact. It was depressing, disconcerting, and frightening. It was a sinking feeling, much like the movie moment when the curtain was pulled back and Dorothy learned the Wizard of Oz was a fraud. Having invested so much time and energy in the belief that our political system should work, it was devastating to learn that it was broken beyond repair.

In short, I was in the same place as tens of millions of Americans today. I realized that our political system was broken and I didn't know where to turn. I still loved my country and its founding ideals, but I was deeply concerned about how long it could survive. That concern sent me searching for solutions, and it turned out to be a long journey.

LOSING FAITH IN POLITICS: THE FIRST STEP ON THE JOURNEY

Losing faith in our political system was only the first step on that journey, but it was the most important one. In fact, if you want to help move the nation forward, it's the most important step you can take as well. Once you do, you'll be amazed at how much better things seem when you look at them from a different perspective.

Many years ago, my wife, our young sons, and I participated in a service day with our church. Our task, along with a few others, was to empty an 18-wheeler filled with yams. We were to separate the yams that could help feed a hungry child from those that were rotten. In the heat of a North Carolina summer day, the overwhelming fragrance from that truck full of yams provided an additional challenge.

As the day progressed, we could take one of two approaches. If we looked back in the truck, we saw that hours of work barely dented the supply of yams we were to sort. It was depressing. If we looked the other way, however, we saw a huge pile of yams in front of us that would soon be feeding people who might otherwise go hungry. It was exhilarating.

Eventually, we all found a position to work that let us see the progress being made. And that encouraging perspective kept us working to provide more food for the hungry.

Over the last decade or two, as my confidence in the political system collapsed, I took a similar approach and tried to position myself to see where progress was being made in our nation. The more I shifted my view away from politics and official Washington, the more my mood improved. It was a healthy reminder that the country and its government were not the same thing.

Even more important, it quickly became apparent that there was a lot of progress being made throughout the nation.

LOOKING OUTSIDE OF POLITICS

Silicon Valley and the tech industry exude so much optimism it's contagious. There is an industry-wide desire to solve the planet's most difficult problems and a belief that they can do it. A fairly typical conference I attended discussed ideas to make driving safer, feed the poor, empower ordinary citizens, provide opportunities for women, personalize manufacturing, lead to healthier lives, and so forth. The new technology was viewed as a tool for democratizing everything.

But it's not just what the tech industry hopes to do in the future that's so encouraging; it's what they've already done. "The devices and connectivity so essential to modern life put unprecedented power in the hands of every individual," according to Harvard's Nicco Mele. This is "a radical redistribution of power that our traditional institutions don't and perhaps can't understand." As if that wasn't enough, he adds, "Radical connectivity is toxic to traditional power structures."[1]

Every American with a smartphone today has access to more information than the president of the United States could command just a generation or two ago. The wide distribution of information is leveling the playing field and chipping away at the information advantage enjoyed by the elites.

There are challenges with the new technology, particularly in the areas of privacy rights, economic transitions, and social standards. But the 200 million smartphone users in the U.S. represent the most powerful force for change in our nation's history. While few recognize it yet, this redistribution of power means that middle-class and lower-income Americans are on the verge of being empowered as never before.

Great as the technology is, it won't solve our problems for us. That requires people committed to making the world a better place and helping their neighbors. Fortunately, there are plenty of Americans who want to do their part. And, as is always the case, it is the younger generation that leads the way with a fresh burst of enthusiasm and idealism. That's why I've come to see the millennial generation as another reason for optimism.

Veteran reporter Ron Fournier captures the essence of what I've seen in a 2013 article noting that millennials "are fiercely committed to community service." At the same time, "they don't see politics or government as a way to improve their communities, their country, or the world."

Fournier "spent two days at Harvard, and couldn't find a single student whose career goal is Washington or elective office.... To Millennials, the world is filled with injustice and need, but government isn't the solution. They have apps for that."[2]

The millennials I work with make it clear that this is not an anti-government attitude, it is simply a matter of pragmatism. They've grown up in a world with so many choices that if one path doesn't work, you try another. If one app doesn't work, you delete it and download another.

This is a generation willing to rely upon government when it makes sense, but also willing to work around government when it doesn't.

Fournier, a well-established and respected member of the political class, is troubled by a generation looking to solve problems outside of government. He calls it "[r]evolutionary, maybe worse."

For me, this perspective is something to celebrate and another reason to be impressed by millennials. They recognize that politics often offers little more than the choice between the lesser of two evils. There is some value in helping the lesser evil win but also an awareness that electing the lesser evil is not enough to address the nation's challenges. For those who truly want to make the world a better place, the solutions will have to be found elsewhere.

As an aging baby boomer, I recognize that I am just catching up to the younger generation! Twenty-somethings already know that we need to find solutions outside the political process.

A HERITAGE OF INDEPENDENCE

Actually, that's something our nation has always known. Change always takes place from outside the political realm.

On February 1, 1960, four black students walked into a Woolworth's store in Greensboro, North Carolina. Nobody knew it at the time, but Ezell Blair Jr., David Richmond, Franklin McCain, and Joseph McNeil were about to make history. The students from North Carolina Agricultural and Technical College bought a few things, sat down at a segregated lunch counter, and politely asked to be served. They were refused, but did not back down. They stayed all day until closing. Within days, more than 300 students joined the protest in Greensboro.

In the 97 years since the signing of the Emancipation Proclamation, the political system had done nothing to end segregation. Within a few months of the Greensboro Four's sit-in, the first black customers were served at that Woolworth's lunch counter. The reason for the change was simple and it had nothing to do with politics. Black consumers boycotted the store. The sit-ins and publicity surrounding them drove away other customers. The store simply got tired of losing money.[3]

The sit-in movement spread throughout the South. There was, of course, resistance. Often it was the political system that led the resistance. But, in the end, it was action outside of politics that brought integration to American lunch counters and other facilities.

Unfortunately, journalists and historians generally write about politics more than anything else. They talk about candidates' visions for the future, presidential legacies, and the promised impact of legislation. That gives us a distorted image of how change really comes about and makes the political process seem more important than it really is. While journalists and historians focus on political leaders, lasting change in America always takes place from the bottom up.

That's been true since the founding of our nation.

We celebrate the signing of the Declaration of Independence as the birthday of our country. The eloquent words drafted by Thomas Jefferson have become what professors Sid Milkis and Marc Landy call the "American Creed." The scholars note that "no other country has a set of key principles and statements to which its citizens adhere to the same degree that Americans adhere to the principles of 'life, liberty and the pursuit of happiness.'"[4]

At its core, that Creed is a belief that we all have the right to do what we want with our own lives so long as we don't interfere with the rights of others to do the same. It is an attitude still embraced by the American people today, brimming with optimism about what a free and self-governing people can accomplish. We cherish our freedom but recognize its greatest value can be found when we use that freedom to build community. As some friends of mine say, liberty loves company.

The Declaration of Independence is the clearest expression of that Creed and certainly worthy of praise. Without a doubt, it deserves its place as one of the most important documents in the history of the world. But the Declaration did not lead the nation or inspire people to take up arms and begin a revolution—the revolution came first.

Six years before Jefferson wrote his famous words, a black man named Crispus Attucks was shot during the Boston Massacre and became the first fatality of the War for Independence. In 1775, 15 months before the Declaration of Independence was drafted, the fighting began in earnest with the battles fought at Lexington and Concord.

Historian Kevin Phillips points out that most of the royal governors had been forced to flee the colonies in 1775. Colonial authorities "began to exercise power twelve to eighteen months before" the Declaration was approved and they had already achieved a "de facto independence." In fact, by the end of 1775, "a few square miles of Boston represented the sole remaining seat of British occupation, authority, and might."[5]

Long before colonial politicians declared the nation's independence, men like Levi Preston had already made it a reality. On April 19, 1775, an 18-year-old Preston joined hundreds of his neighbors standing up to the British in what became known as the Battle of Lexington and

Concord. Seven decades later, historian Mellen Chamberlain tracked down Preston to find out what led him to fight on that day.

The historian assumed it might have been the Stamp Act or Tea Tax, but Preston said he never saw a stamp or drank any tea. "The boys threw it all overboard." Trying a different approach, Chamberlain asked about the writing of "Harrington, Sydney, and Locke about the eternal principles of Liberty." Preston must have thought the young man daft: "I never heard of those men." He added, "The only books we had were the Bible, the Catechism, Watt's Psalms and Hymns, and the almanac."

At this point in the discussion, the young historian must have been a bit frustrated. So he again asked, why did a teenage Preston choose to fight? "Young man," Preston replied, "what we meant in going for those Redcoats was this: we always had been free and we meant to be free always! They didn't mean that we should."[6]

This passion for freedom "acquired strength in the United States from the fact that it did not develop simply within a single sphere of life. Rather, it permeated every aspect of the behavior of the whole society." Respected historians Oscar and Mary Handlin noted that "American freedom possessed a political aspect." It "was also social in character . . . and gave people of every sort a conviction that they had an important stake in the freedom of the communities." And, critically important, "the evolution of voluntary religious, economic, cultural, and philanthropic organizations offered alternatives to state action."[7]

It was this attitude, deeply embedded in the colonial culture, that inspired the revolution. The politicians followed. "Jefferson's contribution was to state compellingly ideas and beliefs that had already worked their way into American political culture."[8] He put into words what the American people already believed.[9] The Continental Congress merely confirmed what had already taken place.

POLITICS IS DOWNSTREAM

The culture—not politics—leads the nation. That was true in the 18th century, and it's true today.

To take just one example, Jackie Robinson broke the major league color barrier in 1947, a huge moment in American civil rights history.

Congress didn't pass a major Civil Rights Act until 1964—17 years later! During those 17 years, there were many heroes of the movement who worked to persuade the nation's politicians that it was time to act. Some, like Rosa Parks and Martin Luther King Jr., are now household names. Others labored in obscurity as Levi Preston had done in an earlier time.

King was a visionary leader who clearly recognized that change comes from outside the political process: "What lobbying and imploring could not do in legislative halls, marching feet accomplished a thousand miles away."[10]

He described the movement's great victories like this: "The 1960 sit-ins desegregated lunch counters in more than 150 cities within a year. The 1961 Freedom Rides put an end to segregation in interstate travel. The 1956 bus boycott in Montgomery, Alabama, ended segregation on the buses not only of that city but in practically every city of the South. The 1963 Birmingham movement and the climactic March on Washington won passage of the most powerful civil rights law in a century."[11]

The strategy worked because it didn't focus on changing laws, but rather focused on changing the culture. The then-new technology of television covered all of these events and showed untold millions of viewers the gap between America's rhetoric and the reality of segregation. It challenged the nation to live up to its high ideals.

The Civil Rights Act of 1964, just like the Declaration of Independence, remains an important historical document. But it was not a document that led the nation into a new civil rights era. Congress did not lead the nation. It avoided the subject until there was overwhelming public support for the measure.

The popular culture led the nation forward and the politicians followed a couple of decades behind. Another great example of this phenomenon is the digital revolution itself.

During the 1970s, journalists covered everything from Watergate and Vietnam to stagflation and energy crises. Nobody paid any attention when Bill Gates and Steve Jobs dropped out of college to launch Microsoft and Apple. Looking back on it, just about everything that the politicians and media talked about in the '70s seems irrelevant today. It was Jobs and Gates—and the companies they created—that changed the world.

Since those tech entrepreneurs dropped out of college, eight men have served as president of the United States: Ford, Carter, Reagan, Bush, Clinton, Bush, Obama, and Trump. Historians will long debate their impact on the nation. But Jobs and Gates did more to shape the world we live in today than the combined legacy of all those presidents.

Politics and politicians don't lead change. They follow. That's their job. At their best, they rise to the level of Jefferson, giving magnificent voice to the best and most noble attitudes held by the people at large. They play a necessary role in society, but they are not the leaders of society.

For me, stepping back from the toxic world of politics and regaining that sense of perspective was a big step in my journey to find reasons for hope. Added to the encouragement I found from the tech industry and millennials, my depression about the failure of our political system was beginning to ease.

COMMUNITY COMES HOME

Something else was needed before I could truly be optimistic about our nation's future. Ironically, the final piece of the puzzle came to me in the aftermath of one of the worst days of my life. March 13, 2010, is a day my family and I will never forget.

Shortly after five in the morning, we heard noise outside. At 5:15, a police officer knocked on our door and told us to prepare for evacuation. The hotel next door was engulfed in flame. By six, despite the amazing efforts of volunteer firefighters, our house was gone. And, when I say gone, I mean completely. The appliances melted. There was nothing left. Everything physical that we had accumulated for more than 20 years of marriage was reduced to ashes.

We escaped with a laptop computer, the clothes on our back, and a few guitars carried out by my musician son. Fortunately, I stuck my wallet in my jeans so we had some credit cards and cash. Standing outside a few minutes later and watching the blaze consume our home, a longtime family friend simply put his arm around me. There was nothing to say.

I still have a shopping list from that morning showing that we had to buy shoes for my son because he left the house in slippers. I needed a jacket because it was cold out. We had prescriptions that needed to be replaced along with toothbrushes. A local hotel gave us a room until we could figure out what was next. We spent over $800 at Target that day and $700 at Walmart the next. The insurance adjuster told us to keep our receipts and gave us a healthy advance.

The blaze took out a B&B, a hotel, and six houses. More than 200 firefighters worked tirelessly in a chilly Nor'easter to contain the damage. A local Christian organization opened its doors, the Red Cross set up shop, and our community grieved. But, we all recognized how lucky we were since nobody died or was seriously hurt.

My faith helped me through months of shock and rebuilding. So did my community.

The outpouring of support was unbelievable. I can't tell you how many people offered us clothes, food, or a place to stay. Some belonged to our church. Others did not. Some I had never before met. Restaurants offered us free meals. It got to be so much that we had to remind everybody we were okay; we had good insurance and our health. People in Haiti needed help more than we did.

It was emotionally exhausting.

On that chilly day in March, and in the months that followed, we needed our local government, our insurance company, our church, local businesses, our neighbors, and the kindness of strangers to get through something I hope you never experience. It was truly an all-hands-on-board effort. Nothing else would have sufficed.

During the 20 months it took to sort things out and rebuild our home, it became clear to me that the community response was another reason for optimism. Each day brought new reminders of how people working together in community roll up their sleeves and get things done. It wasn't really a surprise since I've been involved with volunteer activities all my life. Still, volunteering and community work was so natural that I never really thought about just how powerful it could be.

I began to see the power of community in a new light. That reality shifted my view of politics as well. I couldn't help but notice how empty and off-base the national political dialogue seemed. Listening to the political rhetoric felt like the annoying experience of being seated next to a stranger talking loudly on their cell phone. The conversation makes no sense because you're only hearing half of what is said. And most of the time, you don't really care.

Partisan bickering about the size and role of government in America represents only part of the conversation. It doesn't make sense unless you include the other part—the way that communities, families, businesses, churches, charities, sports teams, civic clubs, and neighbors work together to create the society we live in.

When a young mom first brings home a newborn from the hospital, neighbors sign up to bring meals and help the family out. Carpools become a part of life as young families seek to transport kids to an ever-expanding set of activities. Parents coach Little League and make costumes for local drama productions. Churches provide food banks and other assistance for those in danger of slipping through the cracks. When someone dies, family and friends gather to comfort and support those who are left behind.

This reality helped me put the political process back in its proper perspective. Politics is about power and money—and using one to get the other. Community is about the things that really matter in life. My speeches and writing began pointing out more forcefully that nobody in America cares about limited government. They, do, however, care deeply about the kind of society that a limited government can create.

That's why the political dialogue often seems so irrelevant—politicians talk obsessively about how to make the government better and how their plans will solve our problems. The rest of us are more concerned about how to make society better and don't care who gets it done. Even more, most of us are excited about the opportunity to chip in and become problem-solvers ourselves.

Getting involved in politics may make you feel like you need to take a shower when you finish, but working together as a community is an uplifting and rewarding experience.

As these thoughts were beginning to clarify, we got another chance to witness the power of community up close. Less than a year after moving into our new home, Hurricane Sandy hit our area with devastating force. Since we had a brand new house, our damage was limited to loss of power for a week and some very cold nights with no heat (we got several inches of snow just days after the hurricane!). While our house survived intact, many of our neighbors weren't nearly so fortunate.

The massive storm affected the entire East Coast, killed dozens of people, and caused more than $60 billion worth of damage. Close to home, one neighbor had four and a half feet of water pour into their basement in just 30 minutes. Others had the entire first floor flooded (one assured us that they had moved their kayaks to the second floor, just in case). Images of piers, houses, and amusement rides washing out to sea highlighted news coverage.

In the aftermath of that storm, the Associated Press reported that "friends, relatives and neighbors were cited the most often as the people who helped them make it through." Those who lived in the affected areas "overwhelmingly said the Oct. 29 storm brought out the best in their neighbors, who shared generators, food, water and other supplies."[12]

Highlighting the value of community solutions, the AP reported that far fewer people reached out to government agencies than to family, friends, churches, local businesses, or insurance companies for help. And, the newswire added, family, friends, and neighbors turned out to be the most helpful.

The community involvement was so important that "neighborhoods lacking in social cohesion and trust generally had a more difficult time recovering."[13]

This did not suggest that there was no role for the government. State and local officials clearly had important tasks during both the preparation phase and the recovery efforts. But the government role was not a solo act, it was not even the lead; the government effort was one part of a larger community solution. That's the way America is supposed to work.

As if to emphasize the disconnect between the political class view of the world and reality, a bizarre episode took place as we were digging our way out of the storm. President Barack Obama, in the week before he was re-elected, came to New Jersey for a photo op and was greeted warmly by Republican Governor Chris Christie. Many Republicans were outraged.

At the time, we had no electricity and were jealously guarding our cell phone and computer usage. To my amazement, I started getting calls asking what people in New Jersey thought of Christie's embrace of

Obama. Did I think it would impact the election, or the turnout, or whatever? Talk about missing the point! Our area was among the hardest hit by Sandy and we had more important things to worry about.

We needed an all-hands-on-board approach to community problem solving that included families, neighborhoods, churches, businesses, charities, and government. To the degree that the government had a role to play, we didn't care whether the help came from a Democratic president or a Republican governor.

When there is work to be done, focusing on politics and the role of government misses the point. We need to take advantage of all the resources at our disposal. It's not about the government, it's about the kind of society we want to live in. It's about relationships and problem solving.

Ultimately, it's about figuring out the best way we can work together to find solutions.

CLEAR PERSPECTIVE AT WORK

Ironically, it took a terrible fire and devastating hurricane to confirm for me that the path to a bright future for America was found in the power of community.

All of the pieces began to fit into place. Losing faith in the political process freed me to explore other perspectives and use my energy in a more effective manner. The tools of the tech industry have created the most powerful force for change in our nation's history and the millennial generation is rekindling our idealism. The culture, not politics, drives the nation and communities drive the culture.

Armed with a full dose of optimism, I began to see community problem solving all around me.

Sometimes, the best community solution comes from a single person who acts rather than complains. That's the story of Kenny Thompson, a mentor and volunteer at an elementary school in Texas. Thompson found that 60 children at the school were being fed a cold sandwich rather than hot lunches because their parents had fallen behind on the payments. Making things worse, some of the kids were skipping lunch entirely because they were embarrassed.

Rather than complain that somebody else ought to do something; rather than demanding action from the school board or calling his congressman; Thompson solved the problem himself. He wrote a $465 check to bring the accounts current and the students were able to get hot lunches like everyone else. Thompson said it was the best money he'd ever spent. While politics in official Washington is discouraging and dysfunctional, people like the 52-year-old "lunch angel" provide a ray of hope.[14]

Another example took advantage of the new opportunities for community action driven by the internet. In early 2014, a petition drive was launched by Sarah Kavanaugh on Change.org. The 17-year old athlete from Hattiesburg, Mississippi, liked Gatorade but was concerned about one of the ingredients in it—Brominated Vegetable Oil (BVO). Rather than stop drinking it, she wanted to make it better.

Kavanaugh's petition called for PepsiCo to remove BVO from its products, and more than 200,000 people signed on in support. Within months, the corporate giant agreed to remove the controversial ingredient from all their drinks. Not only that, rival Coke followed suit as well.

USA Today reported it this way,

> Coca-Cola and PepsiCo have stood by the safety of the ingredient, which is used to distribute flavors more evenly in fruit-flavored drinks. But their decisions reflect the pressure companies are facing as people pay closer attention to ingredient labels and try to stick to diets they feel are natural. Several major food makers have recently changed their recipes to remove chemicals or dyes that people find objectionable.

Kavanaugh's response? "It's really good to know that companies, especially big companies, are listening to consumers."[15] What's exciting to me is that Kavanaugh has grown up in a world where the tools exist for her concerns to be heard.

Stories like these are common in America. Still, many people believe that community involvement and volunteerism is all well and good, but they don't think it applies to the really big problems.

What I've come to learn is that it's the only way to solve those really big problems. One dramatic example involved a tourist attraction on the island of Kauai, Hawaii. Polihale State Park was closed when flooding destroyed an access road and damaged the facilities. The state estimated repairs would cost $4 million and take several years. Instead of waiting, the community responded. As CNN described it:

> "Their livelihood was being threatened, and they were tired of waiting for government help, so business owners and residents on Hawaii's Kauai Island pulled together and completed a $4 million repair job to a state park — for free."[16]

According to the government agency that was bailed out by the volunteers, the free bridge repair and improvements included "welding surface pieces in place, pouring concrete access segments, installation of vehicle barrier rails, clearing accumulated debris below to re-establish ability for natural flow under the bridge, and adding structural supports."[17]

Volunteers also repaired four roadway washouts. This included "grading four miles of roadway, and portions covered in silt run-off or scoured out, repair of the road accessing the park water well and pump, repair of the broken water line to four comfort stations, and blocking off vehicle access to the fifth comfort station that was severely damaged."[18]

That's the kind of community engagement that provides hope for America's future.

Community problem solving, fueled by the digital revolution and inspired by the millennial generation, has the potential to overcome the dysfunction of our failed system of politics and government. We may not be able to make government work better, but that won't stop us from making society work better.

CHAPTER 2

THE POWER OF COMMUNITY

AFTER READING an early draft of the first chapter, a friend liked the community problem-solving theme. But he confessed that his first reaction was wondering what policy initiatives we should pursue to support it. "Then, I realized I was missing the point," he laughed. "What you're saying is politics is not the answer."

More precisely, what I'm suggesting is that politics alone is not the answer. It's important to vote and play some role in the political process. But it's even more important to help build a brighter future by working together in community. For America to succeed, we need an all-hands-on-board approach that unleashes the creativity and resources of individual Americans, families, community groups, churches, entrepreneurs, small businesses, local governments, and more.

Politics has a role to play in governing our society, but it is not the lead role.

I recognize that this is the opposite of the message we receive every day from the news, political activists, and government officials. Our society is constantly drenched in the notion that every challenge must have a political solution. Rather than acknowledging the reality that community and the culture lead while politics and government lag behind, the daily chatter builds a mistaken narrative that 21st-century America is guided by a top-down system of governance.

This narrow ideological view is constantly reflected in the news coverage on Fox, CNN, and MSNBC. Every story and every event becomes a battle between conservatives and liberals, Republicans and Democrats, private sector and public. Political activists of all persuasions create talking points to "prove" that they hold the moral and rational high ground. They convey a sense that anybody who disagrees with them is either stupid or corrupt. Public polarization and cynicism are the natural result.

CREATING FALSE EXPECTATIONS

The media narrative suggesting that political battles will determine the fate of the nation makes many people fighting mad and fills them with a burning desire to beat the other team. Far too many nice and reasonable people get so riled up by the partisanship that they do rude and obnoxious things. Friends begin to tune them out and avoid them because their intensity and single-minded focus is tiresome. Then, when the campaigning is done, they learn the ultimate futility of engaging in politics as usual. Even when your team wins, nothing really changes and the anger increases.

Passionately fighting political battles may help vent your rage, but it will not set things right.

When an individual focuses exclusively on politics and government to solve our problems it can be frustrating. But when a society does it, it is very dangerous.

Half a century ago, the brilliant political scientist Aaron Wildavsky wrote of "a simple recipe for violence: promise a lot, deliver a little. Lead people to believe they will be much better off, but let there be no dramatic improvement."[1] He wrote those words in 1968 while America was engulfed in race riots and anti-war protests. It was the year both Martin Luther King and Robert F. Kennedy were assassinated and just five years after Lee Harvey Oswald gunned down President John F. Kennedy. Suffice it to say that Wildavsky did not use the word "violence" lightly.

Sadly, his words from long ago eerily describe the politics of 21st-century America.

Promising a lot and delivering little is what politicians do all the time. To take just one example, Republican politicians have been promising to cut federal spending for generations. Yet, federal spending has gone up in 47 of the last 50 years.[2] The three exceptions were not even real declines in spending. Instead, they were merely accounting flukes in the aftermath of the bank bailouts. As if that weren't bad enough, spending is projected to keep going up every year for as long as anybody has bothered to project. There's no reason to believe that anything will change anytime soon. Republicans will keep promising spending cuts and spending will continue to increase.

Wildavsky observed that this dangerous political game started when the promises made by politicians were paired with proposed solutions that were too small to accomplish the goal. President Donald Trump, for example, said during the 2016 campaign that he would balance the budget without cutting programs by eliminating waste, fraud, and abuse.[3] Many Republicans over the years have said the same thing. The problem is that even if you eliminated every penny of wasteful and fraudulent spending, the savings wouldn't come close to balancing the budget. Federal spending overall would continue to keep going up year after year. The promises appeal to voters and the proposed solutions make it look easy. It's great for campaigning but lousy for governing.

Reducing inequality is a hot issue for many Democrats and raising taxes on the rich is presented as the solution. The power of the issue almost led Vermont Senator Bernie Sanders to an upset victory for the presidential nomination in 2016. But the promised solution doesn't measure up. Research from the left-leaning Brookings Institute shows that such a policy would have only "a small effect on overall inequality."[4] The Brookings research team included Peter Orszag, a man who served as President Barack Obama's budget director. Still, despite this reality, Democrats keep pushing their symbolic issue just as Republicans keep talking about cutting spending.

This political gamesmanship is one of the big reasons Americans distrust their government. By raising expectations while presenting no substantive solutions, the process ensures that just about all voters will end up being disappointed.

For example, what happens if Democrats win an election by promising to reduce inequality? Right off the bat, Republicans will be disappointed and fearful. But if the newly elected Democrats fail to raise taxes on the wealthy, they will deeply disappoint their base voters. On the other hand, if they actually pass the tax hike, it could be even worse for the

Democrats. Why? Because "it soon becomes clear that nothing has changed."[5]

The same dynamic works in both parties. "You have a lot of people who were told that if we got a majority in the House and a majority in the Senate, then life was gonna be great," said Nikki Haley, the Republican former governor of South Carolina. What happened after her party got those majorities? "What you're seeing is that people are angry. Where's the change? . . . They're saying, 'Look, what you said would happen didn't happen.'"[6]

Wildavsky describes this vicious cycle as "minus-sum games in which every player leaves the contest worse off than when he entered."[7] At the very least, these games create a recipe for deep disappointment. We need to break this cycle before it escalates to Wildavsky's feared recipe for violence.

For many who grew up believing in the idealized virtues of our political system, the natural reaction would be to fix the political process. Let's demand that politicians promise real solutions as big as the promises they make! Earlier in my life, I would have said the same thing. The only problem is that it can't possibly work.

For example, imagine a true believer who unabashedly promises to implement a single-payer, government-run, health care program. That might be considered a big enough solution for the problem as some people see it. Very liberal voters would love it and candidates making that promise could win elections in heavily Democratic areas. But if the cry for government-run health care became the dominant theme and issue for the national Democratic Party, it would lead to a Republican landslide.

That reality is how we ended up with Obamacare. Most of its supporters wanted a single-payer system; most Americans did not. So Obama took a different approach. To get the bill passed the president had to make all kinds of promises that couldn't be honored. Most famously, he promised, "If you like your doctor, you can keep your doctor." The promises made it possible to pass the law; breaking the promises ensured the law will never become popular. Ultimately, the 2016 election ensured that much of the law will not even survive.

Politicians don't make promises big enough to solve the problems they identify because they cannot possibly deliver on such promises.

WORKING WHERE WE HAVE CONTROL

This deeper problem has been identified by Jonathan Rauch, one of the most insightful observers of the American political scene. The Brookings scholar wrote what has become a classic book in its field, *Government's End: Why Washington Stopped Working.* He describes a process that over time leads more interest groups to accumulate influence and effectively clog the arteries of government. The government then loses the ability to adapt to a changing world. We are far along in this process.

The end result, according to Rauch, is that never again "can the electorate exert more than marginal control over the vast political biosphere that Washington has at last become."[8] That's a strong statement, and one we really don't want to hear, but we see evidence of it all around us. Voters no longer have the ability to control the federal government.

If Rauch is correct, and I believe he is, voters need to look at politics and government differently. We will continue to be disappointed in government until we lower our expectations for what can be accomplished through the political process. Rauch sees this as "nudging ourselves toward accepting government as it is."[9]

As a young man in the era before video games, I spent perhaps too much time and money playing pinball. At some neighborhood gathering, I was excited about how many free games I had won on a single dime. An adult overheard me and asked what I got out of it. Mistakenly assuming that he didn't understand how pinball worked, I patiently described how long I got to keep playing without putting in any extra money. Plus, of course, there was simply the thrill of winning. The adult in the room then showed he had a better understanding of the game than I did: "In my view, you've already lost once you drop the coin in the machine. You can never get it back."

When we view politics and government as the only way to solve problems, we've already lost. The problems cannot possibly be solved by politics and government alone. That's especially true when our political system is broken beyond repair. In times like these, there's a special need for other approaches to do the heavy lifting.

Fortunately, other approaches are available including entrepreneurs and small business, charities and religious organizations, civic clubs, social movements, and more. These are the building blocks of community problem solving. These institutions—independent of government—also form the underpinnings of grassroots democracy.

These are the institutions that provide ordinary citizens with some level of empowerment to help control the society they live in. They provide citizens with many ways of working together to create a better society. If one approach doesn't work, we are free to try another. They are so intertwined with the governance of society that a 19th-century observer called them "a sort of irregular government within our constitutional government."[10] A 20th-century historian noted, "Day in and day out, this irregular government, by enlisting the constant participation of its members, stirs more interest and often possesses greater reality than the constitutional authority."[11]

That last point highlights the importance of independent groups making democracy work. They are so absolutely essential that political scientists have identified "the absence of private, nongovernment organizations" as one of the key defining elements of a totalitarian state.[12] In other words, you cannot have a free and vibrant society without a healthy sector of independent community problem-solving organizations.

The fact that these groups attract more loyalty than the formal government is good for the nation, but it makes elected politicians uncomfortable. Thomas Jefferson, drafter of the Declaration of Independence, expressed this fear himself. Once the revolution had passed and his team was in charge, Jefferson recalled that such associations had been necessary when "the government had combined against the rights of the people." But he also "feared that the proliferation of voluntary associations would lead again to revolution, this time against legitimate republican governments."[13]

More recent critics have worried that when people are involved "with service oriented volunteering, political energy is being used." Since they are so busy helping their neighbors, the thinking goes, they don't have time or energy left for political advocacy. In this perspective, "volunteering actually prevents needed social changes from occurring."[14]

In other words, Kenny Thompson should not have given generously so that poor students in his school could enjoy a hot lunch; he should have launched a political crusade instead. This attitude reflects a narrow ideological perspective that politics and government alone is responsible for problem solving. That's the attitude we need to reject.

Rather than relying on politics and politicians, we need to recognize that the so-called irregular government has repeatedly led the nation in ways the formal government could not imagine. Most Americans greatly underestimate the ability of these independent efforts to overwhelm the political process.

In recent times, this has been demonstrated by the existence of 89 million 401(k) retirement accounts holding $4.5 trillion worth of assets.[15] Congress had no intention of creating such accounts when it passed a tax bill back in 1978. If you read legislative summaries of the bill at the time,[16] you would have learned that its so-called highlights included reducing the top corporate tax rate from 48 percent to 46 percent, increasing the standard deduction from $3,200 to $3,400, and cutting the effective capital gains tax rate from 35 percent to 28 percent. In short, there were no lawmakers running to the microphones to claim credit for creating a great new benefit for middle-class Americans.

But the lawmakers didn't count on an employee benefits consultant with a passion for "helping those who need it the most." At the time, Ted Benna was unhappy with his job, which involved designing retirement plans for top professionals while ignoring lower-paid workers. "I had been thinking of getting out of consulting and working for a ministry of some type and that's where the prayer came in. It was during this period that the 401(k) hit out of the blue."[17]

Benna got into the act by actually reading the law that Congress had written. He then applied his own creative interpretation to paragraph 401(k). Benna thought he had found an opportunity for the little guy to set aside some retirement savings. Many others were skeptical, to say the least. In fact, the first client he pitched on the idea decided not to take a chance. Who could blame him? Nobody in official circles said that the law was designed to create flexible personal retirement accounts. It was just one private citizen's interpretation of what the law said. Perhaps he read it wrong. Perhaps it was sloppily drafted and would soon be corrected. Besides, what company needed to pick a fight with the IRS?

Benna was confident enough to launch a 401(k) program at his own firm. "My approach was that if the code doesn't say thou shalt not, then thou should be able to."[18] Once the IRS clarified that Benna read it right, things really took off. Today, more than 88 million Americans have such accounts.[19]

This is far from the only example of a law working out differently than the politicians expected. The creation of 401(k) accounts was the power of community at work. The entrepreneurial insight of Ted Benna combined with the financial planning desires of middle-class Americans completely revised the revenue act of 1978. And it was all done without a single vote being cast.

While rarely acknowledged by political elites, entrepreneurship is a vital way that people can work together to solve societal needs. Benna wasn't looking to change the world. He was just trying to serve his clients and create some opportunity for middle-class Americans. By serving, rather than fighting, he changed the world of retirement planning.

Only a few entrepreneurs like Benna bring sweeping change to America. Sometimes it's accidental and sometime it's part of a well-thought-out plan. Ray Kroc built McDonald's into the world's largest chain of fast food restaurants and revolutionized the fast food industry. Sam Walton changed the way Americans shop with his chain of Walmart stores. Fred Smith created the overnight delivery service with FedEx. But these are the exceptions.

THE SOCIAL POWER OF THE ENTREPRENEUR AND INDEPENDENT ORGANIZATIONS

Most entrepreneurs operate on a smaller scale by providing a needed service in their own community, support for their families, and jobs for their employees. They work longer hours and face more challenges than other working Americans, and our nation would be lost without them.

Few who are fed up with politics recognize what a powerful force this innovative segment of the population has become. There are 27 million citizens starting or running their own business today.[20] To put that in perspective, there are more entrepreneurs than government employees. That's true even if you add up all the federal, state, and local government workers, including teachers, police, firefighters, soldiers, tax collectors, and everyone else who receives a government paycheck.[21]

Importantly, these entrepreneurial community servants survive only by serving their customers. That keeps them innovating in ways that really make a difference in the lives of everyday Americans. It's also part of the formula that makes people feel more connected to the so-called irregular government than to the politicians in the formal government.

While entrepreneurs provide innovation, the nation's nonprofit organizations are also an important part of the independent community problem-solving approach. They provide vital efforts to meet human needs that cannot be addressed through the political process. As with the entrepreneurial process, Americans tend to underestimate the potential impact of these independent organizations.

More than one million charitable groups have arisen to meet all sorts of vital needs.[22] On top of that, more than 300,000 religious congregations also provide important community services.[23] These organizations were supported by over $373 billion in voluntary donations in 2015. More than 70 percent of that money ($264 billion) was given by individuals.[24] To put those staggering numbers in perspective, American voluntary giving is just slightly under the International Monetary Fund's estimate of the gross domestic product (GDP) of Norway with private giving exceeding the GDP of Finland.[25]

And it's not just the quantity of giving that sets American charitable giving apart.

According to the groundbreaking research of Arthur Brooks in *Who Really Cares,*

> There is so little private charity in Europe that it is difficult to find information on the subject—so irrelevant is it that few researchers have even bothered to investigate it recently. . . . These data, however, show a huge charity gap. No Western European population comes remotely close the United States in per capita private charity. . . . Even accounting for differences

in standard of living, Americans gave more than twice as high a percentage of their incomes to charity as the Dutch, almost three times as much as the French, and more than five times as much as the Germans, and more than ten times as much as the Italians.[26]

Other research shows that "the value of American philanthropy...is equivalent to 5.5 percent of the national GDP—the highest in the world, by far (in no other country did it equal even 2 percent of GDP)."[27]

In addition to financial support, 62.6 million Americans give of their time by volunteering with community organizations every year. Americans are more than five times as likely to volunteer in their community as to volunteer for a political or issues campaign.[28] The estimated value of the volunteer time contributed was $184 billion in 2015.[29]

Such financial and personal support has created a few massive organizations that highlight the impressive impact of charitable outreach. Feeding America and its partners provide meals to 46 million Americans.[30] More than 5 million people live in homes built by Habitat for Humanity.[31] But, as with the entrepreneurial sector, most of the charitable community efforts are much more modest and closer to home.

The Independent Sector, a networking group for the nonprofit world, believes that "what's most impressive about America's charitable community is the variety of programs it offers...":

- **Arts, culture, and humanities**, such as museums, symphonies and orchestras, and community theatres;

- **Education and research**, such as private colleges and universities, independent elementary and secondary schools, and noncommercial research institutions;

- **Environmental and animals**, such as zoos, bird sanctuaries, wildlife organizations, and land protection groups;

- **Health services**, such as hospitals, public clinics, and nursing facilities;

- **Human services**, such as housing and shelter, organizers of sport and recreation programs, and youth programs;

- **International and foreign affairs**, such as overseas relief and development assistance;

- **Public and societal benefit**, such as private and community foundations, civil rights organizations, civic, social, and fraternal organizations;

- **Religion**, such as houses of worship and their related auxiliary services;

- **Mutual/Membership Benefit**, such as professional societies and associations, fraternal societies, and pension and retirement funds.[32]

On top of all that, of course, tens of millions more volunteer informally to help family, friends, and neighbors through the challenges of life. This community problem-solving spirit reflects a bottom-up form of democracy that is consistent with our nation's founding principles of freedom and self-governance.

"Americans believe that direct action like volunteering can be particularly effective," according to an Allstate/*National Journal* Heartland Monitor Poll. In fact, most "think that their day-to-day life would be more positively affected by an increase in community volunteerism than having a President that agrees with them on the issues."[33] This is an encouraging finding indicating that most Americans are able to keep politics in its proper perspective.

That same survey shows that, when it comes to major issues, two out of three Americans see community groups and small businesses helping the nation. When it comes to addressing the major issues and challenges facing the nation, very few see a negative impact from these groups. Also receiving very positive results are church and religious organizations along with average Americans.[34] In other words, most people instinctively recognize that these independent community problem-solving organizations are the vehicles for bringing about positive change.

That's why it's important for everyone to understand the vast scale of the entrepreneurial and nonprofit worlds. We have 63 million volunteers and 27 million entrepreneurs actively engaged in community problem solving. The resources and loyalty they command are needed to overcome our dysfunctional system of politics and government.

At the other end of the spectrum, "Americans reserve their lowest rating for the federal government and the business and political elite."[35] This broadly negative assessment includes lobbyists, political parties, large corporations, political activists, and public-private partnerships between government and business.

State and local governments earn mixed reviews: much better than the federal government but not as strong as community groups, small businesses, religious organizations, and average Americans.[36]

Despite these attitudes, there are signs of concern. The percentage of Americans volunteering has been trending down to a new low in 2015.[37] The number of new charities getting started is also declining.[38] A similar dynamic is observed in the entrepreneurial sector. Not only is the number of entrepreneurs heading in the wrong direction, it's getting harder and harder to start a business.[39]

This is possibly evidence of what Robert Putnam reported two decades ago when he published *Bowling Alone*. His writing warned "that our stock of social capital—the very fabric of our connections with each other, has plummeted, impoverishing our lives and communities."[40]

Putnam's work struck a nerve, inspiring a wide range of both supporters and critics. Some who disputed his conclusion believed that our social capital was not really declining, just taking on different forms. In the digital era, we do things differently than we did in the television era. Before television, there was an entirely different type of social capital. Putnam himself described the many different ways of building the fabric of our connections.

> Barn-raising on the frontier was social capital in action, and so too are e-mail exchanges among members of a cancer support group. Social capital can be found in friendship networks, neighborhoods, churches, schools, bridge clubs, civic associations, and even bars. The motto in Cheers "where everybody knows your name" captures one important aspect of social capital.[41]

It's difficult to precisely measure social capital in such a dynamic society. The difference between a 19th-century small-town community and a 21st-century online community cannot be compared with any set of numbers. Regardless of whether our stock of social capital is holding steady or declining, it is vitally important to recognize the value of social capital:

> The central premise of social capital is that social networks have value. It...emphasizes not just warm and cuddly feelings, but a wide variety of quite specific benefits that flow from the trust, reciprocity, information, and cooperation associated with social networks. Social capital creates value for the people who are connected and–at least sometimes–for bystanders as well.[42]

Building up social capital is important because it helps bring us closer together. It "creates places where we learn to work out our differences face-to-face and come together in common cause," according to William Schambra of the Hudson Institute. Fortunately, "Americans are still prompted by and still seek to sustain our small, 'human scale' associations, which gently draw our hearts and minds out of self-absorption and into the larger channels of public life."[43]

That's why we need to spend more time serving our neighbors rather than fighting political wars. For our system of politics and government to work properly, every institution must do its part. That includes entrepreneurs, charities, volunteers, and every independent association that serves our diverse communities.

It's similar to something I experienced after having surgery on my left shoulder. Both before and after the surgery, I overworked my other shoulder to the point where it was in a great deal of pain. I began each and every morning with an ice pack on my right shoulder even though the injury and surgery were on the left. The doctor and physical therapist never wavered in their diagnosis—the only way to relieve the pain on the right shoulder was to build up the left so that it could carry part of the workload. It wasn't always the message I wanted to hear, but in the end they were right.

The same dynamic applies to American politics today. Balance needs to be restored to the "body politic." We must build up our networks of independent community organizations so that they can carry an appropriate share of the workload. Until we do, our system of politics and government will remain broken beyond repair.

A good starting point is to recognize that the independent groups of society are competitors to the system of politics and government. That's probably a strange concept to most Americans, but it is a part of our national heritage. In *Dimensions of Liberty*, Oscar and Mary Handlin noted that voluntary associations have always "helped set limits upon the use of political power without depriving society of services considered essential to its welfare."[44]

Examples of independent groups today competing with government are so common that we rarely notice. FedEx was founded as, and remains, a competitor to the U.S. Postal Service. Uber competes with both public transit companies and government-regulated taxis. Food banks and other charitable groups compete with government social welfare programs.

It's not that independent groups are perfect. Because humans are involved, they're not. For example, "most evangelical voluntary societies of the 1830s and 1840s explicitly attacked the Catholic Church and its vision of charity."[45] Even worse, there have been despicable organizations such as the American Eugenics Society, which promoted the idea of improving the human race by selective breeding. It is often associated with the idea that reproduction among the "lower classes" must be stopped. There are also too many stories of fraud, embezzlement and other forms of personal enrichment associated with some charities.

While real, these and similar stories do not represent the main thrust of voluntary associations in the United States. These independent organizations play a critical role in leading the nation forward.

A HERITAGE OF PRAGMATIC PROBLEM-SOLVERS

On the eve of the American Revolution, the Pennsylvania Abolition Society was formed at the Rising Sun Tavern calling for the end of slavery.[46] Eventually, more than 1,000 abolition societies were formed, growing largely out of Northern churches.[47] The societies used a variety of tactics and had a fair degree of success in the North over a period of decades.

Then, "the American Anti-Slavery Society (AAS) took their campaign to a new level with what could be called the first use of a direct mail campaign. . . . They mailed a number of anti-slavery newspapers and printed materials to religious and civic leaders in the south."[48] The Southerners reacted with hostility, and the abolition society found itself fighting the federal government.

Postmasters in the South refused to deliver the mail and there were public burnings of the mailers. "In his 1835 annual message to Congress, President [Andrew] Jackson . . . called for a national law barring "incendiary" materials from the mails. . . . When Congress did not pass the law, Jackson imposed it administratively, ordering postmasters to remove antislavery material from the mails. Jackson's action drew little opposition."[49] Not only that, "a series of state laws [were] created to criminalize sending such 'inflammatory' and 'seditious materials into southern states."[50]

Sadly, it took another generation and a bloody Civil War before slavery was abolished in the United States. But abolition would have been delayed even longer if it had been left to the politicians. While the abolitionists were forcing the issue into the national debate, Congress was constantly searching for compromises that would make the issue go away. That's typical of the way social change moves the nation forward: groups outside of politics leading the way and politicians struggling to protect the status quo.

Another great example of change coming from outside the political process is the life of Samuel Slater. Depending upon which side of the Atlantic you lived on, Slater was known in his day as either the "Father of the American Industrial Revolution" or "Slater the Traitor." Regardless of what you call him, Slater changed America while George Washington, John Adams, and Thomas Jefferson were president.

He fled Britain and came to America in the year that Washington took office (1789). Slater had memorized plans for British textile factories and was intent on launching a business for himself. He found a wealthy partner to back him, and the team opened its first mill in Pawtucket, Rhode Island, a year later. From these humble beginnings, a great

American industry was born. Slater's business grew and many others followed his lead. By the time Slater died in 1835, the U.S. cotton trade was processing 80 million pounds of cotton annually.[51]

But Slater's impact on the nation was much greater than the numbers indicate. "Manufacturing broke with traditional artisan ways," a change that had profound social implications. The Industrial Revolution launched by Slater "shifted American values from republican simplicity to capitalist consumption," according to Holy Cross Professor Edward T. O'Donnell.[52] In 1820, about 7.2 percent of Americans lived in an urban setting. A century later, that figure had grown to more than 50 percent.[53]

O'Donnell described the sweep of the cultural impact like this:

> It changed the role of women in society, separating the spheres of home and work for the first time. Public education was born out of the factory town and the need for trained labor. Industrialized printing of everything from books to sheet music changed the face of entertainment . . . We can even say that the Industrial Revolution led to the invention of time, at least our disciplined sense of it.[54]

All of this change came from outside the political process. To be clear, it wasn't all from Slater any more than victory in the American Revolution can be attributed solely to General Washington. But both men played indispensable roles in the way that history unfolded.

So, while Slater's factory model created the modern sense of time, Jefferson was stuck in the past. The third president created an elaborate and grand clock for his home at Monticello. Jefferson's clock, visible to this day on the front of his historic mansion, didn't even bother with a minute hand. Such precise measurement of time was unneeded in the agrarian society Jefferson wanted to create:

> Let us never wish to see our citizens occupied at a work-bench, or twirling a distaff . . . for the general operations of manufac-ture, let our work-shops remain in Europe. It is better to carry provisions and materials to workmen there, than bring them to the provisions and materials, and with them their manners and principles.[55]

What's especially ironic is that Slater's system really took off during the time Jefferson was in the White House. Slater and his brother built an entire mill village called Slatersville. It even included Sunday Schools for children and became a wildly successful model followed by many others.

Those who follow only politics and government would say that Jefferson ran the country from 1801 to 1809, but the truth is that Slater's world won out during those years. He didn't change the world by getting engaged in politics; he changed it by meeting the needs of American citizens for high-quality, affordable cotton.

The unfolding of the Industrial Revolution launched by Slater dominated America for nearly two centuries before it was recently overcome by the digital revolution. But because historians and journalists overemphasize the role of politics, his story is little known.

On the other hand, Washington, Adams, and Jefferson have become legends. But even as larger-than-life-legends, they did not lead the change that swept over America when they were formally in power.

I say this not to disparage the roles of our first three presidents, but to put them in perspective. All three men played leading roles in creating and leading a government that allowed people the freedom to solve problems on their own. "Secure in the knowledge that the role of the government did not encompass every aspect of life, Americans created an apparatus of free institutions with which each group of them could seek its own goals without coercion."[56]

America's Founders set up a system where each group could pursue its own dreams, and because of that our nation has grown to become a wonderfully diverse society of more than 300 million people. That's an accomplishment worthy of legends. But it's not the same as leading the country.

Washington in particular is worthy of praise because he could have taken over as king following the War for Independence. Instead, he walked away. His chief adversary, King George III, could not believe that any man would do such a thing. Told by an American that Washington would return to his farm after winning independence, the British king replied, "If he does that, he will be the greatest man in the world."[57]

Like Washington, Adams and Jefferson had their greatest impact on the nation before they became president. Fortunately, they then created a system in which independent organizations can compete with government for our time, our money, and our loyalty. These organizations provide more flexibility and experimentation than can be found in the formal process of government. This competition contributes to the healthy functioning of a free society.

That same reality exists today. People feel more connected to family, community groups, their jobs, and their faith than they do to government. In times of trouble, they are more likely to reach out to these groups than to politicians and government.

Recognizing that the voluntary organizations of society are part of the governing process—and are also competing with the formal structures of government—is essential for those who want to move the nation forward. If you keep looking only at politics and governance, you will be filled with despair. But if you look in the other direction—just as my family did with the pile of yams on that long-ago day in North Carolina—you will find reasons for hope.

In this view, the choices before us look much different. When it comes to solving society's problems, do we want to be pragmatic community problem-solvers or rigidly ideological in believing that politics is the only option? Do we want to engage 63 million volunteers and 27 million entrepreneurs in the search for solutions? Or do we want to put our faith in Congress and the president? Do we want to fight petty partisan battles that accomplish little? Or serve our communities to build up social capital and move the nation forward?

To meet the challenges facing our nation, we need an all-hands-on-board approach that uses all the resources at our disposal to move the nation forward.

CHAPTER 3

THE POWER TO WALK AWAY

"Your vote is your voice as an American citizen," according to a state of Pennsylvania website and countless other official sources. "It's your opportunity to be heard, to hold elected officials accountable for their decisions and to have a say in important issues that affect your community. On Election Day, every vote matters."[1]

Such messaging is commonplace and amplified by saturation media coverage. A harsher version of the same thought is sometimes voiced in unofficial communications. "If you don't vote, you have no right to complain."

Candidates and the major political parties pile on with sophisticated and expensive get-out-the-vote efforts. Despite all this, and to the dismay of political activists everywhere, voter turnout remains low election after election. For those who live and breathe politics, it's impossible to understand why people won't take the time needed to make their voice heard.

Often, the political elites blame the voters. But Nancy Duarte, an expert in the art of persuasive communication, argues that the failure to connect always lies with the presenter of information, not the audience. "The audience does not need to tune themselves to you — you need to tune your message to them."[2]

In other words, if you want people to vote, you need to deliver a message that gives people a reason to vote. If you want to be a leader, you need to give a message that makes sense and motivates people to follow you. If voter turnout remains low, the blame lies with the politicians rather than the voters.

Look at it from a different perspective. What would happen if we lived in a world where politics really did determine the fate of the nation? What if voting really was a way to hold elected officials accountable? And what if politicians actually delivered messages that were in tune with voter concerns? If we lived in a world like that, voter turnout would be extraordinarily high.

Instead, we live in a world where voters may like one set of campaign promises better than the other, but doubt that any politician will actually deliver. It's a world where voters have little opportunity to hold elected officials accountable because gerrymandering and other election rules are written to protect incumbents rather than empower voters. That's why more than 90 percent of incumbents routinely get re-elected despite deep dissatisfaction with Congress. On top of that, it's a world where the culture leads and the politicians follow. In this real world, voting has become a civic obligation with only a modest real world impact.

This is not to suggest that voting is a waste of time or something to be discouraged. "In view of the fact that citizens vote by the tens of millions," wrote noted political scientist James Q. Wilson, "one ought to be cautious, at the very least, about describing this behavior as mass irrationality."[3]

Still, while voting is not irrational or meaningless, it is not as powerful a tool as the rhetoric claims.

To understand why, consider the remarks made by President Barack Obama to a gathering of young people in Indianapolis. The president, like countless other politicians before him, shared his view that politics is the way everything gets done in America. Tailoring his remarks to the youthful audience, he explained the process this way:

> When you are a junior in high school . . . if you decide you and your friends are going out, you have got to make all kinds of decisions about, where are we going to eat? What movie do you want to see? You take votes, and you are trying to figure out—maybe one of your friends does not have enough money, and we have to chip in to help make sure she can go too.[4]

In reality, even in high school, there's more to this process than voting. Just because a group of students vote to go somewhere doesn't mean the others are obligated to tag along. If five friends vote for pizza and a sixth doesn't want pizza, he or she doesn't have to go. Some of the time the five would enjoy pizza and the sixth could stay home or do something with another group of friends.

Or, if the teen who doesn't want pizza is the coolest of them all, the other five might change their mind to hang with the cool kid!

The point is that voting is only one part of the decision-making process. That's true in high school, and it's true in America.

In the president's example, the real power possessed by each of the friends is not their right to vote, but the fact that they are free to choose what they want to do. The vote cannot force any of the students to go where the majority wants to go. Regardless of the vote, each student has the freedom to walk away. And if one person walks away, it could change the decision of others.

Economist Albert Hirschman explored these themes in an important book, *Exit, Voice, and Loyalty.* He noted that economists like to talk about the power of exit (walking away) more than the power of voice or vote. But political scientists and politicians only want to talk about the power of the vote. In fact, the power to walk away "has often been branded as *criminal,* for it has been labeled desertion, defection, and treason."[5]

This is absurd. The high school kid who stayed home rather than go out to eat with his friends wasn't deserting them, he just didn't want to go where they were going that night. The taxpayer who moves to another state isn't committing treason. He's just voting with his feet.

Politicians may want to ignore or demonize this form of empowerment, but it's a core part of our national heritage. Hirschman reminds us that "the United States owes its very existence and growth to millions of decisions favoring exit over voice."[6] It began with fleeing religious persecution in England. The power of the vote wasn't enough for them. It has continued for centuries with people exiting oppression and seeking freedom.

Empowerment comes from freedom, not democracy.

Think about the reality of elections. Politicians seeking your vote often talk of empowering the middle class or some other group of voters.

But they're really just seeking power for themselves. The good ones may eventually use that power on your behalf, but that's not the same as empowering you. In fact, when a politician uses his power on your behalf, he is working to make you dependent upon his continuation in office.

You cannot be empowered unless you have the freedom to walk away.

FREE TO MOVE

That's a lesson learned over the past half century by Major League Baseball. Up until the 1970s, baseball players were restricted by something known as the "reserve clause." It was a contract provision that restricted a player to one team for life.

In those days, the minimum pay for a ballplayer was $12,000 a year. The average salary was under $29,303 a year.[7]

Then a series of legal challenges reaching all the way to the Supreme Court began in the 1970s and eventually gave players the chance to become free agents.

Today, the minimum salary is $507,500 a year with an average pay topping $4.25 million.[8]

That change, from an average salary of under $30,000 a year to over $4.2 million, didn't come about because the owners decided things were going well enough to share more revenue with the players. It came about because players won the right to walk away and force the owners to compete for their services.

Few of us will ever earn the kind of money that Major League Baseball players command.

However, we all get to exercise the power to walk away on a regular basis. If we are unhappy with a local business, we take our money elsewhere. It doesn't matter what the reason is. We don't have to meet with the manager to try and fix the policies or practices that upset us. We don't have to justify our reason for leaving, provide a cost-benefit analysis, or give them another chance. We just leave. We don't even have to say we're going.

Some people love Walmart while others hate the mega-store. There's no need for a vote; we don't have to agree. People who love it shop there and those who hate it don't. Both sides are happy with their choice. A society where people are free to walk away produces unlimited amounts of diversity and opportunities.

Some people buy only brand-name products while others mock those who spend money that way. Again, it doesn't matter. There's no need to decide which is right or better or smarter. We just choose. And we might choose differently at different points in our life or under different circumstances.

Regardless, the choice is ours. That's what empowers us.

The same logic applies when it comes to charities and nonprofit groups. Whether it's a food bank or a local theater group, their survival depends upon convincing us to give our time as volunteers, our support as members, and our cash as donors. If we don't like their mission or don't think they're effective, we walk away.

It even applies at work. If we are unhappy with our job, we will seek another.

We think of this as our freedom to choose. But those on the other side of the transaction fear it as our freedom to walk away from them. This gives us the power to hold leaders and organizations accountable.

Leaders are "powerfully constrained in their actions" by the need to keep their customers, members, or donors in place,[9] observed Wilson. "All voluntary associations, like all retail firms, compete with one another—they struggle to obtain scarce resources from a population of prospective contributors (or customers)."[10] That competition forces businesses and employers and community groups to pay attention to the public's needs and desires.

While we rarely think about it, the reality is that we all have more power as consumers than as voters. That's the reason we have hundreds of choices of colors and sizes and styles and delivery options for consumer products but generally only one or two real choices on Election Day.

It also explains why we are happier with local government than with the federal government. We get to choose where we live and that gives us the power to hold local government accountable. Just like voluntary organizations and retail firms, communities compete for residents, employers and jobs.

We choose a place to live based upon the lifestyle mix of housing, activities, taxes, and services. The local government influences that balance, but so do other factors such as geography, climate, traditions, entertainment options, and jobs. Sometimes people have a sentimental attachment to a place that makes them overlook other flaws, and sometimes people have the opposite reaction. Wherever they choose to live, most people don't bother to vote in local elections. Fortunately, they have a more powerful tool to hold officials accountable—they have the freedom to choose.

"The act of moving or failing to move is crucial," according to an influential journal publication written long ago by Northwestern University's Charles M. Tiebout. "Moving or failing to move replaces the usual market test of willingness to buy a good and reveals the consumer-voter's demand for public goods."[11]

When we choose a place to live, we are "buying" a particular mix of lifestyle benefits, and the price we pay is determined by housing costs, taxes, regulations, and other factors. If the costs go up or the benefits go down, we might rise up and try to vote in a new team to fix the problem. After all, it's a bit of a hassle to move. But, sooner or later, if the prices keep going up or the services keep going down, we can express our displeasure simply by moving.

The fact that individuals and businesses are free to move places great constraints on the power of local government officials. If, for example, the officials raise taxes too high or cut valued services too low, some people would move away. Others who had been thinking of moving to the community for the first time would re-evaluate their options. Housing prices would decline and the community would become less desirable.

Just as likely, however, is the fact that change could come from totally outside the local government. If a major employer leaves town, that too could encourage people to move elsewhere, which could lead to a decline in city tax revenue, services, and housing prices. So, local officials have the difficult task of finding the right mix of costs and benefits to keep businesses and individuals from moving away. Fortunately, as consumers, we don't have to evaluate all of their policy decisions; we just have to look at the end result.

It's important to note that this is not just a theoretical possibility. Local officials are competing in a very active market. The average American can expect to move about 12 times in their lifetime.[12] According to the

U.S. Census Bureau, 41 percent of Americans no longer live in the state where they were born.[13] That number naturally goes up as people get older. Around 40 million people move each year (one out of every eight Americans). While most moved within the same county, roughly a third of those moves crossed county or state lines.[14]

This reality provides a powerful tool to hold local government officials accountable. But there is no tool that provides the same level of accountability for federal officials.

The market test that comes from voting with your feet produces results that seem to surprise those who are wrapped up in the political world. One example came from a theoretical listing of the best states put together by *Politico,* a publication for Washington insiders. It rated New Hampshire as the best state in the union and found that nine of the 10 worst states are in the American South.[15]

However, if you look at Census Bureau data showing where Americans move to and from, five of the top seven states are from the South, and the worst states are New York, Illinois, New Jersey, and California. Eight of the 10 worst states by this measure come from either the Northeast or Midwest.[16]

No matter where you look, the differences between the two lists are pretty dramatic. *Politico,* for example, places Texas and Florida a mere 36th and 37th on its list respectively, but Americans voting with their feet make Florida and Texas Nos. 1 and 2 respectively. The states most underrated by *Politico* are Louisiana (51st according to theory, 12th according to reality) and South Carolina (40th in theory, third in reality). In fact, the six most underrated states all come from the South.

At the other extreme, the five states most overrated by *Politico* are Minnesota, New Jersey, Wyoming, Connecticut, and Massachusetts.[17]

Generally, but not exclusively, the states most overrated by *Politico* have higher taxes and a more active government than the Southern states preferred by Americans on the move.

What's going on? Why are people moving to states that rate low on the *Politico* scale of good states and moving away from those *Politico* rates highly?

The most likely explanation is that there's something wrong with *Politico's* rankings. They were based upon 14 categories of data from "reputable sources" on "important factors such as high school graduation rates, per capita income, life expectancy, and crime rate."[18] That sounds good and plausible on the surface. But since the end result doesn't match up with reality, it's likely that the list of "important factors" missed the things that really matter.

For example, while the D.C. publication included "per capita income," perhaps it didn't include cost-of-living factors or housing prices. A state like New Jersey may have a higher per capita income but perhaps not high enough to offset the expense of living in the Garden State. Maybe job creation and a big backyard matter more than some of the things *Politico* considered.

More broadly, perhaps the things that seemed important to Washington insiders really aren't so important to mainstream Americans. It's not unreasonable to think that people whose lives revolve around politics and government would be more likely than others to prefer a mix of higher taxes and more government services.

This gap isn't at all harmful so long as all of us have the freedom to choose where we live. Those who prefer a bigger government presence should have states and cities available that offer such an option. As long as states and local governments are free to determine their own mix of costs and benefits, just about everyone will be able to vote with their feet and find a community to call home.

MORE EMPOWERING THAN VOTING

To take this a step further and see how freedom is more empowering than voting, consider a simple thought experiment.

Imagine a land with 50 states that operate independently. Under one scenario, citizens in each state can vote for their leaders and on all-important issues. The elections are free and fair. But, you cannot move out of the state you live in.

Under a second scenario, citizens have absolutely no right to vote but they can move to any other state at any time. Which would you choose?

At first, the ability to vote for everything sounds fair and appealing. It's especially enticing when you think about the possibility of free and fair elections. But the potential problems are enormous. Without any other options, tyranny of the majority becomes the most likely outcome.

If you are a racial or ethnic minority, you might find that the voters place limits on the kind of job you can get or where you can live. If religion is an important part of your life, a majority might ban you from practicing your faith. The list could go on and on. Over time, even the right to criticize the majority view would be eroded and the promise of free elections would disappear.

If this sounds far-fetched, Fareed Zakaria reminds us that it's happened before. "Recall that in the fourth century B.C. in Athens, where Greek democracy is said to have found its truest expression, the popular assembly—by democratic vote—put to death the greatest philosopher of the age because of his teachings." He said things the Athenians didn't want to hear, so they killed him. Still, "the execution of Socrates was democratic."[19]

Once you think about it for a moment, it becomes clear the second scenario is better because it gives you the freedom to choose. Sure, the absence of the right to vote is a big negative, but you can still vote with your feet and leave. That is what empowers you. It gives you the right to move to a state that meets your needs.

Not only that, but in the scenario where people have the power to walk away, they will eventually get the right to vote. Why? Because state leaders will be competing for residents, businesses, and jobs. Sooner or later, some state will offer voting rights to attract new residents. Other states will be forced to follow suit.

History proves the point that "Liberty led to democracy and not the other way around."[20] As Zakaria puts it, "Liberty came to the West centuries before democracy."[21] In America, it was the power to walk away that won women the right to vote.

In 1869, the territory of Wyoming granted women the right to vote, and they retained that right when the territory became a state. Wyoming is not generally known as a progressive state, so why did it lead the nation on suffrage? The answer had nothing to do with politics and everything to do with marketing.

At the time, there was only one woman for every six men in the state. A lot of the men were lonely. "Appeals to justice and equality did not pass the legislation–most Wyoming legislators supported [the] bill because they thought it would win the territory free national publicity and might attract more single marriageable women to the region."[22]

Within a couple of years of Wyoming's action, the movement for women's suffrage picked up some powerful opponents. An Anti-Suffrage League was formed and the liquor lobby became one of the strongest opponents to women's enfranchisement. They "feared women might use their vote to prohibit the sale of liquor."[23] These opponents were very successful at the federal level. A constitutional amendment granting women the right to vote was first introduced in 1878 by a California Republican, Sen. Aaron Augustus Sargent. It was voted on and defeated every year for 40 years.

Things were different at the state level due to the reality of competition. The first nine states granting women the right to vote were Western states, perhaps recognizing the marketing value first acted upon by Wyoming. The process was slow and inconsistent. In some states, women were granted the right to vote only in school elections or municipal elections. In others, they could vote for president of the United States but not state officials.

In 1911, Jeannette Rankin became the first woman to formally address the Montana state legislature. A few years later Montana granted women the right to vote, and Rankin capitalized on that fact to make history in a stunning manner.

The U.S. Constitution gives states the right to determine who is eligible to vote in their state. But it also says that anyone eligible to vote can serve in Congress. Rankin took advantage of this opportunity and became the first woman to serve in Congress. Elected in 1916, she did so before Congress conceded that women should even be allowed to vote. I would love to have been in the room when she walked into the boys' club, with 434 male members of Congress, to represent her district.

Rankin's time in Congress was brief. A pacifist, she voted to oppose the U.S. entry into World War I and that vote led to her defeat in the very next election. Later, she served another single term in Congress and cast the only vote against U.S. entry into World War II. The unpopularity of that vote led to her not running for re-election in 1942.[24] While Rankin served only two terms decades apart, the very fact of her election showed the importance of state-by-state competition.

Congress finally passed the Suffrage Amendment in 1919, five decades after Wyoming got things started. Some might think that Rankin's presence in Congress guilted the male legislators into treating women more fairly, but that wasn't the case. In fact, she had already lost her re-election bid before the amendment passed.

There was, however, a more basic reality at work. So many states had given women the right to vote that a majority of congressmen had become dependent upon women's votes to get re-elected. By 1919, even members of Congress could figure out that publicly opposing suffrage would hurt them with women voters!

It was the power to walk away that won women the right to vote. It was the culture leading and the politicians following. All that Congress did was confirm the inevitable and take credit for it. That's what politicians do.

COMMUNITY WALKOUT

The power to walk away can even be used by people who don't want to go anywhere, a fact that was highlighted repeatedly by the civil rights movement of the 1960s.

On December 1, 1955, Rosa Parks refused to give up her seat on a bus in Montgomery, Alabama. It was her personal "affirmation that she had had enough. It was an individual expression of a timeless longing for human dignity and freedom."[25]

Parks was promptly arrested, fined, and given a suspended jail sentence for violating the segregation laws. However, her quiet stand against an unjust law instantly transformed the department store seamstress into a "heroine" for Montgomery's black community. "They saw in her courageous person the symbol of their hopes and aspirations."[26]

Still, everybody involved knew that there was no chance of changing Montgomery's segregation laws through the normal political process. The city's political leadership was absolutely convinced that there was nothing the black community could do about it.

So, with the leadership of their churches, the black community decided to withdraw their "cooperation from an evil system." In practical terms, this meant "withdrawing [their] economic support from the bus company." The boycott, effective from day one, created financial distress for the bus company since 75 percent of its riders were black.[27]

It also created challenges for the leaders of the boycott. Roughly 17,500 black residents needed to find another way to travel to work and back each day. Initially, "Montgomery's eighteen black-owned taxi companies had agreed to transport blacks for the same fare they would pay on the bus—ten cents."[28] Within days, however, the police commissioner made clear his intention to enforce a city law making it illegal for cabs to charge less than 45 cents per ride.[29]

But the power of community in action could not be stopped. When the cabs were prevented from helping, an incredible system of ride-sharing was developed and maintained. As the boycott dragged on, churches bought cars specifically to support the ride-sharing effort.

The political leadership in Montgomery fought back with every tool they could muster. They harassed drivers and told those waiting for a ride that they could be arrested for loitering. They pressured local insurance companies to stop providing auto insurance for the ride-sharing vehicles. But "T.M. Alexander, a black agent in Atlanta ... found a Lloyd's of London underwriter who agreed to sell the boycotters a policy."[30]

This was the power of community at work, relying upon the power to walk away. As the nation watched this spectacle unfold on the evening news, the ferocious response from white political leaders seemed wildly out of proportion to very modest demands of the black boycotters: courteous treatment on the buses, first-served seating, the hiring of black drivers on black bus routes.[31]

Eventually, the U.S. Supreme Court confirmed that the segregation laws were unconstitutional. But the court order was not enough to make desegregation of Montgomery buses a reality. After the ruling took effect, the houses and churches of black leaders were bombed. Shots were fired at buses with black riders.

Fortunately, throughout the yearlong boycott, the leadership of the black community had continually emphasized the importance of protesting with dignity and not with violence. When the bombings and shootings came, they did not respond in kind. This impressive restraint made it clear who the troublemakers were in Montgomery.

That contrast was devastating for the city's image and business prospects. It accomplished what the court order could not. White business leaders and churches finally called for an end to violence and respect for the new law. The result "fired the imagination of blacks throughout the country,"[32] and boycotts became a powerful tool for accomplishing what the political process could not.

Whether it's Ted Benna providing a middle-class retirement plan that Congress never intended, Samuel Slater bringing manufacturing to the nation when the president was committed to an agrarian way of life, women like Jeannette Rankin gaining for her gender the right to vote despite the opposition of male legislators, or Rosa Parks' courageous effort to challenge the status quo and bring an end to segregation, it is action outside the normal political channels that leads our nation forward.

THERE FROM THE BEGINNING

Using freedom and pragmatic community problem solving to get around an unresponsive political system is a concept deeply rooted in American history. In fact, while it is rarely celebrated in political circles, it may be our nation's oldest and deepest tradition.

The first charity fund-raising drive in colonial America took place in the 1630s, raising funds for a new school—Harvard.[33] Twenty-first-century readers might be shocked to learn that the creation of this elite school was controversial, even revolutionary. Perhaps even more shocking is the fact that they weren't trying to be revolutionary, just pragmatic.

Whatever else it was, the founding of Harvard was clearly illegal.

The need for Harvard so early in colonial life grew out of the high ambitions the Massachusetts Bay Colony had for itself. Future governor John Winthrop famously described that goal on his voyage to the New World: "We shall be as a city upon a hill, the eyes of all people are upon us."[34] With such a lofty goal, "the state would need competent rulers, the church would require a learned clergy, and society itself would need the adornment of cultured men."[35]

Fortunately, the new colony had "the active support of a nucleus of Cambridge and Oxford trained gentlemen." More than a hundred such men had moved to New England and they became the "founders of Harvard, the fathers of the first generation of Harvard students." These men weren't radicals seeking to re-invent education. Quite the contrary, they were trying to "re-create a little bit of old England in America." They wanted the comfort of their traditions and so created "an English college such as they had known at Oxford but particularly at Cambridge."[36]

There was one not so little problem.

Under English law, only the king had the authority to create a college or business. "The power of granting charters was deemed by the crown one of its most precious privileges."[37] The colonists didn't want to ask the king for a charter because they feared he would want some control over the college in exchange. In particular, "they worried that ... the sovereign might interfere with the freedom of the college to teach its preferred religious point of view."[38] This was a big deal for people who had fled England to avoid religious persecution.

So, the pragmatic colonists improvised and created Harvard on their own. They got away with it partly because they were far away and partly because the English king had bigger problems to worry about. The English Civil War broke out just as the new school was getting started. Eventually, however, when the civil war ended and order was restored, King Charles II decided to show the colonists who was boss. He did more than just challenge the creation of Harvard without his permission. In what was presumably designed to be a show of force, he rescinded the charter for the entire colony of Massachusetts.

In practice, however, "the invalidation of its charter proved no burden to Harvard College." They just kept on going without official sanction. Harvard's experience made the founders of Yale cautious, but they eventually followed the same path.[39] Yale operated for more than four decades without a charter. Over time, many more organizations were created in the colonies without the blessings of the Crown. For the British, "It was impossible to control the formation of these spontaneous bodies which had the approval or tolerance of local authorities."[40]

Before the colonies won their freedom, notable community endeavors included the St. Andrews Society in Charleston, South Carolina, "to assist all people in distress,"[41] a public library in Philadelphia,[42] The American Philosophical Society,[43] the Pennsylvania Hospital,[44] the Charleston Museum, and much more.[45]

The growing conflict with England, spurred in part by the colonial practice of ignoring the need for the king's approval, led to another round of community problem solving.

"The Stamp Act emergency of 1764-66 produced a multifarious network ... of citizens who joined together to boycott British manufactures."[46] When the British closed the port of Boston, other "towns and colonies sent money, grain and livestock to aid Boston residents and businesses."[47] And, of course, Levi Preston and the other Minutemen who stood up to the British soldiers at Lexington and Concord were community volunteers. They trained regularly to defend their community at a minute's notice.

This history of voluntary community engagement is every much a part of our nation's founding ideals as freedom, equality, and self-governance. The decision to start a college without getting royal permission was primarily an act of pragmatism. But it was also an act of defiance and independence because it recognized the right of a free people to act on their own.

This was one step in establishing what Oscar and Mary Handlin called "a critical element in American liberty." The historians explained, "By sustaining the conviction that desirable ends could be obtained without calling upon the state, it helped set limits upon the use of political power without depriving society of services considered essential to its welfare."[48]

In fact, it is impossible to understand the American system of politics and government without understanding the role of independent voluntary associations. The men who drafted the Declaration of Independence and the Constitution lived in a world of voluntary associations. They couldn't imagine the world without it.

For example, Ben Franklin "started a subscription library, an academy for the education of youth, and a volunteer company of fire fighters." Not only that, "he also took part in founding a hospital and a fire-insurance company." He also got engaged with a number of business opportunities that included helping "to promote a Western land company."[49]

This life experience was the only reliable guide to draw upon when constructing a government. No matter how well read the Founders were, "History had produced no truly relevant models of representative government on the scale the United States had already attained, not to mention the scale it would reach in the years to come."[50] They could learn from histories of Greece, Rome, and England or from the theories of Locke, Montesquieu, and others. But the only relevant practical experience for leaders of the new nation was the reality of how things had worked in the colonies.

It was natural, therefore, that while drafting the founding documents of our nation, the role of independent associations in problem solving and governance was simply assumed. It would be like 21st-century Americans assuming the existence of smartphones and the internet. Or the way the Founders defined the presidency while assuming that George Washington would be the president.

As a result, they did not design a government to solve all of society's problems. They made the rational assumption that voluntary organizations would continue to play an ongoing role in the governance of society. Americans working together in community has always been one of the distinguishing characteristics of the United States.

Alexis de Tocqueville, an inquisitive Frenchman who visited the United States in 1832, reported that "Americans of all ages, all conditions, all minds constantly unite."

His insightful 19th-century report on *Democracy in America* has become a literary and political science classic. The two-volume report described how Americans created community organizations for just about everything:

> Americans use associations to give fêtes, to found seminaries, to build inns, to raise churches, to distribute books, to send missionaries to the antipodes; in this manner they create hospitals, prisons, schools. Finally, if it is a question of bringing to light a truth or developing a sentiment with the support of a great example, they associate.[51]

Tocqueville also pointed out how this approach was different from other nations. In France it was the government that led "a new undertaking." In England, "a great lord." But in the United States, "count on it," a community association will take the lead.[52]

It was this society, created by the "irregular governance" of independent organizations that provided the framework for freedom to thrive in America. Some scholars go even farther and believe it was the interconnected web of independent organizations that gave our society a sense of national identity.[53]

But there is an ironic twist to the development of this free society that provides an important lesson for those committed to preserving our freedom.

After independence had been won, many leaders of the new nation wanted to forget all that revolutionary rhetoric so that their state governments would have the same rights previously enjoyed by the king of England. In particular, they wanted the government to grant charters so that they could pick and choose which organizations could be created. Like Thomas Jefferson, many of the Revolutionary-era leaders recognized that the independent voluntary organizations had been essential in defeating the British. They also recognized that such organizations could challenge the new governments just as easily.

Not only that, the men in charge "considered all associations and corporations to be public bodies that must serve the common good." In fact, shortly after throwing off British rule, "states justified denying legal privileges or ideological legitimacy to specific associations when they threatened to fragment the community."[54]

In an especially ironic twist, the state of New Hampshire tried to do to Dartmouth College what the king of England had tried to do to Harvard two centuries earlier. Since the state officials were unhappy with the college, they wanted to take Dartmouth's charter away and claim state ownership of the school. That was too much for the U.S. Supreme Court. It ruled against the state and firmly established the concept that these independent voluntary associations had rights that could not be taken away.[55]

Then, as now, change came from outside the political process. "Only once the state backed off and allowed citizens to organize themselves did a truly vibrant civil society—the kind de Tocqueville witnessed—develop. Between the 1810s and 1840s, this vibrant civil society provided the organizational webs that linked citizens together into an imagined community."[56]

The rhetoric of the revolutionary era had been fully absorbed by the American people of that time. The earliest American citizens "opposed public monopolies and pushed for general incorporation laws. They claimed that no group of individuals deserved special legal privileges from the state. If corporations were to be permitted, all citizens should have equal access to corporate privileges."[57] American colonists had resented it when the king forced them to buy their tea from the Crown-chartered East India Tea Company, and they resented similar efforts by their own government to do the same.

The genie was out of the bottle and there was no putting it back. "Freedom thrives in cultural diversity, in local and regional differentiation ... and above all, in the diversification of power."[58] That was the world created when the United States won its independence from Britain. As a result, the new nation's early political leaders had no more ability than the British to prevent free individuals from voluntarily working together. But the fact that they were willing to try is a sobering reminder of how rare freedom has been in the history of mankind.

In the 21st century, freedom is still the key to empowering everyday Americans. But we too often fail to recognize the source of that freedom. It is not the Constitution or the Bill of Rights. The words promising freedom of speech, press, and religion, the right to bear arms, and freedom from unreasonable search and seizure are an important and valuable part of our national heritage. But the words would be meaningless without a society structured to embrace freedom.

Freedom is not something written on parchment; it is embedded in the very fabric of everyday life. It requires "that there be a large and vibrant private society—a society full of families, churches, businesses, charities, clubs, and teams." Importantly, according to Hillsdale College President Dr. Larry Arnn, "all of these operate independently of government and are able to ask, to paraphrase some famous words, not what their government can do for them but what they can do for their government."[59] Without these independent associations, there can be no freedom.

Despite their vital importance, a Harvard research study found that "only a few historians appear to have been interested in the history of voluntary associations in modern societies."[60] The field is so under-researched that there is not even common agreement on how to define such a group. There are differences of opinion, for example, as to whether churches, unions, businesses, or business trade associations should be included.

That Harvard study was published in 1972 and little has changed since. A 2010 publication from the University of Chicago accused political scientists of "too often overlooking the extra governmental organizations that are critical sites for political mobilization and public provision."[61] It suggested a need for scholars to notice the "networked character of American governance in which voluntary associations and nonprofit organizations play an important part."[62]

Scholars offer a variety of reasons for this lack of attention to a key foundation for our system of governance. Whatever the reason, it has contributed to the dysfunction of our political system and the frustration of the American public.

To move the nation forward, we need to regain the recognition that there is more to governing our nation than politics. Americans have always been free to work together in community and used that freedom to get around unresponsive political systems. We need to use our right to vote but recognize that real empowerment comes from the freedom to choose and the power to walk away.

CHAPTER 4

THERE'S A LOT MORE
TO GOVERNING THAN
GOVERNMENT

E D CATMULL, the founder of Pixar, has spent a lifetime unleashing creativity to develop some of the classic movies of our era—*Toy Story; Monsters, Inc.; Finding Nemo; The Incredibles;* and more. He wrote a great book, *Creativity, Inc.,* describing his journey and passing on valuable lessons for the rest of us.

One of the big takeaways was that our own life experiences make it very difficult to clearly see things that are right in front of us. Catmull wrote of how "only about 40 percent of what we think we 'see' comes in through our eyes."[1] Our brain fills in the rest—60 percent—from memories or patterns that we remember or recognize.

That's why two sports fans cheering for different teams can watch the exact same video and come up with exactly opposite views of the referee's decision. They see what they want to see.

On a more substantive basis, this reality raises questions about the reliability of eyewitness testimony in our legal system. It always looks impressive on TV crime shows and has a big impact on juries, but a fairly large number of people convicted by eyewitness testimony have later been exonerated by DNA evidence.[2]

Different lifestyle experiences lead to wildly different public responses surrounding events like the shooting of Michael Brown in Ferguson, Missouri. When such a story enters the public consciousness, we all tend to "see" what we expect to see. Some believe the teen was shot with his hands in the air, saying, "Don't shoot." Others reject that allegation as dangerous and disproven nonsense.

No matter what evidence is presented, most people will never change their mind. Some see racism at the core of the Ferguson story and view both the police and our system of justice as the villain. Others see law enforcement officers doing a difficult and thankless job to the best of their ability. In that view, the poor choices made by Brown and riotous looters are at fault. Sadly, this same dynamic has played out in many shootings over the past few years.

Because so much of what we "see" is filled in by the way we look at the world, an inaccurate understanding of the way things work can lead to horrific results.

For example, doctors of old had little understanding about how the human body actually worked. Not surprisingly, then, the "cure" they offered was often worse than the disease. By the 19th century, though, human understanding was improving. Louis Pasteur had shown the role of germs in causing disease and Joseph Lister began promoting the value of antiseptics.

We know today that their research fundamentally changed the practice of medicine and provided enormous benefits. However, many experts of the time were dismissive. "In order to successfully practice Mr. Lister's Antiseptic Method," one doctor scoffed, "it is necessary that we should believe, or act as if we believed, the atmosphere to be loaded with germs."[3] This failure to accurately perceive reality had fatal consequences for the 20th president of the United States, James A. Garfield.

On July 2, 1881, Garfield was shot at Union Station in Washington, but the wound itself was "not necessarily fatal." Many soldiers were alive at the time who had survived similar wounds during the Civil War.

"The critical difference between these anonymous men and Garfield was that they had received little if any medical care." The president was attended by leading doctors of the age and other experts. Unfortunately, they didn't accept Pasteur and Lister's new ideas. The president's doctors thought it was essential to find and remove the bullet. So they repeatedly searched for the bullet in his body with unsterilized fingers and equipment. The resulting infection put Garfield in the grave three months after he was shot.[4]

The president's doctors made a bad situation worse because their preconceived notions were wrong. Unfortunately, as we seek to fix America's dysfunctional political system, we are stuck in a similar situation. Our public dialogue is based upon a mistaken notion that is making a bad situation worse.

THE PERNICIOUS PERSPECTIVE OF THE PUBLIC/ PRIVATE DIVIDE

The mistaken notion, deeply embedded in our thought process, is that society is naturally divided into public and private sectors. The public sector is thought of as the vehicle for governing society.

Those who work for the government are called public "servants." They are allegedly concerned with the common good rather than merely looking out for themselves. An article published by the American Society for Public Administration put it this way: "Individuals are drawn to careers in public service, primarily, by a unique set of altruistic motives such as wanting to serve the public interest, effect social change and shape the policies that affect society."[5]

Republicans and Democrats in Washington agree upon very little, but they do agree on this self-serving view of their work. "Public service is a noble endeavor," according to an editorial written by former advisors to Republican George W. Bush and Democrat Edward M. Kennedy. "Most people...get involved because they genuinely want to make a difference for their communities and our country."[6]

This attitude builds on centuries of elite reverence for rulers and disdain for the private sector. That's why it seems so natural. Aristotle thought of politics as a noble profession. Roman rulers became statues and demigods while merchants were low in status. In the Middle Ages, royal families and aristocrats looked down their noses at those who earned their living in the trades rather than toiling in the feudal system.

Part of this was a coping mechanism for the aristocrats. As merchants became wealthy on their own, they had little reason to pledge loyalty to a king or prince. Over centuries, the rise of a merchant class played a key role in undermining the feudal system and stripping royalty of power and privilege. Add in more than a touch of arrogance among those who lived at the top in a *Downton Abbey* world, and it's easy to see why rulers would convince themselves that they were serving the greater good in a way the "nouveau riche" of the private sector could never match.

The for-profit sector is therefore described in less flattering terms. Synonyms for the word "profit" currently include "exploit," "take advantage of," and "make a killing."[7] Karl Marx famously played off such attitudes in his efforts to remake the world. Many intellectuals have shared similar views, helping create the worldview that work in the for-profit sector was somehow less honorable than the government and nonprofit world.

To be fair, the perception of dishonorable private sector activity has been aided by far too many unscrupulous hucksters over the years. Men like Bernie Madoff, whose brazen Ponzi scheme stole billions from investors, do immeasurable damage to the image of the private sector. So do companies like Volkswagen when they cheat on emissions testing.

Such incidents help the myth of the noble public servant persist. One D.C. journalist recently went so far as to suggest that "public officials are the people society trusts to solve society's ills."[8] That's an astounding claim in an era when trust in government officials is at an all-time low. It's also a great example of the fact that most of what we "see" is in fact based upon what we expect to see.

Outside the Washington bubble, we live in a world where people turn to family, friends, and community organizations for help in the aftermath of house fires, hurricanes, and other disasters. It's a world where Americans tend to see community groups, small businesses, and churches as having a positive impact on solving national issues.[9] In terms of helping the country, the public reserves the lowest ratings "for the federal government and the business and political elite."[10]

This is not a new phenomenon. Public cynicism about the real motives of public officials has a long and rich history. Mark Twain famously observed that "it could probably be shown by facts and figures that there is no distinctly native American criminal class except Congress."[11] Most Americans also believe that their own representative in Congress trades votes for cash, that bureaucrats do favors for companies that later reward them with a big contract, and that government workers tend to be underworked and overpaid.

In such a world, how can anyone possibly believe Americans trust public officials to solve society's problems? The answer is that official Washington fills in 60 percent of what they see with a mistaken—and self-serving—notion of how society works. They view themselves as noble public servants guiding the nation and have a hard time seeing the world in any other way.

The truth is that those who work in the "public" sector are no more or less noble than those who work anywhere else.

Collectively, government employees may have a preference for more security and less risk-taking than other workers. Compared with others, they probably have a greater preference for order and a smaller appreciation for the value of freedom. Entrepreneurs and bureaucrats have completely different mindsets (to put it mildly). But those differences do not make one group nobler than the other. Corruption and greed can be found in both the public and the private sectors. So can community spirit and self-sacrificing service.

The problem with dividing the world into public and private sectors is much deeper, however, than just pretending that public servants are somehow superior to those who work in the private sector.

BLURRING THE LINES

One part of the problem is that private companies often provide public services, and public entities often compete in the private sector. Google, for example, enables more people to have more access to information than all the libraries combined in the history of the world. It's a private company providing a public service. Public leadership can also come from the private sector. Samuel Slater, Martin Luther King Jr., Steve Jobs, and Bill Gates all led the nation more than the presidents of their era. None of them ever held a job in the public sector.

On the other side of the coin, the Tennessee Valley Authority (TVA), a government-owned corporation, operates in the private sector by selling electricity to millions of residents in several southern states. What's especially ironic about the TVA is that the core idea was initially proposed as a private venture by Henry Ford. In 1921 he visited Muscle Shoals, Alabama, with his friend Thomas Edison and announced, "I will employ one million workers at Muscle Shoals and I will build a city 75 miles long at Muscle Shoals."[12]

But Senator George Norris from Nebraska hated the idea of a private development effort.[13] "Every stream in the United States that flows from the mountains through the meadows to the sea has the possibility of producing electricity for cheap power and cheap lighting. This natural resource was given by an all-wise Creator to His people and not to organizations of greed."[14]

The Nebraska senator saw a noble public sector and a greedy private sector. Even "where the private sector could help bring the economy back," Norris and other "New Dealers often suppressed it." He felt so strongly about it that he blocked private development efforts and the resulting jobs for more than a decade. Then, "the creation of the Tennessee Valley Authority snuffed out a growing—and potentially successful—effort to light up the South."[15]

You don't have to agree with Norris to recognize that private and public sector entities often provide similar services and compete with each other for the right to do so.

Sometimes, in fact, the lines between the private and public sectors get even blurrier. In Boston, city officials work with Uber, the innovative ride-sharing company. The firm provides a more convenient option to traditional taxi service by allowing customers to order a ride from their smartphone rather than standing in the street and hailing a cab.

In what is likely to become a trendsetting partnership, Uber tracks data on potholes and other traffic issues to help Boston city officials better maintain the roads. The company even draws upon its extensive database to provide information as to when the repairs can be completed with the least disruption to traffic.[16] The end result is that residents get better public service made possible by private technology. Englewood Cliffs (N.J.) Mayor Mario Kranjac describes this as the new normal: "It's only a matter of time until good technology leads to good government."[17]

Such blurred lines between public and private sectors lead to an entirely different perspective about who is more of a public servant. Is it the politician who enriches his friends with special favors or the entrepreneur whose app helps millions take better care of their health? Is it the volunteer at a local food bank or the bureaucrat who proposes new rules to benefit a favored corporation? The answer lies in the service you provide rather than the place where you work.

The single most destructive aspect of dividing the world into public and private sectors, however, is the implication that governing is the responsibility of government alone. Those in politics have a personal interest in promoting this view. By excluding other groups from the governing process, politicians enhance the power of government.

It is in the interest of society at large, however, to have a more complete view of the governing process.

Historically, the word "govern" comes from a nautical Greek term meaning "to steer or pilot a ship." Synonyms include words like "sway, influence, conduct," and "supervise."[18] Such roles are played by both private and public sector entities, along with many personal relationships.

Dictionary definitions of what it means to govern convey the same sense:

- to control or guide the actions of someone or something
- to control, direct, or strongly influence the actions and conduct of
- to exert a determining or guiding influence in or over (income must *govern* expenditure)
- to hold in check
- to prevail or have decisive influence
- to exercise authority[19]

Clearly, there's a lot more to governing than government!

If we are married, our spouse may "control, direct, or strongly influence" our "actions and conduct." Other close family and friends also hold us "in check" and accountable. Their views, too, often "prevail or have decisive influence." At the same time, of course, they also support us, encourage us, guide us, and lend a helping hand when needed.

Moving beyond the family circle, our commitments to employers and community groups play important roles in our lives but also in terms of governing society. They often "exercise authority" and "exert a determining or guiding influence." These relationships help us to be productive members of society.

That's true whether the associations we form are community groups in the traditional geographic sense, online communities, or a workplace. Some groups are as informal as meeting co-workers after work for a beer on Friday afternoons or starting the morning on a power walk with friends. Others are more formal, everything from churches and charities to sports leagues, theater groups, and garden clubs. And, of course, we're just beginning to understand how Facebook groups and other new forms of community fit into this process.

Few think of these ties as having anything to do with governance, but they are absolutely vital to the governing of society. "Communities endowed with a diverse stock of social networks and civic associations are in a stronger position to confront poverty and vulnerability, resolve disputes, and take advantage of new opportunities,"[20] according to *Bowling Alone's* Robert Putnam. Studies have also shown that "social networks, both formal and informal, reduce crime" and have "powerful effects . . . on physical health."[21]

These benefits flow naturally from the associations and relationships of the "irregular" government, and they are the place where community problem-solving reigns supreme. The absence of such community involvement in governing society has clearly negative consequences. After Hurricane Sandy, "neighborhoods lacking in social cohesion and trust generally had a more difficult time recovering."[22]

Additionally, these formal and informal associations are places where people learn about, process, and begin to act upon the news of the day. That includes everything from what the president said the night before, to which companies are hiring or moving away, and who is sick and needs some help to get through. When there is an emergency, these are the groups that mobilize the community by spreading the word and offering a plan of action.

Obviously, there is a need to connect this community governing process with larger state and national policy issues. But as we do so, we must never lose sight of the fact that most governing of society takes place closer to home. On a day-in and day-out basis, the "irregular" government of community relationships plays a bigger role in governing our society than the rules, regulations, and policies of the formal government.

SELF-GOVERNMENT

The differing perspectives were highlighted in a *Washington Post* blog feature a few years back. The author, an assistant professor of political science at George Washington University, quoted me and challenged one of my core beliefs—that the American people don't want to be governed from the left, the right, or even the center. The American people want to govern themselves.

"Do Americans really want to govern themselves?" professor John Sides asked. "There is reason to be doubtful." He cited research showing how unhappy people are with politics as usual but claimed "they don't embrace self-governance." One focus group participant was quoted as saying, "How many of us here want to make a change by going to the government or how many of us can?" Polling data was provided supporting a similar theme.

"There is no question that Americans have lost trust in government," the professor concluded. "It is far less certain, however, that they want to take responsibility for governing themselves."[23]

The fact that people don't want to go to government to make a change is more an indictment of our political process than a commentary on our desire to govern ourselves. Who wants to try and "make a change by going to government" when we know that the system is rigged at every level to benefit political insiders and their friends?

"Evidence of the people's desire to avoid politics is widespread," according to political scientists John R. Hibbing and Elizabeth Theiss-Morse. But political junkies "still find it difficult to take this evidence at face value." The scholars add that "participation in politics is low because people do not like politics even in the best of circumstances."[24]

Just because we don't want to endure the toxic nature of 21st-century politics does not mean that people are unwilling to embrace self-governance. Most Americans are simply unwilling to beat their heads against the wall for nothing. They'd rather use their time in more productive pursuits.

Self-governance is not about going to government and asking someone else to solve your problems. It's a pragmatic all-hands-on-board approach that draws upon family, community groups, businesses, and government to all play a role in governing society. It's focused on working together and getting things done. We all have a role to play and evidence shows we are more than willing to do our part.

The *Washington Post* blogger highlighted just how misleading it can be to view the world narrowly in terms of private and public sectors. It is a mistake to define governing as the responsibility of government alone. Only when you realize that all organizations in society are part of the governing process can you appreciate the self-governing reality of 21st-century America.

In practical terms, self-governance moves with the culture to lead society. Formal governance is simply not designed to play such a role. This reality was highlighted in a 20-year plan released by the Minnesota Department of Transportation in 2013. Not surprisingly, it called for building a lot more roads to handle the state's growing population.[25] However, the report never once mentioned "driverless" or "autonomous" cars. As one local writer noted, that "may turn out to be akin to ignoring horseless carriages in a 20-year transportation plan written in 1903," the year that the Ford Motor Co. was founded.[26]

Looking ahead, research from Columbia University gives a hint of just how much autonomous cars will change public infrastructure needs. It suggests that the next stage in automobiles will allow roads to handle nearly four times as much traffic as they do today with less congestion and more safety.[27]

We don't know if autonomous cars will dominate the market in five, 10, or 20 years. We also don't know what they will do in terms of people's willingness to commute and other lifestyle choices. Perhaps people will move further and further away from center cities as drive time can be put to use productively. Or perhaps they will move to cities as parking issues become less of a hassle. Such details are impossible to predict. What is clear, however, is that the change will come from outside the world of politics and government. Whatever plans the Minnesota Department of Transportation makes will end up in the dustbins of history as the irregular government of community associations shapes the future.

In a world where change comes from outside the political process, it's dangerous to pretend that the "public sector" is guided by noble servants specially ordained to lead society. Political leaders who ignore this reality are as dangerous to our nation as the doctors who ignored the reality of germs were to Garfield.

Evidence of just how dangerous things have become can be found in the high levels of polarization in our political system today. One measure of the polarization is that half-a-century ago "only 5 percent of Republicans, and only 4 percent of Democrats, said they would be upset" if their child "married a member of the other political party." Today those numbers are 49 percent and 33 percent respectively.[28]

Think about that! Republicans today are ten times more likely to be upset by a marriage across party lines than they were a couple of generations ago. Democrats are eight times more likely to be upset. Other data shows similar trends suggesting the partisan opinion of the "other" party have fallen dramatically. Both Republicans and Democrats tend to believe that their own party's actions are motivated by love while the other is motivated by hate.[29]

It's as if many Americans have gone from seeing the other side as a loyal opposition to seeing them as an evil opposition. That was certainly the experience in 2016 when most Americans had an unfavorable opinion of the two leading presidential candidates. The candidates were described as hateful, ruthless and deceitful, and both were accused of criminal behavior by the opposition.

This intensity and vilification of the opposition, the polarization of politics, is the natural result of believing that the world should be divided into public and private sectors. When you believe that the public sector is solely responsible for governing, "'unregulated' is more or less synonymous with 'illegal,'" according to Daniel Hannan, a British representative to the European Parliament. In Parliament, Hannan frequently asks why some new regulation is needed. "Because, comes the answer, there isn't one."[30]

"There seems to be an iron law of bureaucracy," says sociologist Robert Nisbet. "Bureaucrats only tolerate their own processes, and they are inwardly driven to expand them into every corner of social life." They are "secular missionaries with their own handbook for redemption, one which is underpinned by a doctrine of rigorous documentation, calculability, step-by-step itemized planning, and accountability."[31]

The drive of these secular missionaries to expand into every corner of social life pushes politics and government into a larger role in our daily lives. Partisanship doesn't matter so much when the formal government is a distant abstraction and we are generally free to live our lives as we see fit. It matters a lot when the change of government from one party to the other impacts our day-to-day life. It matters even more when nothing can be done to prevent the bureaucrats from imposing their own hand-book for redemption. The more that government assumes sole responsi-bility for governing, the more polarization will increase.

Such polarization is a powerful ingredient in Aaron Wildavsky's "simple recipe for violence." Politicians will always "promise a lot, deliver a little."[32] That's what they do. The false imagery of a public-private sector divide means that politicians have to pretend they are leading the nation and must promise to bring about positive change. But the reality that change comes from outside the political process means that all elected politicians can do is hope the change happens while they're in office.

President Barack Obama learned this lesson on the energy front. He campaigned in opposition to John McCain's call to "Drill Baby Drill." He symbolically rejected the Keystone XL Pipeline and reduced the amount of federal land available for leasing to oil companies. Despite his opposition, new technologies emerged and U.S. oil production soared to record levels during his presidency. Falling oil prices helped the economy, but that benefit was not a result of government leading the way.

If we want to reduce the dangerous intensity and polarization infect-ing our political process today, we need a more balanced and holistic understanding of how society is governed. There is nothing to be gained by arguing about the proper role of the public sector when the entire concept of dividing society into public and private sectors is deeply flawed. We need a different understanding that more accurately fits a world where communities lead and politicians follow. Searching for that understanding became a key part of my journey from pessimism about our political system to optimism about our nation.

I quickly found that many people could accept the idea that the public-private sector imagery does more harm than good, but I had a hard time describing the alternative that I felt in my gut. It wasn't enough to simply highlight the virtues of community problem solving or that the power to walk away is more valuable than the right to vote. I needed something that acknowledged there is more to governing than government without denying the vital importance of government.

CHAPTER 5

FOLLOW THE MONEY

MY SEARCH FOR A HEALTHIER WAY to view society took a giant step forward after discovering the work of William Kornhauser, a former sociology professor at the University of California, Berkeley. His 1959 book, *The Politics of Mass Society*, explored the conditions needed to preserve freedom and democracy and the vulnerabilities which could lead to totalitarianism. To ensure freedom and democracy, he stressed the importance of intermediary organizations between the federal government and individual citizens.

Kornhauser's influential work envisioned three broad levels of society. The first, most basic, level is the very personal—family and close friends. It's our core community. The third level is, essentially, the federal government. The second level is everything in between, even including "local government and the local press."[1] If you were to picture this as a hierarchy, there would be more than 300 million American citizens in the first tier, millions of social networks, companies, towns and associations in the second tier, and a single government (with countless agencies and departments) at the top.

TABLE 1

THE KORNHAUSER MODEL
Federal Government
Intermediary Groups
Family, Friends, Core Community

Kornhauser believed the second tier plays a vital role as a buffer between individual citizens and the government. That seemed to make a lot of sense, and it was confirmed by the views of others. "Some distance between representatives and represented, what George Will refers to as 'constitutional space,' is not a bad thing," according to University of Nebraska professors John Hibbing and Elizabeth Theiss-Morse.[2] Sociologist Robert Nisbet added that "this array of intermediate powers in society" is the only protection we have to maintain "personal freedom and cultural autonomy." Nisbet had an interesting and revealing term for the intermediate powers. He called them "private sovereignties."[3]

Nisbet's terminology gives a quick insight into why those in government get frustrated with such independent groups. Many in Washington believe the federal government deserves all of our sovereign loyalty, but we prefer to share our allegiance with many others. At different times and in different situations, our top loyalty might be to our faith, spouse, job, friends, local community, state, or nation. And, of course, some of the time our top loyalty is also given to the federal government.

While these conflicting loyalties frustrate those at the highest levels of government, having a multitude of diverse private groups is essential. "The great cultural ages of the past were, almost invariably, ages of social diversity, of small independent communities and towns, of distinct regions, of small associations which jealously guarded their unique identities and roles."[4]

The presence of "private sovereignties" drives progress because of their "ceaseless competition for human allegiance."[5] That competition forces every independent organization to meet our needs or else we will walk away. It's what gives us the ability to control private associations large and small. It's also why we have iPhones and Android phones today rather than BlackBerrys.

THE POWER OF CONSUMER CHOICE

BlackBerry was a pioneer in the mobile communications world and introduced the concept to tens of millions of people. For a few years, the company's devices were more than just a means of keeping in touch; they were a status symbol. To have a BlackBerry meant you were important!

Then Apple introduced the iPhone in mid-2007, and consumers soon figured out that the Apple product was better than BlackBerry's. Google entered the competition as well with its Android platform. The result was devastating for the former industry leader. "In September, 2009, Black-Berry led US mobile marketshare [sic] with more than 42 percent." By July 2015, "it had plunged to 1.5 percent."[6]

This sort of thing happens all the time. "Any number of companies that have been said to 'control' a majority of their market have not only lost that market share but have gone bankrupt within a few years of their supposed dominance," according to economist Thomas Sowell. Sometimes, it's changing technology that leaves the company behind. Smith Corona, for example, sold over half the typewriters and word processors in the United States in 1989, but just six years later, it filed for bankruptcy, as the spread of personal computers displaced both typewriters and word processors.[7]

Sometimes it's not new technology, it's just that new competitors offer better products.

Even the biggest of giant corporations can be tamed by consumers demanding a better product.

In 1967, General Motors sold 49 percent of all cars purchased in the United States. John Kenneth Galbraith, a Harvard professor of economics, wrote that GM's position was so dominant that it could no longer be constrained by either consumers or competitors. Galbraith, who served in four presidential administrations, made that claim in a celebrated book, *The New Industrial State*. In his view, the auto firms would never compete with each other because they shared a common interest in soaking the consumer by raising prices.

Eleven years later, Galbraith updated the book and repeated his claim that no other auto company would be foolish enough to take on GM. Why? "Everyone knows that the survivor of such a contest would not be the aggressor but General Motors."[8] The auto giant's market share was still a remarkable 46 percent at that point. It never again reached such lofty heights. In fact, GM's share of the market declined for 29 of the next 36 years, eventually leading it into bankruptcy and a government bailout. It went from selling 46 percent of all cars in 1978 to 35 percent a decade later, 29 percent a decade after that, and just 17 percent in 2014.[9]

What happened? Apparently firms like Toyota, Honda, Nissan, and Hyundai didn't read Galbraith's warning of how they would surely lose by taking on General Motors. In 1978, those firms had a combined 8 percent of U.S. auto sales. Within a decade, that share had doubled to 17 percent and has since doubled again to 35 percent.[10] In recent years, Toyota alone has sold more cars worldwide than GM.[11]

In terms of governing society, consumers with the power to walk away forced manufacturers to build better and safer cars.

WHO'S ON TOP?

There's much more to Kornhauser's middle tier of society, of course, than just competition between corporate giants. There's competition between Little League baseball and soccer, between Presbyterians and Methodists, and between all kinds of organizations desperately seeking our allegiance. In fact, there's even competition across categories. Not only do Presbyterians compete with Methodists, they also compete with Little League baseball and soccer. There is a constant competition for our time, talents and treasure because they need us more than we need them.

The sheer variety of these "private sovereignties" is staggering. The mix includes for-profit companies, nonprofit corporations, and government agencies. It encompasses everything from the local theater group and community blogger to Walmart and Google. But in all cases, large and small, it is our ability to walk away that holds these entities accountable.

As I explored the issues and thought it through, there was much to like about Kornhauser's concept of dividing society into three tiers. It was certainly an improvement over the flawed private-public sector divide, but a couple of things bothered me about it. First, it's upside down. We live in a land where the people are supposed to be sovereign. They should be on top.

So, I flipped Kornhauser's model upside down and expanded the description of the middle tier, as shown in the following table.

TABLE 2

PUTTING PEOPLE FIRST MODEL OF GOVERNANCE
Family, Friends, Core Community
Intermediary Groups, Private Sovereignties, Social Networks, Companies, Local Governments, and Associations
Federal Government

As soon as I saw the "Putting People First" model, I loved the fact that it visually presented the federal government as a foundation upon which a society can be built. That intuitively makes a lot of sense when you think about the foundational role of providing national security, Social Security, and a rule of law that should apply equally to everyone. Without a solid and stable foundation, no society can flourish. This approach defines a vitally important role for government, but it is not the lead role.

With the federal government providing the foundation, the top two tiers represent the places where we do most of our living. With our family, friends, and core community we laugh, love, play, cry, and share. With other groups we work, shop, serve, and go about the business of living. People aren't looking for the feds to make daily decisions for them, but it's reassuring to know that the basics are covered and we are free to build upon that foundation any way we see fit. This intuitively makes sense.

The "Putting People First" model conveys a pair of important truths about a self-governing society.

- First, by putting people and core communities on top, it correctly conveys the truth that "man is not made for the state; the state is made for man."[12] The government exists to serve us, not the other way around.

- Second, the federal government is more distant from— and less responsive to—the American people than every other organization and relationship in society. To empower everyday Americans, we must shift decision-making authority closer to home and further away from the federal government.

The "Putting People First" model highlights the way things work in a free and self-governing society. Everyday Americans are at the top of the decision-making process; distant national politicians and bureaucrats are at the bottom. That's the opposite of what we hear every day from the media and political elites, which is one more reason why the general political dialogue seems out of touch with reality.

As much as I liked the imagery and clarity of the "Putting People First" model, something still seemed incomplete.

REFINING THE MIDDLE

I was troubled by the vast differences between the size, purpose, and structure of organizations in the second tier. How do you define a category that includes local governments, the Salvation Army, and Federal Express? They're the same in some theoretical sense: all are independent of the federal government and all must compete for our attention. But the notion of discussing a local swim club in the same category as the New York Yankees seemed a bit odd. How could they fit together as an alternative to the flawed view of a public sector-private sector divide? How could they help accurately fill in the 60 percent of the world we don't see with our eyes?

On top of that, it soon became apparent that some private businesses really didn't seem to fit in the middle tier. For example, it's hard to call defense contractors like Northrop Grumman independent of the federal government. The firm "derived 90 percent of its 2012 revenue from the U.S. government."[13]

The same is true of General Dynamics, which earned at least two-thirds of its total revenue from U.S. defense contracts. Another 10 percent or so comes from allied defense contracts.[14]

I encountered similar challenges when I looked at nonprofit groups. The Corporation for Public Broadcasting, for example, was created by Congress and receives 96 percent of its funding directly from the federal budget.[15]

Can something owned and funded by the government really be considered independent just because it's set up as a nonprofit corporation?

Any reasonable analysis would suggest that Northrup Grumman, General Dynamics, and the Corporation for Public Broadcasting are more like extensions of government rather than independent organizations.

As if that wasn't enough confusion, the federal government has some agencies that might belong in the middle tier. The U.S. Postal Service and national parks are subsidized through the federal budget but derive significant portions of their revenue from customers.[16]

An even more dramatic example is the Tennessee Valley Authority (TVA). It is a government-owned corporation that does not receive any federal funding. The TVA pays its bills by selling electricity to millions of customers just like a private utility company.[17]

FOLLOW THE MONEY

As I was struggling to make sense of this, official Washington was working itself into a frenzy about the "sequester." This was a program that arose from the fact that our political leaders couldn't agree on a federal budget. They eventually set a deadline so that if no budget was approved, automatic spending "cuts" would go into effect. Actually, the sequester was just a reduction in the growth of federal spending but that was enough to scare both Republicans and Democrats in Washington. Half the growth in spending reductions were to come from defense programs and half from other "discretionary" spending.

Ultimately, no budget deal was reached and official Washington panicked. President Barack Obama warned of "economic catastrophe" if the sequester was allowed to happen. "Yet some of the most influential business organizations ... adopt[ed] a decidedly blasé attitude," according to *Politico*, a publication for Washington insiders. The financial "markets don't seem to care much either."[18]

Why wasn't the business community engaged? "Nobody in America thinks you can't take a couple percentage points out of the federal budget," according to John Engler, president of the Business Roundtable. "If you get five miles outside the Beltway, it's hard to find somebody that cares very deeply about this."[19]

Engler turned out to be right. The sequester was implemented and nobody outside of political circles noticed. The economy didn't collapse.

But one incident in the sequester debacle highlighted the absurdity of dividing the world into public and private sectors. It also helped me figure out how to articulate a more realistic alternative.

A press release claiming an "unprecedented joining of groups across all sectors" of society had joined together to oppose the sequester. The release was issued by a coalition including the giant defense contractor Northrup Grumman, the Association of American Universities, and the Association of Public and Land-grant Universities. Also on the list was a group called NDD United, claiming to represent "diverse interests ... including education and job training, public health and safety, law enforcement, science, natural resources, housing, social services, and infrastructure."[20]

The release echoed the alarmist tone of Obama and other Washington insiders. Sequestration would, they claimed, "threaten to send the economy reeling back into recession and destroy more than two million American jobs." It even suggested that these reductions in spending growth would "cause the United States to fall far behind other nations" like China and India.[21]

The coalition between private businesses and public sector agencies makes no sense for those who believe the mistaken perspective of a public-private sector divide. But it's easy to explain based upon the old adage of "follow the money."

It doesn't matter whether an organization is in the private sector, public sector, or nonprofit sector. It doesn't matter whether it's a corporation, a partnership, a coalition, or a government. It doesn't even matter if it's formally organized or not.

What matters is who writes the checks and provides other support to keep it going. Organizations that depend upon consumers, local volunteers, and individual contributions will serve consumers, local volunteers, and individual contributors. Their loyalty is to the community.

On the other hand, organizations that depend upon the federal government for support end up serving national politicians and bureaucrats. That's what their job requires. Their loyalty is to the government.

WHOM DO YOU SERVE?

This follow-the-money recognition of reality has been part of our nation's history from the beginning. In 1772, as tensions were rising between Britain and its North American colonies, the empire "issued a pair of regulations that altered decades-old practices by ordering that the salaries of governors, judges, and other law officials would henceforth be paid directly by the Crown rather than by the colonies."[22]

Rather than celebrating the fact that the king was going to pick up the tab for these officials, colonial leaders recognized that something more important was at stake. The colonists appropriately feared "that such a change in the source of colonial officials' salaries would lead to a similar shift in the direction of colonial officials' loyalties."[23]

The significance of this threat led colonial leaders to create Committees of Correspondence, a community organization which ended up playing a vital role in winning the War of Independence.

The recognition that he who pays the bills writes the rules goes back a lot further, of course. Jesus taught, "No one can serve two masters. Either you will hate the one and love the other, or you will be devoted to the one and despise the other. You cannot serve both God and money."[24]

We may not like to think of the world in this way, but it's the reality that comes from following the money. The CEO of a defense contractor must keep politicians and bureaucrats happy. The same is true for the CEO of the Corporation for Public Broadcasting.

The CEO of Walmart, however, serves a different master. His job is to keep customers happy. Those who run a local theater group or sports league need to keep their donors, volunteers, and paying customers happy.

In the case of the sequester story, most Americans didn't care too much about it, so the businesses they supported didn't get too excited about it. But the businesses, universities, and trade associations that depended upon the government for funding sounded just like the politicians they served in talking about the evils of the sequester.

The lesson seemed clear. Rather than thinking about the form of an organization—public sector or private—we should be thinking about the substance of whom they serve—community or government. And, we could easily identify whom they serve by following the money.

When I combined this "follow the money" approach with the "Putting People First" model, a more nuanced view of the middle tier emerged. Perhaps something like this:

TABLE 3

PUTTING PEOPLE FIRST MODEL OF GOVERNANCE—VERSION 2
Family, Friends, Core Community
Organizations Heavily Dependent on Community and Consumers ... Organizations Dependent on Mix of Community, Consumers, and Politicians ... Organizations Heavily Dependent on Politicians With Consumer Input
Governments and Associations
Federal Government

In contrast to the phony public-private sector divide, the "Putting People First" model provides a much clearer view of how society is actually governed. It provides a much better way to fill in the 60 percent of any story we can't see with our eyes.

This framework highlights the reality that the core community and the federal government are competing for the loyalty of all the groups in the middle. Whom do those groups serve? Whom do they treat as the sovereign authority?

Some are very responsive to community control because they are dependent almost exclusively on individuals and core community groups. Others are much more dependent on the federal government and are therefore less responsive to community control. Many have mixed loyalties.

Moving decision making to higher levels of authority in a self-governing society means moving it to a larger share of community control.

As the importance of this guiding principle became clear, I began to realize the need to think through how different types of organizations fit into this competition. The result is provided below:

TABLE 4

FOLLOW THE MONEY LEVEL OF COMMUNITY CONTROL		
ASSOCIATION	**TIER**	**COMMUNITY CONTROL**
Family, Friends, Core Community	1	Complete
Local Businesses, Nonprofits, Clubs, Associations, Social Networks	2	Very High
Larger Businesses Dependent Upon Private Customers	2	High
Local Government	2	Moderate to High
Larger, Donor/Consumer-Supported Nonprofits	2	Moderate to High
Businesses Dependent Upon Local Government	2	Low to Moderate
State Government	2	Low to Moderate
Nonprofits Dependent Upon State Government	2	Limited to Moderate
Businesses Dependent Upon State Government	2	Limited to Moderate
Federal Agencies Dependent Upon Private Consumers	3	Limited
Federal Government	3	Very Limited
Nonprofits Dependent Upon Federal Government	3	Extremely Limited
Businesses Dependent Upon Federal Government	3	Extremely Limited

Once again, individuals and communities have more control over organizations near the top of the table. Politicians and bureaucrats have more control over organizations near the bottom.

I suspect that "Follow the Money" table makes intuitive sense to most readers. We have more control over organizations when we have the freedom to choose. We have more control over smaller entities than larger. Groups in the middle have mixed allegiances. State governments, for example, have some degree of responsiveness to the community because people can leave the state. But state governments also depend upon the federal government for 30 percent of their revenue.[25]

This "Follow the Money" table should be viewed as a rough approximation rather than rigid guidelines. For example, smaller local governments may be more responsive than even mid-sized businesses. Those who can run into the mayor at the grocery store know that their voice can be heard! On the other hand, governments of giant cities like New York may be less responsive than many state governments.

The "Follow the Money" table shows clearly that the public-private sector distinction is simply irrelevant. It shows that both public and private sector organizations can be found at all levels of community control. What matters is whether the organization is dependent upon the core community or the federal government for support.

THE DIFFERENCE IT MAKES

This is much more than just a semantic difference. It's a fundamentally different way of looking at the way society is governed. It's the difference between believing that germs were a myth and recognizing the reality of a need for sterilization. A better grasp of reality would have saved President James Garfield's life, and a better grasp of reality is needed today if we want to save our nation.

We must reject the mistaken view that delegates the responsibility for governing society to those in politics and government. We must replace it with an all-hands-on-board, community-driven approach that engages every individual, relationship, and organization in the governing of society.

The contrast is clear and dramatic:

- The traditional, but mistaken, view of public and private sectors implies a top-down system where politicians and designated experts write the rules for everyone else to follow.

- A more realistic view envisions an inclusive democracy guided by countless overlapping social networks that link individuals and families to society at large. These social networks are the key to governing society. They hold companies, organizations, and governments accountable and also provide the platforms needed for us to work together and create a better world.

A second fundamental difference grows out of the recognition that all organizations play a role in governing society.

- In the traditional view, it is simply assumed that those at the top of the public sector pyramid will make the key decisions. The only question that matters is what they decide.

- In the community problem-solving model, all relationships and organizations play a role in governing society. The question of who decides is often more important than what is decided.

These two views are complete opposites. The traditional view places politicians and bureaucrats at the top of the heap and everyday Americans at the bottom. The community-driven approach puts everyday Americans in charge.

The "Putting People First" model and "Follow the Money" table highlight the reality that "who decides?" is the most important question to ask. A free and self-governing society is one where most decisions are made by organizations subject to high levels of community control.

While that concept is clear, in practical terms there is no magically "proper" mix as to who should decide what. Every generation experiences new technology, different economic and lifestyle issues, and a shifting set of global threats. Does it really make sense to base our view of who should decide what upon the model that worked during the Great Depression or World War II? Do we honestly believe that decision-making routines from the snail-mail era should remain unchanged in the 21st century?

WHO DECIDES WHO DECIDES?

Asking not just "'who decides?' but 'who decides who decides?' has been a central theme throughout American history," according to Professor of law Alison L. LaCroix. The University of Chicago scholar shows the debate goes back at least to the 1760s and colonial attempts to "draw the line between the supremacy of Parliament and some modicum of colonial legislative authority."[26] Over the years, as our nation has changed, "the boundaries between proper and improper use of political power were neither rigid nor immutable; they were subject to frequent adjustment."[27] More adjustments are needed today.

Deciding who decides is so important that it's appropriate to look at how the traditional view of top-down governance differs from community-driven governance in a real-world situation.

Consider the upcoming challenge of regulating autonomous cars. The entire concept makes many people nervous, especially older Americans. Currently, only about one out of four Americans are willing to ride in a driverless car.[28] But younger folks are more open to the technology that is about to completely change the automotive landscape.

In fact, the change has already begun. In September 2016, Uber introduced a small fleet of self-driving Ford Fusions for service in Pittsburgh.[29] About six months before that, I enjoyed my first ride in an autonomous car.

In the weeks leading up to my ride, the anticipation was like that of a kid waiting for Christmas morning. But when I shared my enthusiasm with friends and colleagues, many thought I was crazy. A few warned me to make sure my life insurance was paid in full before getting into the car. Others seemed to think I was boarding something like the Starship Enterprise and perhaps envisioned Captain Picard saying "Make it so" as we began the ride.

In reality, the Audi A7 I rode in looked pretty much like any other car on the road. The most amazing thing about the experience was how un-amazing it was. When I thought about it, it seemed a little odd for the car to change lanes on the highway all by itself. But the actual experience of changing lanes was at least as smooth as with any human driver.

In fact, rather than seeming like a great leap forward, the hands-free highway driving felt like just another baby step in a line of continuous progress. Long ago, we made the switch from manual transmissions to automatic. More recently, we've benefited from lane assist technologies and self-parking cars.

I'll admit to being a bit disappointed at how normal it all seemed. I'm ready for a car with no steering wheel and a conference table in the back. But that's the tech geek in me and it'll be a long time before most people are ready to go there. Still, it's easy to recognize that a generation from now, self-driving cars will be the norm. And they will probably look and perform unlike anything we can readily imagine.

The question is how do we get there from here? Obviously, there is a need for some new rules of the road, but who should set them?

The questions involved are complex and, until we have a lot more practical experience, the answers unknowable. Since early testing shows that autonomous vehicles are safer than cars driven by humans, Tesla CEO Elon Musk bluntly asserts that slowing down the introduction of this technology "will kill people."[30] Others, however, worry that moving too fast might reveal a deadly glitch that could have been prevented by more testing.

Beyond safety, other benefits are clear but hard to value. How much is it worth, for example, to increase the mobility of elderly and disabled Americans who are unable to drive on their own?

Who should decide?

History provides limited guidance. "The feds have traditionally regulated the car; the states, the driver," according to Mitch Bainwol, CEO for the Alliance of Automobile Manufacturers. "With autonomy, the car is the driver." That new reality "creates static between federal and state obligations."[31]

The auto industry would like to see the federal government play a bigger role. It's fairly standard for giant corporations to prefer a single set of national rules. Unfortunately, as the "Follow the Money" table shows, there is Very Limited community control over the federal government.

And, as the businesses become dependent upon federal rule-making, community control slips even further to the Extremely Limited level.

Fortunately, the states have generally been taking the lead. "Nevada was the first state to authorize the operation of autonomous vehicles in 2011," according to The National Conference of State Legislatures. "Seven other states—California, Florida, Louisiana, Michigan, North Dakota, Tennessee and Utah—and Washington D.C. have passed legislation related to autonomous vehicles. Governors in Arizona and Massachusetts issued executive orders related to autonomous vehicles."[32] Additionally, some states simply allow the new cars to operate without passing new laws.

Since the states are forced to compete for residents and businesses, this form of regulation allows higher levels of community control. And the benefits of such competition are already visible.

California passed regulations requiring that a passenger must be able to take "immediate physical control" of any autonomous car. In other words, there would have to be someone sitting behind the steering wheel who could take over at any moment to grab the wheel or step on the brakes. On one level, that sounds like a reasonable precaution. On another, though, it represents a major threat to innovation. Google is building cars with no brake pedals and no steering wheel.[33] Such cars are not on public streets in California.[34]

To some, this seems like a reasonable precaution with no downside. That's partly because they're thinking of cars the way they've always been designed.

But there is a huge potential downside to this cautious approach. In the Google vision, people would be freed from the duties of driving and able to focus on more productive activities while moving down the road. Is that something people would want or value? At the moment, there's no way of knowing. There's also no way of knowing whether requiring a human driver to sit behind the wheel would increase or decrease safety. It's certainly possible to imagine that a human grabbing the wheel in a panic could make a bad situation worse.

The California ban on the cars that Google wants to build created an opportunity for Texas. "Google's been testing its cars in Austin, Texas, which welcomes the company's presence and hasn't proposed any rules to restrict it."[35] That's good news, because the only way to measure the potential consumer appeal and safety of Google's approach is through ongoing practical experimentation. Just as iPhone learned from BlackBerry and built a better phone, autonomous car makers will learn from earlier, more limited versions of the product. If the process is governed in a manner that allows for community control, the result will be cars doing more than we can imagine today and doing so with far fewer accidents.

The competition, by the way, has already forced California to allow a little more innovation. A business park wanted to use a completely driverless shuttle bus on a two-mile route that crossed a public road. The California legislature passed a bill allowing for this to take place.[36] It's hard to imagine that would have been done without competition from Texas and other states. And, as the competition heats up, we're likely to see more and more exceptions offered in California over time.

When a state places excessive limits on innovation, it can be held accountable by competition from other states. But there is no such accountability at the federal level, providing lobbyists with a great opportunity to abuse the regulatory process. If all the autonomous driving regulations were written in Washington, D.C., Google's competitors would use the process to gain an advantage over the tech giant. Tesla, for example, is building autonomous cars that fit within California's proposed rules. So, the future design of autonomous cars might come down to a battle between the lobbyists from Google, Tesla, and other auto manufacturers.

Since consumers would only be able to choose from the types of cars approved by regulators, we'd have no way of knowing whether we'd end up with the autonomous car equivalent of a BlackBerry or iPhone. In fact, it's not even clear the standards would measure up to the BlackBerry level of customer satisfaction.

A LIGHT BULB GOES OFF ON REGULATION

That reality was demonstrated a few years back on a far less significant issue—the effective ban on traditional light bulbs.

Advocates of the light bulb regulations claimed that, over the long run, the new bulbs would save money for consumers. Sure, they would cost quite a bit more up front, but experts promised that ongoing energy savings would more than make up for it. One industry group claimed that the new bulbs would save the average U.S. household $100 per year.[37] It's hard to know how such projections addressed the wildly fluctuating cost of energy and many other factors. But the claim raises a key question: If the new bulbs really did benefit consumers, why was a government mandate needed?

If the savings were real, consumers would eventually figure that out and buy the halogen bulbs on their own. Some advocates dismissed this logic by implying that consumers were too stupid to understand. Opposing efforts to repeal the ban, Energy Secretary Steven Chu described it as "taking away a choice that continues to let people waste their own money."[38] Other defenders of the law believed that energy efficiency was such an important goal that our nation couldn't wait until consumers figured it out on their own.

But the real reason for the government action was crony capitalism. It was "pushed by light bulb makers eager to up-sell customers on longer-lasting and much more expensive halogen, compact fluorescent, and LED lighting. When customers balked at paying more for home lighting, General Electric, Sylvania, and Philips did what corporate behemoths always do: They turned to the government for regulation that rigs the market in their favor."[39]

This sort of activity makes society poorer. Jonathan Rauch believes using lobbyists to exact special favors is, from an economic point of view, "like hiring people to steal cars." The scholar explains that "If I hire workers to build cars, the result is new jobs and new cars. But if I hire someone to steal existing cars, I have merely moved a job out of the productive sector and into the car-theft sector."[40]

We all suffer when giant corporations divert resources from the productive sector to stealing from the community by using the power of government. GE and other light bulb producers could easily have introduced the new light bulbs without buying government protection. They could have used their formidable marketing skills and budgets to make the case to consumers that the new bulbs really were better. That would have let everyday Americans and the community at large see for themselves if the promised savings would materialize in the real world. But the companies were apparently unwilling to take such a risk and found it far cheaper to buy government protection. Top-down governance frequently leads to big government and big business working together against the rest of us.

STATE COMPETITION

America, of course, will not stand or fall based upon our ability to buy incandescent light bulbs. But this sort of behavior highlights a larger problem with dividing the world into public and private sectors. By implying that government alone is responsible for problem solving, corporations are encouraged to influence the government rather than serving consumers.

That's why it's important to reject the top-down model of the public-private sector divide and replace it with the more inclusive community problem-solving model. Rather than turning over the key decisions on autonomous cars to distant federal regulators and corporate lobbyists, we should engage state and local governments, private businesses, social networks, and consumers in the decision-making process.

We should be happy that "some states . . . have similar testing regulations to California's. Other states have decided not to regulate autonomous cars for now."[41] California, in effect, adopted Tesla's view that "regulations—or a lack of them—could hinder widespread use of the technology." Other states, for now, have adopted Google's view and "questioned why extra regulations are necessary." In this view, special rules aren't needed "if the vehicles are following existing traffic regulations, and can be demonstrated to do so better than human drivers."[42]

There's no reason to believe state regulators are any wiser or less subject to temptation than their counterparts in the federal government. But the power wielded by state regulators is subject to greater community control than the federal government. The reason is simple: There's competition between the states—competition that gives businesses and residents the power to walk away.

While state-by-state competition is a good start, there's no reason to keep local government out of the action. This is an area where community control is in the Moderate to High range. It's impossible to tell precisely where this would lead, but the possibilities are limitless.

If a state allows autonomous cars but local residents are fearful, towns and cities could be included in the decision-making process by having the ability to ban or restrict the vehicles on local roads. Some local government might create autonomous car only lanes on selected roads or allow driverless cars to operate only in certain parts of the city. If, as some experts predict, autonomous cars would reduce road congestion, cities and towns could encourage their use by making some on-road parking space available only for cars that can park themselves. Others might deploy autonomous cars as the backbone of a more efficient public transportation system. Cities and towns would learn best practices from other communities and shift the rules as experience dictates.

Looking even further down the road, it's possible to envision local control heading even further in that direction. Someday, a big city like New York might even choose to ban human drivers completely.

Entrepreneurs and private companies will have a role to play as well, because every organization plays a role in governing society. It's easy to envision rental car companies and ride-sharing services offering a variety of options. Your ride-sharing app may ask if you want a driver at one price or a driverless car at another price. Rental car companies may charge you one rate for insurance if you do the driving and another if the car drives itself. Insurance companies will set rates based upon actual safety track records. Consumer advocates will watch closely to see whether rates are higher for cars with or without drivers.

Some believe things will go even further and can see cars driving without passengers! Jon Ziglar, the CEO of ParkMobile, believes private parking garages will be the first place most people totally let go. He believes that many people will enjoy the convenience of dropping the car off at the entrance to the garage and letting the car navigate on its own inside.[43] Some garages will allow it, some will ban it, and some will require it. Malls and shopping centers would set their own rules about what kinds of cars they would allow. The rules will change in response to the actual performance of the cars and changing community attitudes.

As things progress, cities might even encourage drive-and-drop policies where the cars drop off their passengers at work and then move to a lot outside the city limits until needed.

All of this information and more will enter into the public domain through the sharing of data, anecdotes and personal experiences across a variety of social networks and community groups. Consumer Reports and other ratings agencies will issue their own assessments. Nonprofit advocacy groups like Mothers Against Drunk Driving may weigh in as well. Who knows? Maybe the AARP will become a leading advocate for autonomous cars because of the safety and mobility benefits they offer to senior citizens.

Importantly, all of these experiments by entrepreneurs, companies, and nonprofit groups will take place in the context of competing for the allegiance of everyday Americans. That provides a Moderate to Very High level of community control. That's what you want to see in a self-governing society. It's an approach that stands in sharp contrast to the Very Limited level of community control that comes from the federal regulatory process.

Obviously, it's impossible to know how this new technology will develop and be adapted. That's really the point. Even if the federal regulatory process were pure, untainted, and completely free of corruption, there's no way any one organization in society could have enough information to wisely govern this process. Public safety could be put at risk by regulators moving either too fast (allowing dangerous technology on the roads) or too slow (preventing safer cars from being allowed on the roads). Other benefits and risks will be ignored or overlooked.

THE PRETENSE OF KNOWLEDGE

When we look at an issue like the regulation of autonomous cars, the key is not the way we view the technology, it's the way we view the governing process. With so much at stake, it's important to move the decision making as far up the ladder as possible toward community control.

This approach makes people who believe in traditional public-private sector divide nervous. Cass Sunstein, who served as White House Office of Information and Regulatory Affairs administrator, is so committed to top-down governance that he opposes the ability of judges to limit the actions of the president. "The interpretation of federal law should be made not by judges but by the beliefs and commitments of the U.S. president and those around him."[44]

The former regulatory czar frequently writes about "Why Paternalism Is Your Friend"[45] and similar themes. "Government does not believe that people's choices will promote their welfare, and it is taking steps to influence or alter people's choices for their own good." This suggests that it's a mistake to let ordinary people decide for themselves (just like Energy Secretary Chu's comments on the light bulb ban). In fact, Sunstein states directly that if we're really concerned about what's best for everyday Americans, "soft paternalism might be required, not forbidden."[46]

The belief that federal experts should be required to alter our decisions for our own good reflects an arrogant, aristocratic view of the world and is a complete rejection of the American Creed. That Creed is a belief that we all have the right to do what we want with our own lives so long as we don't interfere with the rights of others to do the same. It is an attitude still embraced by the American people today, brimming with optimism about what a free and self-governing people can accomplish. "No other country has a set of key principles and statements to which its citizens adhere to the same degree that Americans adhere to the principles of 'life, liberty and the pursuit of happiness.'"[47]

On the other hand, community problem solving is entirely consistent with the Creed recognizing that freedom's greatest value can be found when used to build community.

One explanation for why so many in the political elite have come to reject the American Creed's embrace of self-governance is provided by economist Sowell. "Many intellectuals and their followers have been unduly impressed by the fact that highly educated elites like themselves have far more knowledge per capita . . . than does the population at large."[48] They are better educated than most of us, so they mistakenly believe that they will make better decisions for the rest of us.

Sowell notes, however, that "they have often overlooked the crucial fact that the population at large may have vastly more total knowledge . . . than the elites." The challenge is that the "knowledge is scattered in individually unimpressive fragments among vast numbers of people."[49] There are also different types of knowledge. The elites clearly have more book smarts than everyday Americans, but it's a mistake to dismiss the great value of street smarts and common-sense wisdom learned from practical experience.

When we limit decision making to experts, we ignore the vast majority of information available to society at large. Whether it's autonomous cars or any other topic, the elites simply don't have the knowledge they need to make practical decisions.

An all-hands-on-board approach that engages all the resources of the community produces better results because it taps into the vast amount of knowledge that exists collectively among more than 300 million Americans. Fortunately, we live in a time when technology is making the crowdsourcing of information more practical on a day-to-day basis.

Only one essential step is required to put this knowledge to use: We must prevent a federal monopoly on the regulation of autonomous cars (and other issues). In the top-down, public-private sector way of looking at the world, this is called limiting government or deregulation. In the more realistic community problem-solving view of the world, those terms don't apply.

EXPANDING GOVERNING, NOT GOVERNMENT

Preventing the federal government from monopolizing the regulatory process is not limiting government; it's expanding the governing process by drawing all sectors of society together to regulate an industry. It's giving us a chance to tap into all the knowledge of society rather than the limited knowledge of government-appointed experts. It's shifting the responsibility for governing from an arena with virtually no community control to an arena with high levels of community control.

This approach accepts the reality that only 40 percent of what we see comes in through our eyes and that we need to work together to grasp the whole picture. It creates a learning environment where we constantly gain new knowledge through experimentation. As different businesses, nonprofits, and governments try different things, we will eventually learn and implement best practices.

On an issue like autonomous cars, most states will eventually adopt similar guidelines to create a national standard. But there's no need to force common guidelines before we know what the best practices are and what the standards should be.

For those who like everything tied up neatly in a logical manner, this will seem a bit chaotic along the way. People will laugh at states that lag behind and express concern over states that are moving a bit too fast. Even when a national standard emerges, there will almost certainly be some states with quirky exceptions to the national norm. For example, I currently live in New Jersey, one of two states (the other being Oregon) that prohibit individuals from pumping their own gas. It's a bit odd, but not that big a deal. The only real impact is that when driving in other states, I sometimes sit in the car waiting for someone to come fill the tank. After a moment of embarrassment, I get out and do it myself.

In the interest of maintaining a learning society, it's better to allow such minor oddities rather than demanding a single set of rules imposed by the organization least responsive to community control—the federal government.

When we accept that all organizations and relationships play a role in the governing process, we see the world in a much more realistic light. By following the money, we can see which organizations serve everyday Americans and the core community, and which organizations serve politicians and the federal government.

Whenever possible, we should push decision making to the highest possible level of community control. That allows us to tap into all the knowledge of society and move decision making to the people with the most relevant information. It also adds to our store of knowledge through the process of experimentation and competition.

At the same time, we must recognize that some decisions are inappropriate for community control. Military deployments are but one obvious example. Additionally, there is a natural tension in the process. Politicians and bureaucrats will always prefer to drag the decision-making process away from the accountability that community control provides. Sometimes the political desire for more control will be legitimate, sometimes it will be self-serving, and sometimes it will be driven by well-connected corporations seeking special favors. Regardless of the motive, those who believe politics should decide everything will promote the false claim that government alone is responsible for governing.

The result is that the most important governing question on any issue is the question of who decides. If we get that right, everything else will fall into place. That's true whether we're discussing autonomous cars, light bulbs, the minimum wage, education, health care, or any other issue.

This community-driven approach explains how I can be optimistic about our nation while being so pessimistic about our system of politics and government. It's because most of our day-to-day living is done in organizations where community control is highest. These are the relationships and organizations on the front line of governing society—our ties with family, friends, and our core community. It's filled with the places we work, shop, play, learn, worship, celebrate, and hang out.

No matter how unresponsive our political system becomes, these organizations remain responsive to everyday Americans. This vibrant mix of community organizations is also a powerful force moving the nation forward. It's the same force that in our nation's past led to independence, women's suffrage, the civil rights movement, the creation of 401(k) plans, smartphones, and the entire digital revolution.

CHAPTER 6

THE GREAT TURNAROUND THAT GOT US MOVING IN THE RIGHT DIRECTION

S OCIETAL CHANGES take place so slowly that we rarely see them unfold on a day-to-day basis. Our culture and lifestyles adapt so quickly to new technology that we soon can't remember life without the latest innovation. But when we look back over any significant period of time, the scale of change is truly breathtaking.

My grandfather was born at the dawn of the age of electricity and automobiles. Airplanes and radio had yet to be invented, but he lived to see a man land safely on the moon and watch the event broadcast live on television from Tranquility Base. Before he left this earth, I was even able to show Grampa my first "portable" computer—a Compaq machine so "small" it could fit under the seat in front of me on an airplane (barely)!

That scale of change in a single lifetime used to stun me.

Now, along with other baby boomers, I've reached the age where I can look back and see a similar transformation during my own life. I grew up in a world without email and where mobile phones were found only in Dick Tracy's comic strip or in Maxwell Smart's shoe. Boomers like me also remember record players before stereo, black-and-white television, and waiting three days for photos to be developed. In the days when I transitioned from a teenager to young adult, most communities had one newspaper and maybe three television stations. Only 6 percent of all households had cable TV,[1] and it wasn't even available in about a dozen states![2]

Living through the '70s, we had no idea what was coming next. As Apple and Microsoft were being created, my college computer science class was still teaching us to use punch cards! A special machine punched holes on these stiff 7 3/8-inch-by-3 ¼-inch cards to essentially write a single line of code per card. The cards were then placed in a stack and fed into a computer through a card reader in a giant lab. Scheduling lab time was nearly impossible, so turnaround times for even the simplest of programs were measured in days or weeks.

Archaic as it seems, IBM claims its cards held "nearly all of the world's known information for just under half a century."[3] Still, by the end of the '70s, it was possible to see faint hints of the changes to come—I had an Atari "computer" in my home and used it to play primitive video games. Overall, about a million personal computers were in use before the decade came to an end.[4]

At the time, we saw baby steps—the transition from pinball to pong—but couldn't imagine the bigger picture. With our three local TV stations, we could not begin to conceive of today's world where the average household receives 189 channels and routinely watches 17.[5] We weren't the only ones who didn't see it coming. In 1977, the head of a leading computer firm famously declared, "There is no reason anyone would want a computer in their home."[6]

Only in retrospect did it become clear how completely the new technologies would reinvent every aspect of our lives. In the '70s, without knowing it, we were experiencing the end of the Industrial Revolution and the beginning of the most significant cultural change in American history. The digital revolution kicked off what I call the Great Turnaround:

For two centuries leading up to the 1970s, the trend was for everything in America to get bigger, more centralized, and more homogenized.

- For two centuries leading up to the 1970s, the trend was for everything in America to get bigger, more centralized, and more homogenized.

- After the '70s, however, cultural trends moved in the opposite direction with everything becoming more niche-oriented, decentralized and personalized.

This Great Turnaround moved us from the industrial world, kick-started by Samuel Slater, to the digital world birthed by Steve Jobs and Bill Gates. In a world where culture leads and politicians lag behind, it is virtually impossible to overstate the significance of that change. Political leaders were happy to follow society at large when it led to a growing government with more power and money. They are not nearly as enthusiastic about the ongoing decentralization that is constantly shifting power from the dysfunctional political system to vibrant centers of society.

For me, though, coming to grips with this Great Turnaround helped overcome my despair about the fact that our political system is broken beyond repair. The more I realized power is shifting to other organizations and relationships, the more optimistic I became about America's future. That was especially true as I realized that the Turnaround had put our nation back on the path to realizing our highest founding ideals.

Thinking about it in terms of the "Putting People First" model, the centuries of growing centralization shifted power away from everyday Americans and put more of it in the hands of distant politicians and bureaucrats. By the 1970s, governing power was concentrated in a dangerously small number of hands.

But since the '70s, decentralization and the tools of the digital revolution have reversed that trend and are shifting power back up to higher levels of community control. That's a tremendously important and often underappreciated benefit of the new era.

It's essential to recognize that these trends were deeply rooted in every aspect of society, not just the world of technology.

What, for example, could be a better measure of the popular culture than beer? In 1876, the U.S. had 4,131 breweries to quench the national thirst. However, the forces of consolidation and centralization drove that number down steadily for a full century. In the pivotal decade of the 1970s, the number of breweries sank to just 89, an all-time low. But, then society's Great Turnaround kicked in and the number of breweries began to grow again. Rather than just choosing between one of a few national brands, beer drinkers today have a dizzying assortment of craft beers and local options. As a result, the nation recently surpassed the 19th-century totals and boasts more breweries than ever.[7]

The graph highlighting these trends is a good approximation for what has happened throughout all of society. Consumers were given fewer and fewer options year-in and year-out until the Great Turnaround began. Since then, however, an ever-increasing number of choices has given everyday Americans more control. That's been the encouraging story of recent decades.

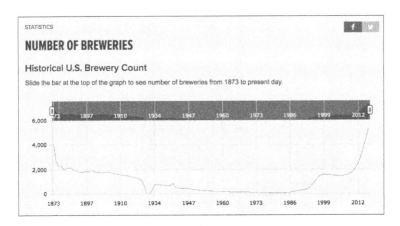

The table above actually understates the explosion of options available to consumers. In addition to the growing number of breweries, more than a million Americans have brewed their own beer at home.[8]

The fact that we now have more options in every aspect of our lives empowers everyday Americans and makes it possible to become the free and self-governing society that our Founders talked about. Obviously, they could never have imagined the digital revolution or the diverse and inclusive society we now enjoy. Our expectations and cultural norms are vastly different from their 18th-century lifestyle and the world of tweets, social media, and Googling would undoubtedly throw the Founders for a loop.

But, despite all the progress and surface differences, the underlying spirit driving the Great Turnaround is the same spirit that animated the founding of our nation. The new tech devices enhance our life, liberty, and pursuit of happiness. By empowering us to both meet our own needs and engage in community problem solving, they help our nation live out what Thomas Jefferson long ago called the spirit of '76. It's the democratizing of every aspect of society.

It took a while, but I eventually realized that the Great Turnaround put us back on the path reaching for our founding ideals because the tech innovators wrestled with the same question as the political innovators who founded our nation—who decides? In the late 18th century, the question was whether decisions should be made in a distant capital or closer to home. In the modern era, it became a question of who decides what the computers will do.

Before the Great Turnaround, computers were the tools of large organizations and huge bureaucracies. In contrast, as Harvard's Nicco Mele observed, the new technology was designed to "empower the individual at the expense of existing institutions."[9] We have the power to decide for ourselves how our own computers will be used. By letting everybody decide for themselves, the tech giants empowered all of us in ways that have fundamentally reshaped society.

As with all societal changes, we have adapted so quickly to the new technology that we have trouble grasping what came before. Before the Great Turnaround, most people first encountered computers in connection with the Census Bureau and other government agencies. They were also a key part of the backstory in the race to the moon.

But when John Glenn became the first American to orbit the earth, there was no computer on board in his Mercury capsule. Why? As NASA historians describe the reality of the early '60s: "Expensive to purchase and operate, the giant computer needed a small army of technicians in constant attendance to keep it running."[10] Such a cumbersome device simply couldn't fit or function in a small space capsule.

The realities of early computers are why economists like John Kenneth Galbraith thought that large organizations like General Motors could never be challenged. For him, technology explained both "the need and the opportunity for the large business organization. It alone can deploy the requisite capital; it alone can mobilize the requisite skills." Galbraith made the case that all innovation would come from such large organizations. In fact, shortly after Jobs and Gates dropped out of college to develop a pair of innovative companies, Galbraith wrote, "There is no case that such innovation will come better from the little man."[11]

Galbraith was not alone. Public perceptions saw computers as giving power to big government and big business to encourage uniformity.

George Orwell cemented this imagery with his classic novel *1984*, which gave us a vocabulary of skepticism still in use today; words like Big Brother, thought crime, memory hole, and Orwellian. The hero of the story worked for the so-called Ministry of Truth. His job was actually to destroy truth by revising history so that it matched whatever the political leaders were saying at the time.

Orwell was far from the only writer stoking such fears. Arthur C. Clarke wrote of alien Overlords who used anonymous computers to administer the earth,[12] while Dennis Feltham Jones envisioned a pair of giant computers controlling the nuclear arsenals of both the U.S. and the Soviet Union. His story eventually became a movie and the computers merged to take over the world.[13] It was a common literary and cultural theme.

Scholars weren't as dramatic, but they also conveyed the message that the United States had become what Cornell's Robert Vance Presthus called an Organizational Society.[14] In that world, the computer and humans alike served the large organization and many feared that meant "people had to change their ways to suit the machines."[15] A University of California sociology professor, Charles Michael Otten, wrote that "the very way we think is dependent upon the products and information processed by large organizations."[16]

Brown University's Steven Lubar observed that punch cards like those I used in computer lab somehow became a "symbol of alienation. They stood for abstraction, oversimplification, and dehumanization."[17] They even earned a prominent place in the storyline of the mid-'60s Berkeley free speech movement. One of the movement leaders, Mario Savio, "wrote that individuals were processed by the university, emerging as IBM cards with degrees."[18] Similar references were commonplace both in the movement and society at large.

In truth, it wasn't really the punch cards or even the computers that were dehumanizing society. It was the bureaucracies they served. Faced with such a powerful foe as the large, computer-driven organization, the response of Savio and many others was to try and break the machine. On December 2, 1964, the 22-year-old student activist gave what became a famous speech from the steps of a building on the Berkeley campus:

> There's a time when the operation of the machine becomes so odious, it makes you so sick at the heart, that...you've got to put your bodies upon the gears and upon wheels...and you've got to make it stop. And you've got to indicate to the people who run it, to the people who own it, that unless you're free, the machine will be prevented from working at all.[19]

As if to confirm everything that Savio and his colleagues feared, he and hundreds of others were arrested following that speech. Not only that, he and his wife were subjected to obnoxious and improper surveillance by the FBI for more than a decade. Newspaper reports years later found that "bureau officials plotted to 'neutralize' him politically—even though there was no evidence he broke any federal law." The IRS piled on as well, illegally turning over his tax records.[20]

Unfortunately, there was nothing Savio and others could do to bring about lasting change in a world where computers served only large organizations. In such a world, Orwell's vision of Big Brother could easily have become reality.

LEVELING THE PLAYING FIELD

Today, of course, we still have problems such as the NSA's unauthorized spying on everyday Americans. But, the playing field is no longer one-sided. Shortly after the revelations of NSA abuse, any concerned citizen could find articles like "10 Apps to Keep the NSA Out of Your Phone."[21] Additionally, Apple and Android phones began offering "smartphone encryption so secure that law enforcement officials cannot easily gain access to information stored on the devices."[22] On top of all that, our devices can also be used to turn the table and keep tabs on Big Brother as well.

This community-driven response to inappropriate government actions clearly highlights the value of having "private sovereignties" that are not dependent upon the government. Then-FBI Director James B. Comey was outraged that Apple and Google served their customers by keeping their smartphone information private, but he acknowledged the public demand for such protection: "Encryption isn't just a technical feature; it's a marketing pitch." Comey complained that by addressing real-world concerns about governmental invasions of privacy, the tech industry "threatens to lead all of us to a very dark place."[23] Fortunately for all of us, Apple and Google are financially dependent on hundreds of millions of people rather than a single government agency.

I have no doubt that Comey was sincere when he said, "Justice may be denied because of a locked phone or an encrypted hard drive."[24]But we live in a world where, among other things, government agents have used their spying power on love interests.[25] Locked phones, a community-driven solution, often prevent the denial of justice and abuse of power. Rather than chastising companies for providing a solution, the FBI director should seek to change the behavior of his agency so that it can earn the trust of those it claims to serve.

Before the Great Turnaround put the power of the computer into everyone's hands, the FBI had no such problems. It was able to do what it pleased with people it considered a threat—anyone from Mario Savio to John Lennon. The Encyclopedia Britannica reminds us that longtime FBI Director J. Edgar Hoover

> habitually used the FBI's enormous surveillance and informa-tion-gathering powers to collect damaging information on politicians throughout the country, and he kept the most scurrilous data under his own personal control. He used his possession of these secret files to maintain himself as the FBI's director and was apparently able to intimidate even sitting presidents by threatening to leak damaging disclosures about them.[26]

But the transition of power away from large secretive organizations took a huge step forward less than six months before Hoover died. While hardly anybody noticed at the time, an ad appeared in the November 15, 1971, edition of *Electronic News* announcing "a new era of integrated electronics."[27] The ad was placed not by some large organization with a dominant role in society, but by a three-year-old innovative start-up named Intel. Their team had created the first commercially available microprocessor. It was "the size of a little fingernail" but "delivered the same computing power as the first electronic computer built in 1946." That first computer had filled an entire room.[28]

The microprocessor was a game changer. It made possible new technology that would bring an end to a one-size-fits-all organizational society. The Great Turnaround was just beginning. Rather than serving giant bureaucracies in government or large corporations, the stage was set for computers to empower everyday Americans.

Without the microprocessor, all someone like Savio could do was try to mess up the gears and prevent the machine from working. But with Intel's innovation, Jobs and Gates were able to bring power to the people through a vastly different approach. Rather than "making it stop," Apple and Microsoft made it possible for everyone to own and run their own machine.

DEMOCRATIZING TECHNOLOGY

It took a long time, of course, before all this became clear. In fact, the first visible impact of the Great Turnaround had little to do with computers. In 1975, RCA (Radio Corporation of America) placed the first commercial geostationary communications satellite into orbit—Satcom 1.[29] Among other things, this innovation dramatically lowered the cost of distributing television programming. When we were launching ESPN, I calculated that it cost less to send a signal around the country via satellite than it cost to send the same signal around a small state like Connecticut via traditional land lines.

Just four years after Satcom 1 was launched, ESPN went on the air, followed quickly by CNN, MTV, and countless other networks. When that satellite was launched, the Big Three networks (ABC, NBC, and CBS) attracted 94 percent of the prime-time audience.[30] Today, that figure is down to less than 15 percent.[31] Confirming the overall trend of decentralization, the audience for network television news peaked when the cable networks arrived and have been declining ever since.[32] Even the much-hyped first debate between Donald Trump and Hillary Clinton attracted a much smaller share of the television audience than the 1980 matchup between Ronald Reagan and Jimmy Carter.[33]

While television was the most visible cultural transformation in the early days of the new era, the larger changes continued to percolate just beneath the surface. Personal computers got smaller, more powerful, and more common. While only about 1 percent of homes had a computer in 1980, that figure quickly grew to 15 percent by 1990.[34] Then, the internet arrived in the mid-'90s and things really took off. By the year 2000, 51 percent had a computer in their home, and 75 percent a decade later.[35]

A different way of grasping the sweeping scope of change is to realize that the initial budget projections I calculated for ESPN were done by hand on paper using 13-column analysis pads. At the time, computers were still in the service of large corporations and entrepreneurs didn't have access to personal computers capable of such a task.

Now, of course, we've moved well beyond desktop computers into an amazing world of mobile communications. YouTube on mobile devices alone already reaches more adults under 50 than any cable channel.[36] We watch what we want, when we want, and on whatever device we want.

And the latest wave of change is just getting started. Legendary internet pioneer and tech investor Marc Andreessen sees a future where even smartphones will be a thing of the past.

> The idea that we have a single piece of glowing display is too limiting. ... In 20 years, every physical item will have a chip implanted in it. ... By then, every table, every wall, every surface will have a screen or can project. ... Hypothetically you walk up to a wall, sit at a table and [talk to] an earpiece or eyeglasses to make a call. The term is ambient or ubiquitous computing.[37]

Regardless of precisely what the world looks like in twenty years, there is no doubt that society will continue to become ever more decentralized and personalized. There will, of course, be efforts by both corporations and governments to steal and monopolize this information, but consumers will find ways to protect themselves with encrypted phones and other innovations. The trends that began with the Great Turnaround of the 1970s will continue to work their way through every aspect of American society for many years to come.

These trends are enabling us to come closer than ever before to reaching the high ideals of America's founding. In terms of the "Putting People First" model, the Digital Revolution helps move decision making away from the federal government up to ever higher levels of community control.

It's important to recognize, however, that the digital revolution did not create the society of the early 21st century. We, the people, created it and are continuing the culture and the society that we live in. For better or worse, it's up to us. All the tech innovators did was give us the tools so that we could decide for ourselves.

EXPERIENCING THE GREAT TURNAROUND

Over the years, friends have pointed out that I tend to be more enthusiastic about new technology than others. I loved NASA's race to the moon in my youth. I am probably a bit of an early adapter and have tapped into new technologies throughout my entrepreneurial career. I'm also aware that most Americans did not have a home computer for a full quarter century after the Great Turnaround began. Many don't connect the cultural changes of recent decades with the more personalized technology that began to emerge in the 1970s.

With this in mind, it's important to acknowledge that what matters is not the technology, but the way it is used. No matter how many tech toys a producer or director has at their disposal, a good movie still depends upon a good story well told. I was working at a local TV station when the very first *Star Wars* movie came out in the late '70s, and I can still remember the awe in our director's voice when she described the special effects breakthroughs of that film. But the special effects don't look all that special today. It was the story of Luke Skywalker, Han Solo, and Princess Leia that made the movie into a blockbuster franchise.

The personal experience is far more important than the underlying technology. An older woman recently welcomed everybody to our local church by excitedly telling us all that her brand-new car parks itself. When describing the excitement of hearing the car ask her to remove her hands from the steering wheel, she put a smile on everyone's face. In addition to the fun of it all, there was also a pragmatic angle to her enthusiasm. We live in a town where almost all parking is done on narrow streets and it's sometimes difficult to squeeze into tight spaces. She no longer had to worry about that particular daily challenge.

It is through people like that woman, not tech geeks, that technology empowers us to reinvent society. In fact, technology only moves the nation forward when it addresses the practical, day-to-day needs of society.

For example, 29 million Americans have diabetes. Most get it as they age, but there are currently 208,000 people under age twenty who will live their entire life with this condition. The implications are significant. "People with diabetes are at increased risk of serious health complications including vision loss, heart disease, stroke, kidney failure, amputation of toes, feet or legs, and premature death," according to the Centers for Disease Control (CDC). But it "can be managed through physical activity, diet, and appropriate use of insulin and oral medications to lower blood sugar levels."[38]

Because the stakes are so high, researchers have long sought ways to monitor the blood sugars of people with diabetes. The first blood glucometer to do so was created in 1969, just before the Great Turnaround. But it was expensive and only available to hospitals and doctors. That helped a bit, but going to a medical center every ninety days to get your blood sugar checked was both inconvenient and not very useful in monitoring day-to-day activities. After the '70s, glucose meters became available for personal use.[39] A woman with diabetes could check her blood sugar throughout the day to guide her insulin intake and adjust her diet. The end result of putting a glucose meter in her hand did far more than just empower better management of her health; it led to a vastly improved lifestyle for her and millions of other Americans.

I know about this firsthand because I was diagnosed with diabetes in my forties and now check my own blood sugar every morning. It had a huge impact on my own health because the self-monitoring helped guide me to a healthier lifestyle. I've lost weight, exercise more, and eat a little better (even if that only means ordering fruit with my cheeseburger instead of fries). Even more, though, I know how much this technology has done for others close to me; people who have had diabetes since childhood. For them, the lifestyle improvements are staggering, aided not only by glucose meters but ongoing advancements including insulin pumps.

The point is that people with diabetes experienced the Great Turn-around without even thinking about Intel, Apple, and Microsoft. Because of their need for better management of blood sugars, the technology was adapted to serve them. This was exactly the opposite of the '60s fear that "people had to change their ways to suit the machines."

THE BLESSINGS OF DECENTRALIZED POWER

The Great Turnaround even made possible countless improvements in areas of life having absolutely nothing to do with technology. Before the turnaround, a top-down organizational society with only three television networks and J. Edgar Hoover's FBI created a one-size fits all homoge-nous culture. In that world, those who didn't agree with the bureaucrats and conform to the dominant culture got harassed.

In 1974, I spent a year selling ladies' shoes in a G. Fox department store. We had a small group of full-time workers and a few regular "con-tingents" who socialized together and became friends. Most were women, but Tony was the first openly gay man I had ever met. Being openly gay in the mid-'70s was definitely unconventional and fairly brave, especially in small-town Connecticut.

In those days, I drove to the Jersey Shore on weekends, and Tony rode along one time so I could drop him off at a friend's. Leaving straight from work, we stopped for dinner at the Howard Johnson's off exit 7 in Dan-bury. It was my traditional stopping point, partly because it was halfway, and primarily because a crushworthy girl from the Shore worked there.

When Tony and I were seated for dinner, a nearby booth full of young guys began mocking and taunting us. I hate to say it, but my first visceral reaction was that they should know I wasn't gay. I was there to flirt with a waitress! But the jerks wouldn't let up and I grew angrier and angrier at the way they were treating my friend. For Tony, it was nothing new. He pretended not to notice and remained classy throughout. So, I followed his lead. We simply had dinner together, continued our conversation, and went on our way.

The worst part of the episode was realizing that the hatred I experienced for a single meal was horrifyingly normal for Tony. In fact, he had experienced far worse. For me, it was an unforgettable lesson.

Fortunately, things have changed dramatically over the past four decades. Tony and I would not experience the same reaction walking into that Howard Johnson's today. We'd be far less likely to encounter people with the same hateful attitude. And, if we did, society has changed so much that they would probably keep their comments to themselves (or risk being humiliated on YouTube).

It's important to recognize that this change in societal attitudes was made possible by the Great Turnaround and decentralization of power.

Whenever any one person or group holds centralized power and sets the rules for everyone else, divergent views and lifestyles are threatened. It is only in a world of decentralized power that we can truly be free to live our lives as we desire. In the words of a recent Android commercial campaign, the Great Turnaround created the environment that allows us to "be together, not the same."[40]

THE TIP OF THE ICEBERG

Like an iceberg, most of the impact from the Great Turnaround is hidden from sight.

In 1974, the world's first Role-Playing-Game (RPG) was created—*Dungeons and Dragons*. It sold only a thousand copies during the first year, but soon acquired a cult following and has grown to generate more than a billion dollars in book and equipment sales.[41] Even more, it sparked an entire gaming industry. *World of Warcraft* was created in 2004, and it has already generated more than $10 billion in sales.[42] Over 100 million people around the world have set up a *World of Warcraft* account, and there are nearly 3 million player trades every day.[43] Interest in the genre is so strong that a crowdfunding site features more than 1,300 independent developers raising funds to create similar games.[44]

Not everyone will view the development of a new gaming genre as a big deal, but it's another part of our modern society that would not have been possible before the Great Turnaround. Rather than an isolated group of people longing for a collaborative story-telling experience, the new technology empowered the creation of large gaming communities without geographic limitations.

I don't particularly enjoy RPGs, but I'm glad those who do have a chance to enjoy the experience. Beyond that, I'm grateful for a spinoff that emerged in the gaming culture. When my older son moved away, he gave me a PlayStation as a parting gift. A lot of my friends found that a bit odd, but it was wonderful. Even though he is in Texas and I'm in New Jersey, we can log on, play a game together, and chat through headsets. It's a great way to keep in touch (and I especially cherish the very rare occasions when I win a game).

The cultural impact of the Great Turnaround goes way beyond issues of improving health, showing respect for people who aren't just like us, or offering more options to relax together and keep in touch. It's felt in every nook and cranny of society. Internet guru Mary Meeker reports that 86 percent of cell phone users have used their device for turn-by-turn driving instructions. Nearly as many have used their phones for breaking news updates and learning about activities in their own community. A third of all workers now engage in freelance work and 65 percent of them say the internet makes it easier for them to find new jobs.[45]

CONCLUSION

For those of us who lived through the '70s though, the most startling thing about the Great Turnaround is that most Americans alive today were born in an era when niche-marketing, decentralization, and personalization were the norm. They never experienced the top-down organizational society that enabled three television networks to control 94 percent of the prime-time audience. They can't imagine a world where network executives tell us what to watch and when.

But an understanding of how much things have turned around is essential to grasping the political dynamics of the early 21st century. Thinking of it from the "Putting People First" model of governance, it's great that the new technologies are shifting power to ever higher levels of community control.

But not everyone appreciates the change. Unfortunately, as Martin Luther King Jr. wrote, "no one gives up his privileges without strong resistance."[46]

During the Montgomery bus boycott, King was arrested for going 30 miles per hour in a 25 miles-per-hour zone.[47] To be clear, he was not fined or given a ticket. He was arrested and taken to jail. King became a convicted criminal, but one who "was proud of my crime ... It was the crime of desiring for my people the unalienable rights of life, liberty, and the pursuit of happiness."[48]

Later, after desegregation of the bus lines was ordered by the courts, the white political leaders of Montgomery responded with spite rather than grace. "New city ordinances make it a crime for Negroes and whites to play together or participate jointly in any sport or game, even checkers, or to use the same parks or playgrounds." [49] And "the newspapers and the politicians" remained the most vocal supporters for "active segregationist sentiment."[50]

We are now witnessing the same sort of response from America's political class. As society becomes more decentralized, the defensive reaction from the elites presents great challenges for all of us.

Understanding those challenges and how we should respond to them is the topic for the remainder of this book.

CHAPTER 7

THE EMPIRE STRIKES BACK

VERYBODY LOVES A GOOD STORY of an underdog beating the heavily favored champion. Everybody, that is, except the heavily favored champion.

The story of America since the Great Turnaround is a wonderful story of underdogs beating champions. Nicco Mele, author of *The End of Big*, captured the flavor of the age in the subtitle to his 2013 book: *How the Digital Revolution Makes David the New Goliath*. He writes, "Our twentieth-century institutions ... are on the cusp of collapse—or, if not outright collapse, of irrelevancy and anachronism.[1]

That's great news for everybody but Goliath.

For example, it's great news that Americans now have hundreds of television channels, YouTube, Netflix, Hulu, and other options for video entertainment. But it wasn't so great for the corporate network executives who used to control 94 percent of the prime time television audience.

It's also great news that Americans now have many alternative sources of news at every level of society. But that hasn't been so great for local newspapers, television stations, and other legacy media companies that used to control the news flow. Thirteen of the top 15 sources for news today were created *after* the Great Turnaround of the '70s.[2]

The increased accountability is good for society, but it wasn't great for Dan Rather. The former CBS news anchor was fired for using fraudulent documents in a hit piece on President George W. Bush during the 2004 election. He was brought down by little-known bloggers who conducted their own research without corporate backing.

The frustration experienced by elites losing power can easily be sensed in the voice of a former CBS executive: "These bloggers have no checks and balances.... You couldn't have a starker contrast between the multiple layers of checks and balances and a guy sitting in his living room in his pajamas writing."[3] As it turns out, the bloggers were just the checks and balances that America needed.

Corporate elites weren't the only ones affected by digital revolution.

"The speed with which outside challengers can maneuver unencumbered by the hierarchy and weight of traditional institutions leaves the political establishment dangerously exposed." Mele believes "this is a good thing, for the political establishment in both major parties has become dangerously corrupt, undemocratic, and divisive in recent years."[4]

But while it's good for America, think of how it looks from Goliath's perspective.

GOLIATH'S PERSPECTIVE

In the old days, a president controlled the flow of information in ways unimaginable during the 21st century. President Franklin D. Roosevelt was paralyzed from the waist down but most Americans at the time never knew it. There are only two known video clips of FDR walking. "Footage of Roosevelt struggling to move is rare because the Secret Service either prohibited or confiscated cameras at the time to minimize the public's knowledge of the devastating effects that polio had had on him. The media complied with the request."[5]

Before the Great Turnaround, a president's team could distribute news to the nation by reaching out to a small group of network executives, wire service reporters, and editors of leading newspapers. With the advent of television, the president could also influence public opinion directly with a national broadcast. Nobody else could come close to matching that bully pulpit.

It's hard to believe now, but in the '70s all television shows were routinely pre-empted when the president spoke. His speech was on every channel. Without any competition, the president drew huge ratings. Most Americans watched President Richard Nixon's speeches live on topics including Vietnam (58 percent of households with TVs) and Watergate (56 percent).[6]

Bounces in support for the president's policies were normal in those days. When a politician and his speechwriters could lay out their case and present it without any opposing views, it was almost impossible not to win converts to their cause. This was such a powerful tool Nixon gave 37 addresses from the Oval Office,[7] an average of more than one for every two months he was in power.

But the president's ability to influence public opinion has dramatically fallen. Most Americans watched President Ronald Reagan's 1981 State of the Union Address (56 percent)[8] and he was repeatedly able to go over the head of Congress to take his case directly to the people. Looking back, that was the end of an era. Audiences for presidential speeches have declined steadily for the past three decades. By 2015, just 20 percent of Americans watched President Barack Obama's State of the Union message.[9]

The decline of the president's ability to shape the debate is even more dramatic than the audience decline. Research published in *Presidential Studies Quarterly* found that members of the opposing party are especially likely to tune out the president these days. "Modern presidents thus find themselves increasingly preaching to their party choir and losing the capacity to influence public opinion more broadly."[10] Today, when the president gives a speech, nobody changes their mind, and there is no bounce in the polls.

The leveling of the communications playing field is good for America, but it's not great for modern presidents. In fact, Bill Clinton, George W. Bush, and Barack Obama all came into office with their party in control of Congress. All three lost control of Congress during their tenure. Never before in American history have voters rejected three consecutive presidents in this manner. And, the president before that—the first President Bush—was defeated in his bid for re-election.

GEORGE LUCAS SAW WHAT THE PRESIDENTIAL COMMISSION MISSED

In every transition, there are winners and losers. In the transition to a decentralized society, the losers are the corporate and political elites. A presidential commission in 1980 recognized this threat way back when the Great Turnaround was just getting started. "The last decade has witnessed the beginnings of a trend away from the centralization of authority." For the politically well-connected commissioners, this was seen as bad news. "The real fear . . . is that society will become so fractionalized as to be ungovernable."[11]

That commission, appointed by President Jimmy Carter, was charged with preparing a "National Agenda for the Eighties." It included scholars, politicians, political activists, business leaders, and union leaders. They disagreed on many things, but agreed on the importance of centralized power. The commission warned that the "ambivalent attitude on the part of the people toward the role of government is self-deluding."[12] And, in case you missed the point, it seemed "evident" to members of the presidential commission that decentralization posed "a significant danger to our democracy."[13]

Stunningly, however, while the commissioners knew something was going on, they had no clue what it was. Especially revealing was their section on "Science, Technology, and Economic Growth." Nine years after the invention of the microprocessor, five years after Microsoft was founded, and four years after the creation of Apple, the president's commission wrote about a technology agenda without even mentioning the word computer.[14]

In a nation where the society leads and the politicians lag behind, it is perhaps no surprise that the most successful film franchise of our time tapped into these themes before the political leaders caught on. *Star Wars* became a cultural icon for many reasons. It was a classic tale of good vs. evil using new technology to enhance the viewing experience. Fans loved Luke, Han, and Leia while appreciating the amazing diversity of the imaginary galaxy.

But the story of a Galactic Empire trying to centralize all power in the galaxy also resonated with movie-goers because it was a timeless story rooted in the reality of our time. It was written while elites worried about losing power in a decentralizing society and the topic of an imperial presidency was a normal part of the public dialogue.[15]

The story survived the test of time because, unlike the political elites, George Lucas recognized the potential of the new technologies. He even envisioned a world where new technology could so empower individuals that a small group working together could overcome Imperial ambitions. And, just as the Imperial leaders missed the possibility that a single X-wing fighter could destroy their Death Star, the experts on the presidential commission completely missed the possibility that personal computers could completely undermine their "National Agenda for the Eighties."

By the time the political leaders figured out what was going on, it was too late. "Nobody in Washington DC took [the Internet] seriously, so it was allowed to happen," according to Mitch Kapor, an early pioneer in the home computer era. "By the time anybody noticed, it had already won."[16]

THE GREAT REGULATOR

In the real world, though, as in the movies, the elites were not going to give up without a fight.

Nixon was president when the Great Turnaround began. He was a man who saw no limits on what the government—embodied by the president—could do. His concept of presidential power was so sweeping that he remains the only president ever to declare a peacetime wage-price freeze on the entire economy. After being driven from office by scandals of his own making, he declared that: "When the president does it that means it is not illegal."[17] His secretary of state, Henry Kissinger, put it this way: "The illegal we do immediately; the unconstitutional takes a little longer."[18]

While Nixon is most remembered for the debacle of Watergate, Jonathan Rauch believes Nixon's "most important legacy was as the "Great Regulator. It was he who built the modern regulatory apparatus." Nixon's lust to centralize power led him to regulate with what Rauch describes as "reckless abandon.... Under Nixon the number of pages in the Federal

Register (which publishes regulations) went from under 20,000 per year to three times that amount."[19]

He created entirely new laws and bureaucracies, giving them great power but few guidelines or limits. The list includes:

> In 1969, the National Environmental Policy Act; in 1970, the Poison Prevention Packaging Act, the Clean Air Amendments, the Occupational Safety and Health Act; in 1972, the Consumer Product Safety Act, the Federal Water Pollution Control Act, the Noise Pollution and Control Act, the Equal Employment Opportunity Act; in 1973, the Vocational Rehabilitation Act and the Safe Drinking Water Act; in 1974, the Hazardous Materials Transportation Act. Nixon opened the Environmental Protection Agency, the Consumer Product Safety Commission and the Occupational Safety and Health Administration.[20]

It is impossible to overstate the significance of these actions. In the context of the "Putting People First" model of governance, this was shifting power as far away from community control as possible. These agencies quickly acquired the power to make large corporations dependent upon their rulings. Lobbying and corruption played an ever-larger role in determining profits and losses. And, as shown in the "Follow the Money" table, corporations dependent upon the government are subject to Extremely Limited community control.

Nixon was the one who presided over the enormous expansion of the regulatory state, but he was supported by a bipartisan consensus of Washington politicians. They were building on more than a century of efforts by corporate and political elites to create a centralized government guided by experts and freed from the meddling of mere voters.

Nixon's role in all this is significant primarily because he happened to be in office when everything began to turn around. Earlier presidents who brought more power to Washington were moving in the same centralizing direction as society at large. Nixon had the misfortune of implementing a huge centralization of government at the very time society was preparing to move in the opposite direction.

For many in the political class, the regulatory regime quickly became the primary means to strike back at a decentralizing world. It was the Death Star of the political class.

THE RISE OF THE REGULATORY STATE

The rise of the regulatory state "represents perhaps the single greatest change in our system of government since the founding," according to George Washington University law professor Jonathan Turley. "Our carefully constructed system of checks and balances is being negated by the rise of a fourth branch, an administrative state of sprawling departments and agencies that govern with increasing autonomy and decreasing transparency."[21]

Chris Demuth, a scholar with the Hudson Institute, agrees. He calls the regulatory state "the most potent institutional innovation in American government since the Constitution. The Constitution was designed to make lawmaking cumbersome, representative, and consensual; the regulatory agency was a workaround, designed to make lawmaking efficient, specialized, and purposeful."[22]

What Nixon recklessly launched has grown to "a massive system of 15 departments, 69 agencies and 383 nonmilitary sub-agencies with almost three million employees." Alarmingly, according to Turley, "Citizens today are ten times more likely to be the subject of an agency court ruling than a federal court ruling."[23]

The Supreme Court has consistently aided this sprint to impose top-down bureaucratic control. In 1984, the Honorables ruled that agency decisions should be given great deference by the courts.[24] Later, the court ruled that agencies should even receive deference in terms of deciding their own jurisdiction. That latter ruling prompted Chief Justice John Roberts to write a strong dissent highlighting significant concerns: "It would be a bit much to describe the result as 'the very definition of tyranny,' but the danger posed by the growing power of the administrative state cannot be dismissed."[25]

It will be interesting to see where the chief justice leads the court on this issue in the coming years. Even before Donald Trump was elected president, the Roberts Court began to rein in some of Obama's executive rule-making. And, clearly one part of the reason for the new president's election was resistance to excessive regulation. Perhaps the court will someday catch up with the decentralizing trends of society at large.

But that hasn't been the case in recent decades. With the blessing of the court, the regulatory explosion has relegated Congress to a more modest role in the rulemaking process. In 2015, Congress passed 224 laws, and 3,554 new regulations were implemented.[26] In other words, Congress had nothing to do with 94 percent of all new federal laws. Instead, they were "issued as regulations, crafted largely by thousands of unnamed, unreachable bureaucrats."[27] These regulators now have a bigger impact on the daily lives of most Americans than Congress, the president, or the nation's courts.

A FUNDAMENTAL THREAT TO DEMOCRACY

That is what it looks like when the Empire strikes back. By placing faith in government and bureaucrats—rather than everyday Americans and community organizations—the regulatory state is fundamentally a threat to American democracy and self-governance. Voters, of course, don't have the power to walk away from the regulators. Their right to vote doesn't help much, since the regulators aren't accountable to Congress either. Yale University's Jonathan G.S. Koppell summarized the problem this way: "An 'unaccountable' government, insulated from the public and their elected representatives, threatens the very legitimacy of a democratic political system."[28]

He's right. It is hard to see how the regulatory state of the 21st century can claim any legitimacy from the consent of the governed.

For many in Washington, however, getting voters out of the loop is the best part of the regulatory state. Presidents as far back as Woodrow Wilson and Herbert Hoover dreamed of turning power over to unelected panels of experts. They expected those experts to make wise decisions without interference from the voters. Whether the decision making by regulators has generally been wise or not is debatable. What is indisputable, however, is that the explosive growth of the regulatory state centralized political power at the very time that American society was decentralizing.

Back in the 1970s, few Americans recognized the radical implications of this power grab. Partly, that's because the nation was dealing with the Vietnam War, rioting in many cities, the resignation of a scandal-ridden president, a troubled economy, and the first Arab oil embargo.

Another reason people didn't grasp what Nixon was doing is that societal changes unfold slowly and it takes a while before the real-world effects can be seen. It's the same reason that we didn't grasp the beginnings of the technology revolution while we were living through it. But as we saw how things played out, most Americans embraced the empowering trends of the technology revolution while growing frustrated by uncontrollable regulatory bureaucrats.

For example, in 1977 the federal government began aggressively steering Americans away from whole milk. A massive propaganda campaign was launched and whole milk was banned in school lunch programs. All this disruption was done at high cost in the belief that it would reduce heart disease.

Reducing heart disease was a noble goal. Who could object? In fact, most Americans signed up for the campaign. At one level, it was a success—sales of low-fat milk soared while sales of whole milk plummeted. But it didn't produce the expected health benefits. As time went on research failed to confirm that "this massive shift in eating habits has made anyone healthier." Even worse, the *Washington Post* reported, "millions might have been better off had they stuck with whole milk." Contrary to what the government bureaucrats expected, "people who consumed more milk fat had lower incidences of heart disease."[29]

The "campaign to reduce fat in the diet has had some pretty disastrous consequences," according to Walter Willett, dean of the nutrition department at the Harvard School of Public Health. University of Texas professor Marcia Ott added, "What we have learned over the last decade is that certain foods that are high in fat seem to be beneficial."[30]

THE CENTER OF A STORM

When it was first suggested, the idea of the government issuing health guidelines about whole milk seemed fairly harmless. After a few decades of practical experience, the reality of having rules set in Washington by bureaucrats with an agenda became clear. Fortunately, in a world with hundreds of millions of smartphone users, the government officials couldn't hide the truth. Just like Dan Rather, they were held accountable because alternative news sources were available. People were freed to consider a wide variety of expert opinions, chat with family and friends, and decide for themselves.

With more reliable information available, including practical experience, consumers shifted gears and sales of whole milk began to increase again (though not returning to earlier levels).[31] For some people, whole milk was healthier. Others are better off with low-fat options. In either case, we live in a world where one-size-fits-all solutions don't make any sense.

Episodes like this make clear to the general public that there is real danger in giving even the smartest of people decision-making power without adequate information and with no community control. But despite the evidence, the regulatory state continues to grow.

"Bureaucracy and representative government are at the center of a storm,"[32] according to William Niskanen Jr., an economist who served in several presidential administrations from Kennedy to Reagan (he was unhappy with all of them). It is a storm created by the fact that political and corporate elites are doing all they can to resist giving up power.

Back in 1971, he wrote an influential book, *Bureaucracy and Representative Government,* noting that bureaucracy has been around a lot longer than democracy: "from the ancient kingdoms of Sumer and Egypt to the modern nation-state." As a result, "most of the literature on bureaucracy, from Confucius to Weber, proceeds from . . . a concept of a state for which the preferences of individuals are subordinate to certain organic goals of the state."[33]

It's a view that people exist to serve the government, rather than the other way around. Sadly, that view has always found many supporters among the political elites. Theodore Roosevelt, for example, complained that we needed to stop talking about the rights of the people and start talking about their duty to government.[34]

From Roosevelt's time onward, bureaucratic government has been on a collision course with America's founding ideals. As Niskanen put it, "the parallel growth of bureaucracy and national government [has created] confusion about whether the people or these institutions are sovereign."[35]

This is the real conflict of our time. It is a conflict about what noted scholar Martin J. Sklar called "the central principle of the American political tradition, namely the supremacy of the society over the state." In his history of the progressive era, Sklar noted that in America, government is supposed to "adapt to, and serve, the freely developing society." The end result should be that "society commanded the state, not the state the society."[36]

THE LAST REFUGE

Unfortunately, our corporate and political elites don't like that answer. "Like all elites, they believe that they not only rule because they can, but because they should," according to *Bloomberg's* Megan McArdle. "If they think there's anything wrong with the balance of power in the system we all live under, it is that [they] do not have enough power to bend that system to their will."[37]

The elite movers and shakers say, and probably believe, that they will use their power "for the good of everyone else. ... Not that they spend much time with everyone else, but they have excellent imaginations." McArdle sums it up by reminding us that "all elites are good at rationalizing their eliteness, whether it's meritocracy or 'the divine right of kings.'"[38]

The regulatory state has become the last great refuge for political elites trying to hold back the tides of decentralization. "Who benefits from the growth of complex and cumbersome regulation?" asks Niall Ferguson, a noted author and professor of history at Harvard. "The answer is: lawyers, not forgetting lobbyists and compliance departments. For complexity is not the friend of the little man. It is the friend of the deep pocket. It is the friend of cronyism."[39]

While the digital revolution is empowering everyday Americans, the elites have struck back by shifting power to organizations with hardly any accountability to society at large. As shown in the table on the following page, giving more power to regulators also means limiting the independence of groups more subject to community control.

Limiting the power of groups subject to community control is bad for self-governance, but it's been very good for America's political class. Their resistance to following the public's lead is fueled by the fact that the regulatory regime and crony capitalism have been very good for the city of Washington, D.C.

TABLE 5

FOLLOW THE MONEY TRENDS 1970 TO PRESENT		
ASSOCIATION	COMMUNITY CONTROL	CHANGE
Family, Friends, Core Community	Complete	Stable
Local Businesses, Nonprofits, Clubs, Associations, Social Networks	Very High	Reduced Independence
Larger Businesses Dependent upon Private Customers	High	Reduced Independence
Local Government	Moderate to High	Reduced Independence
Larger, Donor/Consumer-Supported Nonprofits	Moderate to High	Stable
Businesses Dependent upon Local Government	Low to Moderate	Stable
State Government	Low to Moderate	Reduced Independence
Nonprofits Dependent upon State Government	Limited to Moderate	Stable
Businesses Dependent upon State Government	Limited to Moderate	Stable
Federal Agencies Dependent upon Private Consumers	Limited	Stable
Federal Government	Very Limited	High Growth
Nonprofits Dependent upon Federal Government	Extremely Limited	Extraordinary Growth
Businesses Dependent upon Federal Government	Extremely Limited	Extraordinary Growth

According to the *Washington Post*, its hometown "has been the beneficiary of a decade-long, taxpayer-funded stimulus package." Federal spending in the capital region—funded by those of us in outlying areas—soared from $29 billion in 2000 to $75 billion" in 2012.[40]

In fact, the median household income in our capital city is 67 percent higher than it is in America.[41] This reality was reflected and exaggerated in *The Hunger Games*, where the capital city lived in lavish excess at the expense of those living horribly in the outlying districts. While the movie presents an extreme example of the problem, five of America's seven wealthiest counties do in fact surround our very own capital city.[42]

COSTS OF THE REGULATORY REGIME

While the centralization of power did wonders for Washington, the experience throughout the nation has been far more controversial. In addition to the fights over light bulbs and whole milk, the regulatory state has turned even the most wholesome local efforts—school bake sales[43] and school lunches—into unpleasant political battlegrounds.[44]

Negative reaction to regulations requiring low-flow toilet flushes forced the EPA to respond with its own spin claiming to sort out fact from fiction.[45] The IRS harassed people who opposed the president,[46] and the Transportation Safety Administration (TSA) has become a regular source of public outrage. With an extraordinary display of arrogance, the TSA even ordered state governments to change the format of their driver's licenses or else they would not be accepted for travel.[47]

Living under such a regulatory regime naturally leads to lots of complaints. Some complain about how expensive it is for businesses to comply with all the new commands. One estimate suggests that it costs consumers nearly $2 trillion annually.[48] Many worry about the fact that regulators end up serving the very corporations they are supposed to regulate. That's one reason it is so common to find the federal government siding with Wall Street instead of Main Street.

Those are all valid concerns and there are plenty of others. But the larger problem is that the regulatory state is a threat to American democracy and self-governance. By placing faith in government and bureaucracy, rather than everyday Americans and community organizations, it is a rejection of the very idea that the people should be in charge.

Do we want America to be ruled by distant bureaucrats with great power and little accountability?

Or, should our nation be ruled by everyday Americans solving problems in community and living with the consequences of their own decisions?

In a nation committed to having a government of, by and for the people—a nation committed to providing everyone with the right to life, liberty, and pursuit of happiness—there can be only one answer.

CHAPTER 8

WINNING BY SERVING

Y JOURNEY from pessimism about our political system to optimism about our nation has been anything but smooth. Along the way, there have been many twists, turns, and bumps in the road.

While I believe the Great Turnaround is a real blessing for our nation, I also recognize that it's been a massively disruptive transition involving every aspect of daily life. After 200 years of everything in America getting bigger, more centralized, and more homogenized, it's proven extraordinarily difficult for our society to do a 180 and enter a world where everything grows more niche-oriented, decentralized and personalized. Even when change is good, transitions are hard.

Along with all the benefits, though, the new technologies raise difficult and novel ethical questions just about every day. Privacy and security issues are in uncharted territory. There are real concerns about automation eliminating jobs and creating mass unemployment. Others worry about the impact of the new technology on social interactions. Are we spending too much time with our phones and not enough time talking to real people?

Making the transition far more difficult has been the *Empire Strikes Back* response from the political realm. Our political system is completely out of sync with the nation it is supposed to serve. "As consumers move faster toward building digital lives, lawmakers are increasingly if spastically putting on the brakes" according to Larry Downes of the Georgetown Center for Business and Public Policy. He notes that bureaucrats and lawmakers want to stuff the digital revolution "genie . . . back into the bottle. And then bury the bottle."[1]

While society is decentralizing, the political class is desperately trying to centralize its hold on power. It has adopted the attitude of a young Anakin Skywalker before he became Darth Vader. Upon being told that he was not all powerful, Anakin replied, "Well, I should be."[2]

If that seems a bit harsh, consider the words of former Regional EPA Director Al Armendariz:

> The Romans used to conquer little villages in the Mediterranean. They'd go into a little Turkish town somewhere, they'd find the first five guys they saw and they would crucify them. And then you know that town was really easy to manage for the next few years.
>
> And so you make examples out of people who are in this case not compliant with the law . . . you hit them as hard as you can and you make examples out of them, and there is a deterrent effect there.[3]

This attitude is so breathtakingly offensive that Armendariz was forced to resign when his comments became public. In America, one of our most cherished ideals is that the law is supposed to be applied equally to all. It's definitely not about hitting a few randomly selected targets "as hard as you can" to "make examples of them."

Even more troubling was his claim that the random targets were "not compliant with the law." Armendariz may have believed that, but he had no legal grounds to back him up. His team simply ruled imperially as judge, jury, and executioner. They didn't worry about core values like the fact that we are all presumed innocent until proven guilty. When the company Armendariz selected for special attention fought back and federal courts demanded evidence, his agency dropped the case.[4]

While most regulatory bureaucrats don't abuse their authority in such a dramatic fashion, the "trend of using regulation to quash political freedom is in place and will only increase."[5] The Hoover Institution's John Cochrane describes the current system as a place where you can have "a good living and a quiet life" if you cooperate. On the other hand, "the cost of stepping out of line is personal and business ruin."[6]

A society where regulators can decide whether you have a good living or face personal ruin is not a free society, a fair society, or a self-governing society.

What can we do about it?

LEARNING FROM DAVID

That's an enormously difficult question and one that I struggled for many years to answer. My own experience dealing with the political realm has made me all too aware of how hard it is to challenge those who write the rules. Why is it so hard for third parties to arise and challenge Republicans and Democrats? Because Republicans and Democrats write the rules. Why is it impossible to pass term limits on Congress? Because Congress writes the rules.

These things are true not because politicians are corrupt and evil. They are true because it's human nature. Asking even the most noble person you know to set reasonable limits on their own power is like asking a toddler to set a reasonable bedtime for herself. It's just not going to happen. "Power tends to corrupt and absolute power corrupts absolutely."[7]

I learned this firsthand during my time in the term limits movement. It was stunning to see how fiercely those in power dug in to resist such a modest reform. The political leaders didn't care that term limits were supported by more than 70 percent of Americans. They did care about protecting the status quo and their place in it. Sadly, we live in a world where the entrenched defiance of the political class can block any attempt by voters to rein in their power.

Experiencing those realities, there were times when I came close to giving up. In fact, for several years I was as pessimistic about the future of the nation as I am about the reality of our political system. Eventually, however, I found encouragement and insight from an ancient biblical tale of another seemingly invincible foe.

Twice every day for 40 days, Goliath dared the Israelite army to find a soldier who would fight him. The giant was nearly seven feet tall and wore armor over his entire body. He carried three weapons—a javelin, spear, and sword. The image was so intimidating that "the Israelites were dismayed and terrified . . . they all fled from him in great fear."[8]

Then, of course, a young shepherd boy named David volunteered and felled the giant with nothing but a sling and a smooth stone. In *David and Goliath: Underdogs, Misfits, and the Art of Battling Giants*, bestselling author Malcolm Gladwell makes the case that we have been misinterpreting that story for generations.

In Gladwell's view, seeing the giant clearly was key to David's success. Like all the Israelite soldiers, the shepherd saw that fighting on Goliath's terms would be suicidal. But he also saw something else. The young boy recognized that Goliath had weaknesses others did not see. The giant's heavy armor slowed him down, his eyesight was not very good, and his forehead was unprotected.

With these insights, David developed a strategy that played to his own strengths rather than Goliath's. Since he knew how to use a sling, all he needed was a smooth stone to aim at Goliath's forehead. When the fighting finally began, the slow-moving giant never saw it coming in time to get out of the way.

By changing the form of combat, David transformed the giant from a ferocious force into an easy target. Gladwell believes that the tale presents "an important lesson . . . for battles with all kinds of giants. The powerful and the strong are not always what they seem."[9]

WEAKNESSES OF THE REGULATORY STATE

America's regulatory state can be even more terrifying than Goliath, and it often appears just as invincible. But as I reflected on Gladwell's book, it became clear that our nation's giant has some major weaknesses. With the right strategy, we can exploit these weaknesses to ensure a great future for our nation.

The first, most obvious, weakness is that top-down rule making simply doesn't work as well as community problem solving. That's true whether the problem is helping a family through a fire, creating 401(k) retirement plans, or founding Harvard College.

"Most sustainable improvements in community occur when citizens discover their own power to act," according to Peter Block, an award-winning author who has written extensively on community building and civic engagement. "Whatever the symptom—drugs, deteriorating houses, poor economy, displacement, violence—it is when citizens stop waiting for professionals or elected leadership to do something . . . that things really happen."[10]

A second glaring weakness is that the regulatory state has never been popular with the American people. In fact, during the entire four decades of the regulatory state's existence, a majority has never trusted the federal government. The longer that people live under the regulatory regime, the less they support it. Over the past decade, the number trusting the federal government to do the right thing most of the time has fallen to 25 percent or less.[11]

Things have gotten so bad that most Americans today believe the federal government is a special interest group that looks out primarily for its own interests.[12] They are right.

Significantly, this decline in trust applies only to the federal government. State and local governments retain much higher levels of trust and approval and have seen little change over the years.[13] It is the federal government alone that has lost the legitimacy to rule, a legitimacy that can only come from the consent of the governed.

I do not lightly make the charge that our federal government today is illegitimate. It breaks my heart to do so. But the regulatory state is a fundamental rejection of America's core values. Rather than celebrating government of, by, and for the people, fans of the regulatory state hail it as "a demonstration of faith in government and in future generations of scientists and regulators to shape policy."[14]

Very few Americans share that faith in government and government experts. That's why they refuse to give it their consent and support.

The regulatory state "is not merely unconstitutional; it is anti-constitutional," according to Gary Lawson, professor of law at Boston University. "The Constitution was designed specifically to prevent the emergence of the kinds of institutions that characterize the modern administrative state."[15] In other words, the rise of the regulatory state over the past four decades has been a hostile takeover of America's government.

"Regulators and politicians aren't nitwits," Cochrane reminds us. There is definitely a method to their madness. "The fact that the regulatory state is an ideal tool for the entrenchment of political power was surely not missed by its architects."[16] Lawson put it this way: "The architects of the modern administrative state did not misunderstand the Constitution. They understood it perfectly well. They just didn't like it."[17]

IT'S TIME TO STOP PLAYING THEIR GAME

We have a form of government that isn't very good at solving problems and is vastly unpopular. On the surface, these two glaring weaknesses should make the regulatory state easy to defeat.

But experience has taught us that the regulators and their friends often defeat the voters, the public interest, and common sense. After the bank bailout debacle in 2008, voters demanded change so that the big banks could never again pose such a threat to our nation's economy. But the regulatory system was more interested in protecting Wall Street than Main Street (perhaps because most senior regulatory officials had worked on Wall Street before and expected to work there again). So new rules were passed, but they did not break up the big banks or end the risk of future bailouts. Instead, the biggest and most dangerous banks grew even bigger.[18]

How can this happen in a nation where the people are supposed to be in charge?

The short answer is the regulatory state wins because we're playing their game. We have been trying to defeat professional politicians and career bureaucrats at the game of politics. That's as likely to succeed as it would have been for David to fight Goliath in hand-to-hand combat.

If we want America to succeed, we need to change the game and find our slingshot.

The need to change the game has also been recognized by Charles Murray of the American Enterprise Institute. The noted scholar has proposed "a declaration of limited resistance to the existing government." He envisions a massive campaign of civil disobedience with small-business owners and others refusing to obey silly regulations. Murray hopes thousands upon thousands of small legal battles could overwhelm the regulators and "make large portions of the Code of Federal Regulations de facto unenforceable."[19]

Murray is careful to define precisely the types of rules he believes are appropriate to ignore. "Civil disobedience must therefore be undertaken in such a way that it is obvious to all who watch with an open mind that they are witnessing free people behaving appropriately—that the problem is not the person who violated the regulation but the regulation or its interpretation by the bureaucrats."[20] He adds that "it is essential that people reading or watching news reports about the trial are overwhelmingly on the side of the defendant."[21]

Civil disobedience is an effective and honorable strategy that has played an important role in American history. The civil rights movement of the 1960s would not have been possible without it. In his *Letter From a Birmingham Jail*, Martin Luther King Jr. reminded us that we have "a moral responsibility to disobey unjust laws." He agreed with St. Augustine that "an unjust law is no law at all."[22] But King also reminded us, with far more than words, that we must be willing to pay a heavy price to pursue such a strategy.

While there is certainly a time and place for civil disobedience, I am more than a little skeptical about the practicality of Murray's plan. How many volunteers would really be willing to put their lives on hold for years while being harassed by government agents and dragged into court? Who would pay the hundreds of millions of dollars in legal fees Murray believes would be needed each year to defend them?[23] How long would it be before someone like Al Armendariz overreacts and decides to "crucify" random volunteers to "make an example of them?"

Though I am skeptical of Murray's approach, I understand the frustration that drove him to that conclusion. It's the same frustration that drove me and millions of others to despair. It's a recognition that our dysfunctional political system cannot possibly solve the problems facing our nation today.

That's why losing faith in the political process was such a critical step in my journey to optimism about America's future.

Only then could I could truly embrace and act upon the reality that community and the culture lead while politics and government lag behind. Once I accepted that, it became clear that I had been looking for answers in all the wrong places. It's not about fixing the government, fighting the government, limiting the government, or electing new people to run the government. It's not about government at all. It's about the society we live in.

A MASSIVE CAMPAIGN OF COMMUNITY PROBLEM SOLVING

We don't need a campaign to resist and limit the government. We need a positive campaign that shows how we can work together to solve problems and create a better world.

Rather than a campaign of massive civil disobedience, we need a massive campaign of community problem solving. That's an approach that is consistent with our highest ideals and deepest traditions. It's an effort that can rally support from the vast majority of the American people.

This is the way America is supposed to work. Our nation has been built on an attitude brimming with optimism about what a free and self-governing people can accomplish. We cherish our freedom but recognize its greatest value can be found when we use that freedom to build community.

Knowing that we have within our own communities the power to solve the problems before us fills me with hope. It is the reason I can be optimistic about the future of the nation despite being pessimistic about politics.

The campaign I envision is an all-hands-on-board, community-driven approach that engages every individual, relationship, and organization in the governing of society. As usual, the American people are far ahead of the politicians. Most already recognize that "their day-to-day life would be more positively affected by an increase in community volunteerism than having a President that agrees with them on the issues."[24]

This strategy draws upon a strength that is difficult for many involved in politics to understand. "The service motive is at least as powerful as the desire for profit or power,"[25] according to Richard Cornuelle. Back in the '60s, Cornuelle left a powerful position in Washington[26] to engage in community problem solving. "I am offended by people who stand around like pop bottles and don't do anything." *Life* magazine noted that Cornuelle did "plenty himself, and what's more, [made] it count." The magazine cited his work to develop a student loan program that outperformed the federal program and a project placing the "hard-core unemployed" in productive jobs.[27]

Cornuelle saw "some people in whom [the service motive was] paramount and overwhelming, just as some men seem to have no other interest than the stubborn pursuit of wealth or power." But Cornuelle believed that he could "see the service motive to some degree in almost everyone."[28] As a result, the answer we need "lies in the vast unused resources of . . . the thousands of foundations, churches, unions, and other nongovernmental organizations who more and more ask, 'What can I do?'"[29]

Community problem solving plays to the service-motivated strengths of the American people. It is our slingshot. Politics is about power and money and using one to get the other. Community is about serving others. We can't beat politicians and bureaucrats in the game of politics, but they don't stand a chance when we compete to serve others and create a better world.

A friend of mine who serves as a Navy chaplain put it this way: "No matter how strong the regulatory state becomes; it will never be more powerful than loving thy neighbor." You don't have to be a Christian to recognize the truth of that statement.

We must all get engaged in the process of creating a better world. That's asking a lot. Even though we already have 63 million volunteers and 27 million entrepreneurs directly engaged in community problem solving, much more is needed.

Unfortunately, at a time when we need more community engagement, the trends are not encouraging. During the nearly half century of American life under the regulatory regime, many traditional community groups and activities have suffered. *Bowling Alone* author Robert Putnam reminds us that "Americans in massive numbers began to join less, trust less, give less, vote less, and schmooze less."[30] Adding to the problem is a decline in both entrepreneurial activity and the number of organizations independent of the federal government.

The timing is no coincidence. It is in the interest of the regulatory state to limit independent community problem-solving efforts. Unchecked "power corrupts not only rulers but also the ruled," according to Columbia University professor of law Philip Hamburger. "It accustoms an otherwise self-governing people to a regime of potentially pervasive control, and it thereby . . . gradually deprives them of their capacity for self-rule."[31]

In other words, as the regulatory state grows, our capacity for self-governance and community problem solving declines.

"For the people *outside* government to be strong enough to hold that force in check requires that there be a large and vibrant private society," according to Hillsdale College President Larry Arnn. That means "a society full of families, churches, businesses, charities, clubs, and teams."[32]

So, we need to reverse recent trends by building up, creating, and strengthening independent organizations that are responsive to the community rather than to the politicians.

CONCLUSION

I am optimistic that we can do this for many reasons.

The first is that the new technology empowers everyday Americans and gives us new tools for working together. It's worth noting that the internet itself flourished only after tight regulations gave way to community problem solving. Prior to the 1990s, commercial use of the internet was forbidden. "It served mostly as a closed club reserved for academics, a handful of technologists and engineers and assorted government bureaucrats."[33] In those days, sending electronic mail "for commercial profit or political purposes" was considered "both anti-social and illegal."[34]

"Undoubtedly," as the Mercatus Center's Adam Thierer notes, "the restrictions on the commercial use of the internet were thought to have served the best of intentions." But, despite the good intentions, there were huge opportunity costs to this regulation. "As soon as the net was commercialized, social and economic activity online exploded in previously unimaginable ways."[35]

When the technology of the internet was restricted to use by elites, it was little noticed and had little impact. When it was freed for development by everybody, it changed the world. The digital revolution is now poised to dethrone the elites of the regulatory state in the same way that it dethroned the media elites over the past generation.

But the technology is just a tool. What matters is how we use it. Another reason for my optimism is that the community problem solving approach taps directly into the idealism of younger Americans today. As journalist Ron Fournier noted, "Millennials believe traditional politics and government (especially Washington) are the worst avenues to great things. They are more likely to be *social entrepreneurs*, working outside government to create innovative and measurably successful solutions to the nation's problems."[36]

This is not an anti-government attitude; it is simply a matter of prag-matism. If one path doesn't work, you try another. If one app doesn't work, you delete it and download another.

Millennials, of course, aren't the only Americans looking to support efforts that produce "measurably successful solutions." But it is a bit harder to see among older Americans. Partly that's because the idealism of many has been worn down over the years by the cares of everyday life. They still want to make the world a better place but need to worry first about paying the bills and getting the kids to rehearsals and practices. Far too many have given up hope. But that idealism and hope can quickly be rekindled as younger Americans lead the way.

The reason that the millennial generation will lead is because they have grown up with the tools of the digital revolution. I once asked the developer of a new tool for online news services how he taught readers to use his service. "People under 30 just figured it out. Those over 40 looked for instructions and took a week or two to get comfortable." That's the way it will be with the campaign of community problem solving. Younger Americans will develop new approaches and new tools; the rest of us will eventually catch up.

That's why I'm so encouraged by the idealism of the millennial gen-eration. They will use—and show us how to use—new technologies to overcome problems in health care, education, poverty, race relations, and more. Along the way, we will all work together through independent community organizations to defeat the regulatory state and end the ability of a bureaucrat to arbitrarily determine whether you have a good life or face personal ruin. We will end the hostile takeover of America's government and strengthen our commitment to freedom, equality, and self-governance.

To make this happen—to launch a massive campaign of community problem solving—we will need to use a strategy of radical incrementalism.

CHAPTER 9

RADICAL INCREMENTALISM

W HEN DEVELOPING ANY STRATEGY, it's vitally important to consider the context. In the business world, this reality has generated a thriving niche industry. Consultants earn big money guiding companies through the PEST approach (Political, Economic, Social, and Technology context), SWOT analysis (Strengths, Weakness, Opportunities, and Threats), or some other method.

In the sports world, a baseball team that has clinched the playoffs might rest its key players while a team fighting for the last spot might start its ace pitcher on short notice. In politics, the candidate with a big lead tries to avoid debates or any unscripted events, while the challenger looks for every opportunity to shake things up. The context determines the strategy.

In moving America forward, the overriding context for us to recognize is the Great Turnaround. The centralized model of the regulatory state was built to serve the 1960s-style organizational society run by giant bureaucracies. It is totally out of step with the decentralizing society of the 21st century. To put this disconnect into Hollywood form, imagine towering, all-powerful regulatory chiefs shaken by earthquakes as their world crumbles around them.

That's probably just how it felt to seemingly powerful political figures who took on Uber. The tech company's innovative app has provided a vastly improved service for those who used to rely on taxis. Rather than wasting time selling its idea to local taxi commissions, Uber simply offered its app directly to customers and then provided over a billion rides within six years.[1]

But the old-fashioned taxi companies didn't like it. Soon they began pressuring the political system to eliminate the competition by outlawing Uber. A number of politicians, including New York Mayor Bill de Blasio, were only too happy to help. The *New York Daily News* properly described the mayor's effort as "a protectionist crusade for an entrenched industry, absurdly claiming to stand for the thousands of New York passengers and drivers who have flocked to Uber."[2] The *New York Post* noted that the beneficiaries of the mayor's plan would have been "a yellow-cab monopoly, and fleet owners who'd donated more than $550,000 to de Blasio's mayoral campaign."[3]

Despite his apparent power over the regulatory process, the mayor was forced to back down. "The consumer demand for the Uber and Lyft kind of services is so great that any politician who gets in the way of that is really asking for trouble," according to Roger McNamee. The co-founder of investment firm Elevation Partners said, "Uber's success is really about consumers demanding the availability of Uber and Lyft cars wherever they are."[4] The consumers demanded it and the politicians were unable to stop it.

In terms of developing a strategy for moving America forward, the Uber story highlights a few key points. The first ties back to the "Follow the Money" table from Chapter 5. The table itself can serve as a useful scorecard for measuring our progress toward restoring a free and self-governing society. Before Uber, taxi companies were local businesses dependent upon local government. That allowed for a low to moderate level of community control. In a big city like New York, community control was low because all decisions were made by unaccountable political appointees. The situation was similar, if perhaps not quite as extreme, in smaller cities. Uber, on the other hand, entered the scene as a business dependent upon private customers. Because those customers all have the power to walk away, the level of community control was high right from the start.

Any time decision making moves from low to high on the level of Community Control, we have moved one step closer to putting the American people back in charge. With Uber, the decision making was transferred from local political appointees to individual consumers. That's a huge step in the right direction.

TABLE 6

FOLLOW THE MONEY LEVEL OF COMMUNITY CONTROL		
ASSOCIATION	TIER	COMMUNITY CONTROL
Family, Friends, Core Community	1	Complete
Local Businesses, Nonprofits, Clubs, Associations, Social Networks	2	Very High
Larger Businesses Dependent Upon Private Customers	2	High
Local Government	2	Moderate to High
Larger, Donor/Consumer-Supported Nonprofits	2	Moderate to High
Businesses Dependent Upon Local Government	2	Low to Moderate
State Government	2	Low to Moderate
Nonprofits Dependent Upon State Government	2	Limited to Moderate
Businesses Dependent Upon State Government	2	Limited to Moderate
Federal Agencies Dependent Upon Private Consumers	3	Limited
Federal Government	3	Very Limited
Nonprofits Dependent Upon Federal Government	3	Extremely Limited
Businesses Dependent Upon Federal Government	3	Extremely Limited

The second key point is that Uber shook things up out of a simple desire to make money. This was not a citizens crusade to reform the taxi commissions. But it was far more effective than any citizens crusade could have ever been. Improved community control over the taxi industry was not the objective, but it was a beneficial byproduct of Uber's innovative technology platform. Change always comes from outside the political process.

The third point is that politicians will instinctively resist any change that limits their control and shifts power to the people. In Austin, Texas, Uber and Lyft provided a valuable service but did so without first getting permission from the local government. So officials effectively forced the ride-sharing services to leave town.

Since the need for ride-sharing was still strong, a Facebook group popped up to meet the need and quickly attracted 40,000 users.[5] Faced with this community response, the city officials declared all ride-sharing illegal. They went so far as to conduct undercover sting operations and confiscate the cars of those who were providing a service to the community.[6] Ironically, this was the exact same tactic used in the 1950s in an attempt to thwart the Montgomery bus boycott and defend segregation.

Uber is far from alone in making life difficult for regulators by shifting power to the people.

Chris Anderson is co-founder of 3D Robotics and former editor of *Wired* magazine. Several years back, his young daughter wanted furniture for her dollhouse. Anderson found some designs online and made them on his home 3-D printer. Because he was doing the work, Anderson customized everything to color-coordinate with the dollhouse.[7] When all was said and done, he got a more customized result, spent less money, had no waiting time, and put a smile on the face of a young girl who saw him as the greatest dad ever.

Not all of us, of course, have a 3-D printer at home. But 278,000 such printers were sold in 2015, with more coming every year. And, even if you don't have one, there are services that will do the printing for you. Just pick a design, click to submit, and your personally designed and customized product will soon arrive. It's a long way from becoming the new normal, but 3-D printing is already a $5 billion industry.[8]

The implications of this technology are revolutionary. "If Karl Marx were here today, his jaw would be on the floor. Talk about 'controlling the tools of production': you (you!) can now set factories into motion with a mouse click."[9] Obviously, of course, this technology could reshape the toy industry and many other industries. Imagine what will happen when, in Anderson's words, "The collective potential of a million garage tinkerers is ... unleashed."[10]

For purposes of this discussion, though, think about the threat this exciting technology poses to regulators. "Technology will always win," says former Intel CEO Andy Grove. "You can delay technology by legal interference, but technology will flow around legal barriers."[11] In the case of 3-D printers, it's relatively easy to regulate big companies and big factories. But it's just about impossible to regulate people sharing designs and building things at home. With other technologies, the details will be different but the impact is the same. The digital revolution is shaking the ground beneath the feet of the regulatory regime.

THE HEAVY LIFTING HAS ALREADY BEEN DONE

This is the encouraging context for launching a massive campaign of community problem solving. We live in a world where the culture always leads and politics lags behind. The tools of the tech industry have created the most powerful force for change in our nation's history, and the millennial generation is rekindling our idealism. Because of the Great Turnaround, cultural trends and new technologies are already doing a lot of the heavy lifting to weaken the regulatory state and strengthen community control.

On top of that, we're already winning in the court of public opinion. Most Americans see community groups, small businesses, religious groups, and average Americans as a positive force helping the nation address major issues and challenges facing the nation.[12] In contrast, they recognize that groups associated with the regulatory state—lobbyists, political parties, large corporations, political activists, and public-private partnerships—tend to do more harm than good.[13]

In this context, we don't need a citizens crusade to singlehandedly defeat the status quo. Instead, we need to capitalize on the opportunities presented by the clash between a decentralizing culture and the centralized political system. Change is coming. Our role is to make sure it reflects our core values of freedom, equality, and self-governance. A key part of the strategy must be identifying steps that everyday Americans can take to do their part. In the fight to restore freedom and self-governance, we all have a role to play.

"It is not always apathy or indifference that keeps people from doing something about social problems," observed anti-poverty activist Richard Cornuelle. "It's a lack of savvy about *what to do*. If a case of need is visible, and the way to help is obvious, you may even have an overkill."[14]

He made those comments back in the '60s, but they are just as true today. Anderson points out that the explosion of web content has been driven by "volunteer labor—it made people happy to be creative, to contribute, to have an impact, and to be recognized as expert in something"[15] If we can make the need visible and the way to help obvious, we can tap into that same desire to be creative, contribute and have an impact. The service motive remains at least as powerful as the motivation provided by a desire for wealth or power.

INVISIBLE GORILLAS

To get started, we first need to see the world more clearly. That need was demonstrated in a fascinating experiment conducted by psychologists Christopher F. Chabris and Daniel James Simons. In the late '90s, they created a film showing two teams passing basketballs. Participants in the study were asked to "silently count the number of passes made by the players wearing white while ignoring any passes by the players wearing black. The video lasted less than a minute."[16] The experiment required a fair amount of concentration because the players were moving and you had to avoid counting passes made by the wrong team.

Ultimately, about three dozen passes were made, but that wasn't really the point. "Halfway through the video, a female student wearing a full-body gorilla suit walked into the scene, stopped in the middle of the players, faced the camera, thumped her chest, and then walked off, spending about nine seconds onscreen."[17] Stunningly, about half the participants in the study never noticed the gorilla! They were so focused on the task at hand that they were unable to see anything else.

The invisible gorilla is a great example of how we only see 40 percent of a scene with our eyes and fill in the remaining 60 percent with what we expect to see. "When people devote their attention to a particular area or aspect of their visual world, they tend not to notice unexpected objects." The scholars concluded that was true "even when those unexpected objects are salient, potentially important, and appear right where they are looking."[18]

A similar form of blindness is holding our country back. Our society is drenched in the notion that every problem must have a political solution. We know that's not true because in reality the culture leads and politics lags behind. But it is the message we hear every day from Fox, CNN, MSNBC, and from the political world. It's the message that comes also from every frustrated citizen who grumbles, "There ought to be a law."

This blindness creates two major problems. The first is that when we devote our attention and energy to finding political solutions, we become so focused on politics that we are unable to see other solutions right before our eyes. Uber improved taxi service far more than any political answer could have done. Kenny Thompson made sure the children at his school enjoyed hot meals. Ted Benna created a retirement program for middle-income Americans. Sadly, the drumbeat of messaging from the political realm encourages us to put on blinders and ignore the community problem-solving gorillas in our midst.

One U.S. senator tapped into the obsession with political solutions by telling supporters, "Many of you have jobs. Many of you have families. Ignore them."[19] He wanted them to devote all energy to his re-election bid. Hopefully it was just a tongue in cheek reference to fire up his team, but the sentiment captures the apparent attitude of many partisan political activists. In any event he had things backwards. Taking care of personal responsibilities like jobs and family are far more important than whether one politician beats another. While we should get involved in the political process, it's important to keep things in proper perspective.

Why on earth would we want to limit our problem-solving options to what the federal government can do? We also have available 50 state governments, 89,004 local government entities,[20] almost 28 million businesses,[21] and 1.5 million nonprofit groups.[22] We are a nation of 27 million entrepreneurs and 63 million volunteers. There is no reason to fight the challenges before us with one hand tied behind our back. Rather than just focusing on politics, we need to take advantage of all the resources at our disposal to create a better world for our children and grandchildren.

HIDDEN COSTS

The second, and equally important, danger is that the blindness can cause us to miss the costs and dangers of political solutions. To take just one example, accepting a federal grant may seem like getting free money. But there are always strings attached, and getting too dependent upon such grants can quickly cause a charitable group to lose its independence.

Recently, that lesson has been painfully learned by our nation's colleges and universities. Fifty years ago, the federal government was not broadly involved in student loans. Colleges and universities were fairly independent, subject to varying degrees of control by a wide range of communities. Some were dependent upon funding from state governments, others relied upon tuition-paying students, and some had wealthy alums. Most had some mix of all the above and more.

Today, there are 4,726 colleges in the nation,[23] and all but about eight accept federal loans to help their students cover the cost of tuition.[24] Federal dollars have become the single largest source of funding for higher education[25] and schools are addicted to the revenue. All that money comes with strings attached, because every school that accepted federal funding also had to accept federal regulation.

Going back to the "Follow the Money" table, this makes virtually the entire system of higher education a nonprofit dependent upon the federal government. That provides extremely limited levels of community control. It's no coincidence that as centralized control has grown, the problems associated with higher education have increased.

The schools that are free of these restrictions are very clear about the importance of academic independence. "Here at Wyoming Catholic College, we don't want the government telling us what to teach our students . . . so, we've decided not to accept federal funds."[26] Hillsdale College and Grove City offer similar perspectives.

The desire to be free from regulations issued by Washington bureaucrats comes at a cost. The schools must raise funds for their own student loan programs. But the benefits of independence are substantial. The Higher Education Compliance Alliance recently reported that "there is every reason to believe that compliance requirements will present formidable challenges for institutions of higher education for years to come."[27]

A bipartisan Task Force on Federal Regulation of Higher Education reported, "Oversight of higher education by the Department of Education has expanded and evolved in ways that undermine the ability of colleges and universities to serve students and accomplish their missions." As if that weren't enough:

> The compliance problem is exacerbated by the sheer volume of mandates—approximately 2,000 pages of text— and the reality that the Department of Education issues official guidance to amend or clarify its rules at a rate of more than one document per work day. As a result, colleges and universities find themselves enmeshed in a jungle of red tape, facing rules that are often confusing and difficult to comply with. They must allocate resources to compliance that would be better applied to student education, safety, and innovation in instructional delivery. Clearly, a better approach is needed.[28]

This loss of independence for colleges and universities has many negative side effects beyond the campus itself. Access to easy money dramatically raised the cost of tuition, which drove students to accept growing mountains of personal debt. "More than 40% of Americans who borrowed from the government's main student-loan program aren't making payments or are behind on more than $200 billion owed, raising worries that millions of them may never repay."[29] By way of comparison, one of the schools that stayed out of the federal program provides student loans on its own. Its default rate is less than 3 percent.[30]

As if that wasn't bad enough, a government plan designed to help give lower-income Americans a better chance has had exactly the opposite effect. Cornell professor Suzanne Mettler has made the case the federal program has actually *increased* inequality and "sabotaged the American Dream."[31]

What's especially important about this example is that there were other options back in the '60s when the federal program began. A privately funded effort to help lower-income Americans get into college was launched and working before the federal program began.[32]"Its dollars were doing over 25 times the work of dollars Congress had allocated to its student loan program."[33] Unfortunately, higher education officials in the '60s were so focused on finding a political solution that they missed the bigger picture. That's why colleges and universities are under the thumb of the Department of Education today.

Whenever we search only for political options, we are blinded both to other approaches and to potential dangers of those political "solutions." That blindness prevents us from pursuing an all-hands-on-board approach that would unleash the creativity and resources of individual Americans, families, community groups, churches, entrepreneurs, small businesses, local governments, and more.

The question, then, is how can we eliminate the blindness and truly see all the options at our disposal?

TAKING THE TIME TO DO IT RIGHT

That's where Radical Incrementalism[34] comes into play. It's a concept recognizing the power of modest changes in behavior to produce significantly different results. The best way to lose weight—and keep it off—is not with a fad diet. It's by making a minor change in your daily routine and sticking with it. If you get up a bit earlier and work out each day, the pounds and inches will eventually melt away. Staying away from desserts can multiply the impact. But, ultimately, it's the persistence of incremental steps day in and day out that brings about radical change.

An important part of the process is keeping the behavioral change manageable enough so that it can become a habit before you quit. For me, starting with twenty minutes and a modest pace on the elliptical was a sustainable change; an hour of intense work each morning was not. After a while, as my new daily actions became a habit, I was able to increase my workout intensity and take it to another level.

This approach makes just as much sense when launching a massive campaign of community problem solving. We can't expect people to give up their jobs, family time, or every available waking moment to community engagement. But most people can find time to do a little bit more and will enthusiastically do so if they believe it can make a difference. And, as they develop new habits, they will be able to increase the intensity of their effort and take it to another level.

In terms of a massive campaign of community problem solving, the first step in the process is simple. We need to start solving the manageable problems before us and encouraging others to do the same.

But, to avoid the civic equivalent of a fad diet, we should also think about gradually building up our community problem solving capabilities. A good start would be to gather problem-solvers for regular meetings that provide encouragement, support, training, and a forum for strategic decision making. Most importantly, by bringing people together for a common purpose, they will strengthen the fabric of community itself.

The meetings should be focused on the larger goal of empowering a massive campaign of community problem solving. To help get things started, an Institute for Community Driven Solutions is being developed at the King's College in New York City. Among other things, it will develop support materials for training, group meetings, and problem-solving approaches. Some groups will use these resources; others will develop their own.

I recognize that getting together for a weekly meeting may not sound as exciting as crusading for the latest hot button issue or beating the other side in a political grudge match. But in any serious competition, preparation is the key to victory. A billboard near my home puts it this way: "Beach bodies are made in winter." In the world of sports, championships are won on the practice field long before they are realized in the big game.

Preparation is essential. As we seek to serve our communities, we will encounter tremendous resistance from those who believe that every solution must have a political solution. Similar meetings played a vital role in the black freedom movement of the 1950s and '60s. The movement's greatest successes could not have occurred without ongoing training in the principles and practices of nonviolence.

In fact, Martin Luther King Jr. said that victory in the Montgomery bus boycott was won during the very first mass meeting. That meeting displayed a tremendous "enthusiasm for freedom" but was also "tempered by amazing self-discipline." The enthusiasm kept them going while the discipline made them effective. The effort filled those present with "a new sense of dignity and destiny."[35]

The meetings for a massive campaign of community problem solving must seek similar objectives: provide enthusiasm that can be directed in a disciplined manner while lifting up the souls and spirits of all who take part.

One set of especially important meetings will be a series of small group discussion forums hosted in homes and online. The Institute for Community Driven Solutions will provide content for these groups, including a video series based upon this book that covers one chapter a week. Meeting participants will watch the video and then engage in a discussion about how it applies to the reality in their community.

The small group model is, of course, far from an original idea. It's been used successfully by churches and other organizations for thousands of years. Part of its value comes from the strengthening of personal relationships that develop through thoughtful and substantive conversation. It's not just talking about community building, it's actually building community.

Another part of the value comes from the underlying desire of each participant to make the world a better place. The meetings are for preparation and training. But every meeting will end by focusing on how each participant can change their own behavior to have an impact on the larger community.

It's hard to overstate the importance of taking the time to increase our community problem-solving capacity, what some call social capital. Long before the colonists sought to create their own country, they had built up the independent organizations needed to make it work. These groups did not rely upon support from King George and therefore were not controlled by him. Just as important, when the British were defeated, these groups made a self-governing society work.

FIRST THINGS FIRST

Many politicians today have this process backward. They believe we need to change government policy first and then hope that the free market will find solutions. A better approach is to follow the example that led to the founding of Harvard. The colonists didn't lobby the king for permission to create the school because it would have been a waste of time. They just did it.

We need to just go about the business of solving community problems and serving society. That means building up, strengthening, supporting, and creating independent groups to solve the problems facing our nation. These are the groups that govern society and will help us through the difficult times when our dysfunctional political system finally breaks down.

No one, of course, will be expected to start a new and independent college after their first meeting. Instead, participants will be encouraged to carve out a little more time for community projects, make most effective use of that time, and hold each other accountable. Those baby steps are an important part of Radical Incrementalism, but as time goes on the small group training will prepare the group for bigger challenges.

The exciting thing about unleashing the creativity, connections, and resources of group meetings and small group participants is that you have no idea where it will lead. Every time one small group succeeds in solving a problem, or shifting decision making to higher degrees of community control, the nation will be one step closer to making its highest ideals a reality.

As we go about solving problems on our own, more and more people will become aware of the power of community, the power to walk away, and the "Putting People First" model of governance. Over time, the false narrative that every problem must have a political answer will be thoroughly discredited.

Again, I recognize that this slow but steady approach will not excite those itching for a political war. It won't connect with those who believe that every solution must have a political solution and that our only hope is finding the right leader. But no amount of political maneuvering can solve the problems before us until the American people recognize that every organization and relationship has a role to play in governing society.

That can only be accomplished by a core group of people willing to take time to think through the foundational concepts of freedom, equality, and self-governance. It draws upon a powerful process described by four signs on the wall at one of my youthful hangouts. I don't remember paying any conscious attention to them at the time, but they were always there and we all knew the words.[36]

"Sow a thought, reap an act."

"Sow an act, reap a habit."

"Sow a habit, reap a character."

"Sow a character, reap a destiny."

That's the way to create lasting change—one step at a time. That's what Radical Incrementalism is all about.

CONCLUSION

It's important to recognize that this campaign will not succeed because of some clever marketing plan or sales pitch. It will come about only because it taps into the core beliefs and idealism fully embraced by everyday Americans. It's wholly consistent with the American Creed: the belief that we all have the right to do what we want with our own lives so long as we don't interfere with the rights of others to do the same. It is built upon an attitude brimming with optimism about what a free and self-governing people can accomplish. We cherish our freedom but recognize its greatest value can be found when we use that freedom to build community. As I mentioned earlier, liberty loves company.

The group meetings are simply a vehicle for helping people think through the practical implications of what they already believe. It's a way of putting the pieces together so that they make sense and can help guide their actions. It's giving them a new way to fill in the 60 percent that they don't see with their eyes.

The real power of the meetings is that those who commit the time and effort will have a massive impact on the world around them. In the experiment mentioned earlier, half the people focused on counting the number of passes missed seeing the gorilla. But if someone is told about the gorilla first, they can't miss it.

The same is true with community problem solving. When our friends and neighbors get caught up in seeking only political solutions, they may be blinded to other alternatives. But if we point out the invisible gorillas in our communities, we can change the world. Once others get in the habit of looking for the whole range of options, they'll never again limit themselves to only political options.

In this way, we will help our communities see the world more clearly. As that happens, the communities will begin to think and act differently to form new habits. The character of our communities will come to embrace an all-hands-on-board approach to meet community needs. Ultimately, these steps will shape the destiny of a nation that is worthy of our highest ideals.

That's the way it worked for Levi Preston. He and his friends did not read the great books or take part in the discussions that guided colonial leaders. But they were influenced by those discussions because Preston and the Minutemen experienced the unbeatable reality of a free and independent society. They felt the power of those ideas deep in their bones. It guided their behavior and gave them the courage to stand up for what was right. "What we meant in going for those Redcoats was this: we always had been free and we meant to be free always! They didn't mean that we should."[37] It wasn't just Preston. The colonial passion for freedom "permeated every aspect of the behavior of the whole society."[38]

Radical Incrementalism, driven by thousands of independent small groups throughout the country, can permeate every aspect of 21st-century America with the understanding that every organization and relationship plays a role in governing society. That understanding will unleash the talent and creativity of the American people in a massive campaign of community problem solving.

CHAPTER 10

CHANGE IS GOOD, TRANSITIONS ARE HARD

WHEN I WAS VERY YOUNG, my Nana worked as a bank teller in Paterson, New Jersey. It was always a great day when I could ride the bus in and have lunch with her! The credit card industry was just getting started and most people paid for just about everything in cash. ATMs were still far in the future, so a crowd of regulars came in to Nana's branch every week to cash their paycheck. They also put money aside each week in a Christmas Club account and transacted other routine financial business in person.

In those days, banks were not allowed to operate in more than one state. In fact, many states didn't even allow branch banking, so there were lots of small local banks around the nation. People dealt with a local bank manager when they needed a loan, a mortgage, or a credit reference. Since there were no FICO credit ratings or Quicken Loans to provide competition, the local bank manager's opinion of you was often decisive. Not surprisingly, the bank manager typically became a big-man-in-town who enjoyed "bankers' hours" to golf on Wednesday afternoons and Saturday mornings.

Those days, of course, are long gone. There are only half as many banks around today and the big banks have gotten much bigger.[1] Just about everything you used to do at a local bank branch can now be done on your smartphone. In fact, the only thing your phone can't do is issue paper money. But that doesn't matter so much when you have phones, digital wallets, and credit cards to pay for what you need.

All of this raises a pretty basic question. Why do we need bank branches?

The answer is that we don't. Sure, they hang on as a comfortable habit for people born before the digital revolution, but they no longer provide an underlying value. Even if you really need or want paper money, you don't have to go to a bank. There are plenty of free-standing ATMs around to meet your need.

A Citigroup report projects that a third of the nation's 94,000 branches could disappear within a decade, taking with them 770,000 jobs. That's from the company that owns more branches than any other firm. Other estimates of the carnage are even higher.[2] Since technology usually pushes transformation further and faster than industry leaders expect, traditional bank branches could soon be extinct in most communities.

This is a prime example of a good change being achieved through a hard transition. The end result will be better consumer service and a more efficient financial system. "The cost of branches and associated staff make up about 65 percent of the total retail cost of larger banks, much of which can be eliminated via automation."[3] For consumers, there will be more choices and fewer hassles.

But that transition will be costly for those who lose their job and for the banks that need to unload tremendous amounts of real estate assets. The ripple effects will spill over and hurt the commercial real estate market as well. As branches are closed, hundreds of millions of square feet of commercial space will become available.[4] In some communities, the closing of a local bank branch may be the final straw that dooms a downtown area. Eventually, the benefits will outweigh the costs, but the process of change is always difficult.

Bankers think that they are ready for all this. A 2014 letter to JP Morgan shareholders warned, "Silicon Valley is coming. There are hundreds of startups with a lot of brains and money working on various alternatives to traditional banking."[5] The bankers may see it coming, but the change is likely to be far more substantial than most can imagine. One study analyzing the impact of millennials on 15 leading industries found that "banking is at the highest risk of disruption."[6]

The generation that grew up with the digital revolution would rather go to the dentist than hear about new financial offerings from their bank.

Instead, millennials would be more excited to hear fresh approaches from Google, Apple, Amazon, or Square.[7] The reason is simple. As JP Morgan's Jamie Dimon puts it, "Silicon Valley is good at getting rid of pain points. Banks are good at creating them."[8]

Just as the journalism industry faced a battle between print newspapers and online services, banks are now caught in "a tremendous battle for the customer interface from fintech providers such as Simple, Moven, PayPal, Venmo and hundreds of others that are unbundling banking."[9] Smartphones have empowered consumers to cherry-pick the services they want, some from a bank and some from other sources. This makes big banks vulnerable to "death by a thousand cuts." CB Insights, an investment research firm, notes that the banks are already under attack "from robo-advisor wealth management services like Wealthfront and Betterment; small business loan companies like Prosper and Kabbage; personal loan startups like LendUp and Oportun; apps that offer new models for banking like Moven and Digit; and many more."[10]

The bottom line is that the digital transformation of the banking industry is just beginning. Before it is finished, the changes will be far more comprehensive than all the changes the industry has experienced since I visited my Nana more than a half century ago.

It's important to clearly recognize that all this change is not coming from politicians, regulators, or other financial firms. It is simply another case of the culture leading and the politicians lagging behind. New technology has shifted power away from politicians and bureaucrats and put it in the hands of everyday Americans. Bankers' hours no longer exist because customers won't put up with it.

It's going to be a very bumpy ride, especially for the biggest banks and those who work for them. But, following a painful transition, the resulting financial system will be much less volatile and less subject to regulatory gimmickry. The new system will serve Main Street rather than Wall Street.

THE AUTO INDUSTRY WILL NEVER BE THE SAME

A similar transition is taking place in the auto industry. As ride-sharing and self-driving cars become the norm, everything about the car culture will change. Overall, the changes will be positive. Studies indicate that ride-sharing companies like Uber and Lyft have already reduced the number of traffic fatalities and DUIs.[11] Self-driving cars will also reduce the number of accidents dramatically, and a McKinsey Report projects a significantly positive impact on the overall economy.[12]

Today, the typical car is actually in use only about 5 percent of the time. It will be far more efficient to share cars than keep them reserved for personal use. One Goldman Sachs researcher suggests, "Instead of owning a car outright, we might start consuming mobility services."[13] In other words, rather than having a car parked in the driveway, we might order a car to take us to work in the morning. The car would drive itself to pick us up and take us where we need to go. A different car might take us home. When we head out with the family for a road trip, we might order still another car, something a little roomier.

Not all of us will do this, of course, but most probably will. Sharing rather than buying saves money and hassle. It provides just the right vehicle for the right trip and all sorts of other benefits. But, just like the changes in banking, the transition will not be pain-free. If most of us are sharing cars, there won't be a need for as many cars. According to one estimate, car sales could fall nearly in half over the next generation.[14] Again, since technological changes usually outpace what industry leaders can envision, the real decline in auto sales may be much bigger and faster.

I know this sounds fanciful to some who can't imagine Americans giving up their love of cars and driving. But we've seen this happen before. It's the same sort of transformational change that took place more than a century ago when cars replaced horses as the primary means of transportation in America.

The ripple effects of the changing car culture will spread far beyond the direct decline in auto sales and loss of those manufacturing jobs. What happens to auto dealers when consumers start ordering rides rather than buying cars? Even the best news will create problems for someone. As auto safety improves, the auto insurance industry will decline. So will the need for car washes, tow trucks, auto parts stores, body shops, and other repair services.

The implications of this shift will be felt far and wide. Some envision the public transit industry being turned upside down.[15] Once we are able to order a driverless car to pick us up at any time, why would we need buses and trains?[16] It's even possible to imagine self-driving cars cutting into the airline business. For shorter distances, working or napping while a car handles the ride may be easier than dealing with the growing inconvenience of air travel.

It's impossible, of course, to know exactly what this will look like in a generation or so. That's the beauty of community problem solving in a free and self-governing nation. Unleashing the creativity of countless individuals and organizations to meet the needs of society will lead to solutions no one can even imagine today. And, while the journey may be unpredictable and bumpy at times, we can take comfort in the fact that the people are in charge of the process, not the politicians. Intentional community problem solving will yield pragmatic changes that really work in day-to-day life.

The same scale of change is coming to two huge sectors of the economy currently dominated by government—education and health care. These vitally important segments of American society consume more than 22 percent of all spending in our nation.[17] Think about that. More than one out of every five dollars spent in America is spent on either health care or education. That's roughly three times as much as the entire financial services industry[18] and more than three and a half times the size of the auto industry.[19]

Education and health care, of course, matter far more than money. However, I emphasize the size of these industries to give a sense of the impact that transformation will bring. The adaptation of self-driving cars and the closing of tens of thousands of bank branches will pale in comparison to the impact of transitioning to new forms of education and health care services.

In both of these fields, the issues involved are so personal and important, they cannot rationally be discussed in a dysfunctional political environment. Change will come from the outside now that technology has empowered individuals to work around traditional bureaucratic institutions.

It will not be easy. With so much money and power at stake, any changes that improve health care and education will encounter significant opposition. The more that patients, health care providers, parents, students, teachers, and everyday Americans are empowered, the stronger the resistance will be from political and corporate elites who benefit from the status quo.

EDUCATION

My mom was an English teacher. So are my son and daughter-in-law. Yet I grew up with a passionate hatred of school. I loved learning, but hated school ("School's Out" by Alice Cooper was my theme song). My wife prayed that our children would be better students than I was, and I'm forever grateful that they were.

Despite my hatred of school, there were a few teachers I will never forget. One in particular was Miss Brewer. Before taking her class as a high school senior, I had no use for history. But she used engaging approaches to reach a disengaged teen and made the subject come alive. Because of Miss Brewer, I learned to appreciate history as the fascinating human story of people both famous and unknown dealing with larger than life events.

It took a while before I finished college, but when I did I had a history degree. Not only that, my love of history played a big role in my polling career by enabling me to put current trends in a larger context. Like many students, it took decades before I fully appreciated just how much Miss Brewer had impacted my life.

Around the time I was learning to love history, 58 percent of Americans had quite a lot of confidence in public schools.[20] The Great Turnaround was just getting started and Americans still had confidence in big bureaucratic organizations. But leading reformers had already figured out that bureaucracy was not a good model for education.

John Holt, a frustrated teacher whose best-selling books sparked a nationwide debate, wrote, "It is a rare child who can come through his schooling with much left of his curiosity, his independence, or sense of his own dignity, competence, and worth." Holt added that schools of that era taught students that they were "worthless, untrustworthy, fit only to take other people's orders."[21]

Since then, public schools have been rocked by the same forces that are shaking up banks, the auto industry, and the routines of everyday life. Only half as many Americans—just 30 percent—now express quite a lot of confidence in public schools.[22] Americans have even come to believe that private schools, parochial (church-related) schools, charter schools, and homeschooling all provide a better education than traditional public schools.[23]

Like the banking and auto industries, the change coming to the world of education is just getting started. It's not a question of whether change is coming; it's a question of how we shape it.

Teachers are stuck in the middle, caught between the needs of their students and the demands of the bureaucracy. Eighty-two percent consider making a difference in students' lives to be one of the most rewarding aspects of the job. But 81 percent believe students spend too much time taking district- or state-mandated tests. Overall, state and district policies that get in the way of teaching rank as the number one concern for teachers. Other top concerns include the constantly changing bureaucratic demands on both teachers and students.[24]

Making matters worse, 76 percent don't believe their professional opinions are factored into district decision making. An even larger number, 94 percent, believe that their views are not considered in formulating state or national education policies.[25] "The joy and reward have been all but sucked out of teaching," according to one teacher. They've "been replaced with unending paperwork, staff meetings, and Professional Learning Community meetings—generally to be completed either before or after school hours."[26]

The good news is that there are still plenty of teachers like Miss Brewer. Not only that, the tools are now available for great teachers to get around the bureaucracy and our dysfunctional political system. New technologies have opened up a world of possibilities for teachers to create an entirely new system of education. The end result will be unlike anything we can imagine today, perhaps as different as the auto industry will look in an era of self-driving cars.

The most likely scenario is for teachers to start new schools—lots of them—just as the early colonists founded Harvard. Some teachers will take the lead; others will sign on to collaborate with their more entrepreneurial peers. The schools will come in a wide variety of shapes and sizes, but all will be focused on serving students rather than bureaucrats. Unleashing the creativity of a million or more teachers to meet the needs of students will lead to solutions no one can even imagine today.

The idea of teachers starting schools to give parents more options is far from a new idea, but it has been gaining ground due to the decentralizing trends of the Great Turnaround.

Charter schools were first envisioned in the 1970s by an education professor at the University of Massachusetts. Ray Budde saw "a necessity of placing more decision-making at the school level, close to the classrooms."[27] Around the same time, the political movement for school vouchers was gaining steam. Nobel Prize-winning economist Milton Friedman promoted the idea that parents should be able to use public funding to choose whatever school they wanted. Another big fan of vouchers was Apple's Steve Jobs. "The problem is bureaucracy. I'm one of these people who believes the best thing we could ever do is go to the full voucher system." Jobs added that if we had a voucher system, "People would get out of college and say, 'Let's start a school.'"

Today, 2.5 million students are enrolled in charter schools[28] and 400,000 attend school through a voucher program.[29] On top of that, the modern home schooling movement was launched in the 1970s, by a teacher, principal, and superintendent of California public schools.[30] Today, 1.77 million students are home schooled.[31]

While these numbers seem big, 50.4 million students still attend traditional public schools.[32] Not only that, many of the other schooling options are still teaching in a somewhat traditional manner. All of that is going to change in the coming reformation of education in the United States.

Instead of a one-size-fits-all debate about, say, whether students should wear uniforms, the 21st-century educational system will recognize that different students have different needs. Some need more structure and rules, while others flourish with more freedom and flexibility. Questions about year-round schooling vs. summer vacations will be resolved by having schools that offer both calendars. In fact, just about every hot-button issue in education today will be resolved by giving teachers, parents, and students more choice.

How much attention and money should be devoted to the arts? Or sports? What books are appropriate? Should schools prepare students for a job or for life in general? Should prayer be allowed? Should students learn about the founding ideals of the nation? Or the history and accomplishments of Western civilization? These questions are best answered by teachers and parents committed to their students rather than distant bureaucrats committed to their ideological agenda.

As teachers are treated like professionals and freed from the bureaucracy, even more change is likely to take place. Maybe some schools will continue to offer a traditional school week while others will have four days of class and a long weekend. Or, perhaps, two long days of class and two days of working on projects at home. Some might simply respond to a substantial body of research showing that high school students would do much better if classes started an hour later.[33]

Some of the schools will be small and meet in the home of students or a teacher. A more innovative option might be for schools to operate in office buildings where Mom and Dad work. That could be a nice employee benefit for leading firms to offer. Some might put all those abandoned bank buildings to use while others could use a church, Y, or Boys & Girls Club. The physical location won't matter as much as the cooperation of teachers and parents to provide a quality experience for each student.

Importantly, this can all be accomplished through community problem solving by focusing on what teachers do best, and what students need most. There is no need for a political crusade because existing rules that empower home schooling and other private education programs can be used to create new schools.

Still, while community problem solving will create the 21st-century system of education, the 20th-century model has created a reality where state and local governments spend more money on education than anything else.[34] The people who control that money are not likely to give up easily. That means political battles will remain part of the ongoing discussion.

Efforts to expand charter schools and vouchers will continue while bureaucrats will fight back harshly. The *Empire Strikes Back* mindset can already be heard in the rumblings of those who believe we should ban all private schooling options. Today, those suggestions come from the political left. Earlier in American history, the Ku Klux Klan and other anti-Catholic groups pursued the same goal in a campaign that was eventually overturned by the U.S. Supreme Court.[35]

But efforts to ban alternatives to traditional public education will not succeed. As one reporter noted following an effort by New York City to cut back on charter schools, "Once you help put kids into better schools, their parents will mobilize to defend them."[36] Some states are likely to temporarily impose more restrictions than others, but eventually the best practices discovered through experimentation will carry the day.

The underlying forces for change are more powerful than the bureaucracy. They will ultimately have a much bigger impact than vouchers and charter schools. Financially, this transformation will be fueled by the fact that we currently spend an annual average of $12,401 per student in K-12 schools.[37] However, parents can buy a full year's curriculum for only a few hundred dollars (or even free in some cases). That gap presents a tremendous entrepreneurial opportunity.

Technology entrepreneurs are already working on this, including efforts that will customize coursework based upon a student's personal interests.[38] In addition to the social value of improving education, entrepreneurs will be enticed by the huge market opportunity: We currently spend more than $600 billion annually on K-12 education.

All the technology and spending in the world, however, cannot change the fact that teachers can add great value to the educational process. From a business perspective, the challenge will be figuring out how to fairly compensate and treat teachers while keeping down the price of a quality education. From a moral perspective, this approach will give parents more control over how and what their children are taught. As an added bonus, all this experimentation and competition will improve traditional schools as well.

Somewhere over the next decade or so, a radical transformation will take place. It will probably occur when next-generation educators consistently provide a superior education at a price working-class families are willing and able to pay. The service will have to be very impressive, because the competing public school alternative will be available for free.

Once that point is reached—when the quality and cost effectiveness of the new schools has been clearly demonstrated on a grand scale—the status quo will crumble and bureaucrats will no longer be in charge of education. Everything we think we know today about how schools work will be turned upside down. Most importantly, students will receive better preparation for life than they do today.

The transition will be difficult, but it will lead to a far more vibrant, relevant, and diverse system of education for American children. The institutions, associations, routines, and best practices of the 21st-century school system will be vastly different from anything we know or can imagine. But while we don't know what the school system of the future will look like, we can take comfort from the fact that it's being developed by teachers and parents rather than bureaucrats and politicians. Students around the world will benefit from the resulting innovation.

HEALTH CARE

America's health care system was broken long before Obamacare was implemented. Michael Porter of the Harvard Business School described the situation bluntly:

> No one is happy with the current system—not patients, who worry about the cost of insurance and the quality of care; not employers, who face escalating premiums and unhappy employees; not physicians and other providers, whose incomes have been squeezed, professional judgments overridden, and workdays overwhelmed with bureaucracy and paperwork; not health plans, which are routinely vilified; not suppliers of drugs and medical devices, which have introduced many life-saving or life-enhancing therapies but get blamed for driving up costs; and not governments, whose budgets are spinning out of control.[39]

Those dreaming of a political solution to this mess are sure to be disappointed. Obamacare didn't fix the problem and its unpopularity helped elect Donald Trump. But the Republicans' efforts to develop their own centralized plan to replace it will not fix the health care insurance mess we have today. According to Porter, "Health care delivery is simply too complex, too subtle, too individualized, and too rapidly evolving to be manageable by top-down micromanagement."[40]

Control by politicians and bureaucrats has created what the Harvard professor describes as "the fundamental flaw in U.S. health care policy" today—"a lack of focus on patient value." Whether the bureaucrats work for insurance companies or the government, patient needs get lost in the shuffle. "The right objective for health care is to increase value for patients. ...Minimizing costs is simply the wrong goal, and will lead to counterproductive results."[41]

Fortunately, the decentralizing forces of the Great Turnaround are poised to shake up the health care system just as they are shaking up the fields of banking, autos, and education.

PC Magazine reports, "Telemedicine and telehealth apps are dramatically making healthcare more convenient, less expensive, more preventative, and in many cases downright better."[42] A National Conference of State Legislatures (NCSL) report sees this as a strategy "to help achieve the triple aim of better health care, improved health outcomes, and lower costs."[43]

To take just one example of the coming transformation, the first working electrocardiogram (EKG) was created in 1903 and earned Willem Einthoven a Nobel Prize in 1924.[44] A standard test for monitoring heart health,[45] EKGs are typically conducted in a hospital or doctor's office and cost more than $100.[46] But this early 20th-century technique has been upgraded for the 21st century. Now, for less than the cost of a single test at the doctor's office, you can enable your smartphone to conduct an EKG at home.[47]

Cardiologist Eric Topol described the shock of receiving an email from a patient with the attention grabbing subject line: "I'm in atrial fib, now what do I do?" Test results were attached. The doctor "immediately knew that the world had changed. The patient's phone hadn't just recorded the data; it had interpreted it."[48]

The value of this upgrade is far greater than saving money or the convenience factor. It's the likelihood of improved health that comes from more regular testing to catch problems earlier. It won't be long until doctors can "discover most heart disease before a heart attack or stroke and address it at a fraction of the cost of care that would be needed following such a trauma."[49] An added benefit is that patients receive instant feedback from their daily testing. Research shows that such feedback leads to better lifestyle choices, which also improves health.

If the idea of self-monitoring and sending the results to a doctor seems a bit strange to you, keep in mind that millions of patients with diabetes have been doing so for years. The health benefits from measuring their own blood sugar levels is incalculable.

Since recovering from the shock of his patient's email, Dr. Topol has written extensively about the many ways that "the medicalized smartphone will democratize health care." You will soon be able "to perform an array of routine lab tests via your phone" and do so "at a fraction of the current cost."[50] In fact, "it won't be long before you can take a smartphone X-ray selfie if you're worried that you might have broken a bone."[51]

These self-monitoring devices will dramatically impact every aspect of the health care industry. Currently, for example, there are more than 200,000 diagnostic laboratories in the country.[52] While there will always be a need for some testing outside the home, the business of medical labs is likely to shrink dramatically. Even when lab tests are needed, the costs will be much lower due to the competition from new technologies. Proving once again that positive changes require painful transitions, many medical lab facilities could go the way of bank branches.

As more preventive testing can be done at home, there will also be less demand for hospital service. The potential financial impact here is staggering. One out of every 14 Americans spends at least one night in a hospital each year with an average stay of five days. Additionally, there are well over 100 million outpatient visits each year.[53] Total hospital spending is estimated at $1.036 trillion.[54]

The reduced need for these services will be good for patients but hard on the industry. "Good quality is less costly because of more accurate diagnoses, fewer treatment errors, lower complication rates, faster recovery, less invasive treatment, and the minimization of the need for treatment." As Harvard's Porter puts it, "better health is less expensive than illness."

The coming change will also drive enormous changes in the relationship between doctor and patient. One relatively modest change—virtual doctor visits—were initially thought of "as a means to reach rural communities, which typically face additional barriers to accessing care." Live videoconferences were helpful when the patient lived far away from medical professionals. As a result, states like Alaska, Arkansas, and South Dakota were early leaders in adopting telehealth initiatives.[55]

But the NCSL report shows that the new techniques are now "being viewed more broadly."[56] One reason for the growing popularity is that you can now have a virtual consultation with a doctor on a moment's notice at any time, day or night. And the cost is only $40.[57] That's not much more than the co-pay for a typical doctor's visit. Once you factor in the convenience and the cost of driving, these virtual visits can seem like a bargain for the patient. In some cases, you can now even have a prescription sent to your smartphone following a virtual checkup.[58]

Once again, though, the painful process of transition shines through. While the out-of-pocket cost for the patient is similar to a typical doctor's visit, the money paid to the doctor is far less. Why? Because in the typical office visit, the doctor also gets paid by the insurance company. Overall, this use of telemedicine reduces costs for the patient by more than $100 a visit.[59] But from the doctor's point of view, that's $100 less income.

Virtual visits, though, are just the beginning of the transition.

As more and more data is provided by patients doing daily checkups at home, no medical professional could possibly analyze all the incoming data. Besides, "much of what physicians do (checkups, testing, diagnosis, prescription, behavior modification, etc.) can be done better by sensors, passive and active data collection, and analytics."[60] The end result is that computers will review the flood of daily test results and draw the medical staff's attention to areas of concern. Or, patients will call in with concerns and their test results will already be in the doctor's hands.

One advocate of the new technology believes that soon "the idea of going down to your doctor's office for a visit is going to feel as foreign as going to the video store to get a VHS tape."[61] Reasonable estimates suggest that computers will eventually replace 80 percent of what doctors do. There will be fewer doctors but they will have more time for patients. On top of that, studies have shown "that 75% of cases can be safely triaged to be treated by RNs."[62] The professionals will continue to play vital roles in the health care process, but their roles won't look anything like they do today.

Despite the tremendous health benefits and cost savings offered by the new technologies, change will be fought every step of the way. Health care in America is a $3.2 trillion industry (an average of $10,000 cost for every man, woman, and child in the land).[63] Because so much money and power is at stake, the nation's health care system is at the epicenter of the battle between the regulatory state and community problem solving. Those who benefit from the status quo will not hesitate to call on the federal bureaucracy to protect their position.

Fortunately, though, that $3.2 trillion will continue to draw entrepreneurs into the process of developing new techniques. In an era of increased personalization and decentralization, their efforts will be devoted to putting more power into the hands of everyday Americans.

Still, the federal bureaucrats have tighter control over health care than they do over education. But, there are cracks in their system of control that increase community control over the developing health care system.

Most significantly, perhaps, the political issues involved in the transition to telehealth initiatives are governed by state law rather than federal regulations. Questions about insurance coverage, issuance of prescriptions, Medicaid rules and more are being explored on a state-by-state basis with an eye toward developing best practices. In some cases, states are working together on the licensing of physicians across state lines or forming compacts to establish similar guidelines.[64]

The possibility of states setting the pace of reform is aided by the fact that "the telehealth field is changing rapidly." The NCSL report acknowledges that "technology may be getting ahead of policy."[65] This is another way of saying patients are taking control by searching for new ways to improve their own health. Whether it's buying a Fitbit accessory or using other apps to guide their own health practices, consumers are taking the lead.

Additionally, despite the frustrations of the current bureaucratic health care system, most medical professionals entered the field due to a passionate desire to serve others. Just as parents and teachers will take the lead in reforming education, the 21st-century health care system will be created by patients seeking better health and health care professionals seeking to serve them. Politicians and bureaucrats will be cut out of the loop.

Eventually, the insurance company and federal bureaucrats will find themselves in the position of children who build sandcastles at low tide. No matter how big a wall they build, the high tide will always wipe out their castle and level the beach. The rising tide of decentralization that began in the 1970s is prepared to wipe out bureaucratic control of health care and create a level playing field for all Americans.

Change will come to the political rules concerning health care, but it will come *after* community problem-solving efforts have already created a 21st-century health care system. As always, it's a mistake to think that our dysfunctional political system can or should lead the nation forward. The only real question is how far behind the politicians and bureaucrats will lag.

THE POWER OF COMMUNITY AT WORK

It would also be a mistake, however, to ignore the role of community problem solving and empowerment in guiding the transformational changes coming to banking, autos, education, and health care. While the technology empowers us as individuals, it is only by working together in community that we can create a better world for our children and grandchildren.

This community-driven approach is perhaps most obvious in the transformation of education. Teachers and parents will intentionally work together in community to create new schools. Those schools will form a larger community of schools collectively offering a wide variety of options to meet the needs of every student. As new approaches are developed, they will spill across the borders and benefit children throughout the entire world. One of the truly exciting aspects of this transformation is that local control will be combined with technology providing access to knowledge, resources, and best practices from around the globe.

The banking transformation will be guided primarily by individual customer preferences, but community norms will be established through discussions around kitchen tables, at the office, and on social media. There will be no shortage of discussion about which apps work, which ones don't, and which ones are scams. The only banking services that succeed in transforming society will be those that meet the broadly defined acceptable standards of a community.

In autos, best practices will be developed as people rapidly adapt to the new opportunities. Guiding power will come both from individual preferences and from state or local government rules.[66] As with everything else in the decentralizing and more personalized world, there will be no one-size-fits-all solution. And, as addressed in Chapter 5, whenever state and local laws guide the process, community control is stronger than it can ever be in the regulatory state.

In health care, it's state laws that will provide guidance as best practices are developed. Community control will shape those laws to serve what one health care strategist describes as "the Blockbuster Drug of the Century"[67]—the engagement of patients in their own care.

Patients engaged in their own health care needs act in community not isolation. They gather information and consider options from a variety of community resources. They also rely on personal networks and community groups for everything from nutrition and workout ideas to finding support during difficult times.

In short, the 200 million smartphones and other new technologies are the greatest force of change in the history of the world. They are already transforming the world we live in by providing ways for people working together in community to get around a dysfunctional political system. The regulatory state is resisting that change and desperately trying to hang on to centralized power in a decentralizing world. But it will not succeed.

CHAPTER 11

STATES DON'T HAVE RIGHTS, PEOPLE HAVE RIGHTS

I N THE SUMMER OF 1619, well over a year before the Pilgrims set sail on the Mayflower, two contradictory strands of American history got their start in Jamestown, Virginia. One strand was noble, the other was shameful.

On July 30, the first representative government in the American colonies was established. The House of Burgesses met in the Jamestown Church "to establish one equal and uniform government over all Virginia."[1] (As with many historical firsts, the event itself wasn't all that great. "It was hot and humid and many of the Burgesses were ill from the extreme temperatures." One of the 22 elected representatives died from the heat and the entire session was concluded after just six days.[2])

Thus began America's long and generally successful experiment with self-governance.

However, in a twist of fate worthy of a Greek tragedy, the first enslaved people arrived in the same town just a few weeks later.[3] They were probably literate and Christian,[4] having been abducted by Portuguese slave traders from what is now Angola. British pirates raided the Portuguese ship, took roughly two dozen captives as their prize, and sold them in Jamestown.[5]

Thus began America's great national sin, a sin that has haunted the nation for four centuries.

These two narratives—one positive and one negative—have competed and interacted to define America ever since. These dueling histories directly impact the way we perceive events today. We see it in the polarized responses that arise every time a young black man is shot by a white police officer. In fact, we see it every time any racially charged event bursts into the news.

The polarized response results from the fact that we see only 40 percent of these current events with our eyes. How we fill in the remaining 60 percent depends upon which strand of history we instinctively accept as dominant. When a story breaks on the national news, those who see our national legacy as noble see something entirely different from those who primarily see the shameful strand.

All, however, recognize that America's history of legalized discrimination calls into question the legitimacy of our more noble traditions. The conflict between the competing strands is so dramatic that some people instinctively try to downplay every reminder of our less appealing history. When First Lady Michelle Obama said that she wakes up in a house built by slaves, Bill O'Reilly responded on Fox News that those slaves "were well-fed and had decent lodgings provided by the government."[6]

O'Reilly's statements were technically accurate but completely off-base. It's true that "America's self-sufficiency in food ... made it possible for masters to provide slaves with a comparatively healthy diet."[7] But the fact that they had a healthier diet than slaves in other countries is hardly something to brag about. Surely the larger issue is that a nation promising life, liberty, and pursuit of happiness to everyone should never have allowed slavery at all. That's the history we need to address.

As we seek to lift the nation up to its highest ideals through a massive campaign of community problem solving, we must recognize that there is another side to our nation's story. Michelle Alexander, author of *The New Jim Crow*, correctly notes that it is "impossible to overstate the significance of race in defining the basic structure of American society."[8]

There's much more to American history than race, of course. But the "ever-raging conflict" between the noble American Creed and legalized racism is a serious moral problem at the heart of our national story. In *An American Dilemma*, Gunnar Myrdal correctly noted that the "moral struggle goes on within people and not merely between them."[9]

Lillian Smith, a white Southern woman raised in the early 20th century, described the reality of this internal struggle. "The mother who taught me what I know of tenderness and love and compassion taught me also the bleak rituals of keeping Negroes in their 'place.'" Smith added, "I learned to believe in freedom, to glow when the word *democracy* was used, and to practice slavery from morning to night."[10]

Because it is so deeply rooted, this conflict has played a key role in defining our system of politics and government right from the start. It even tarnished the Constitution itself.

Our Constitution is appropriately revered and celebrated for placing limits on ambitious politicians through a wonderful system of checks and balances. By protecting the rights and freedom of individuals, it laid the groundwork that enabled our country to become a powerful and diverse 21st-century nation.

But, shamefully, compromises with defenders of slavery added unsavory provisions to the very document that created our government. While the Declaration of Independence lifted up the noble ideal that we are all created equal, the Constitution said that black slaves counted only as three-fifths of a person. And, when it came time to vote, the voices of those slaves were not counted at all.

It took a bloody Civil War to have the racially offensive passages overturned by constitutional amendments; a war directly provoked by the conflict between racism and our founding ideals. When residents in South Carolina fired upon Fort Sumter to start that conflict, they were fighting both to defend slavery and to overturn the Declaration of Independence.

The states that left the union to defend slavery explicitly rejected the great ideals of freedom, equality, and self-governance. John Calhoun, a leading defender of slavery, was frustrated that admiration for the Declaration had "spread far and wide, and fixed itself deeply in the public mind."[11]

Calhoun was far from a fringe figure in American politics. In fact, he served as vice president of the United States under two different presidents and was a U.S. senator from South Carolina. Yet he considered it a "great and dangerous error to suppose that all people are equally entitled to liberty."[12] In his view, black people did not deserve freedom because liberty was "not a boon to be bestowed on a people too ignorant, degraded and vicious, to be capable either of appreciating or of enjoying it."[13]

These views made Calhoun a traitor to America's founding ideals just as surely as Benedict Arnold was a traitor to the young nation in the War of Independence.

Stories like these, and the reality of such treasonous attitudes, make all who believe in the American Creed uneasy. For me, it led to a long personal struggle trying to determine whether the positive or negative version of history is the real story of the nation I love. Eventually, though, I came to understand that such an effort is pointless. Both narratives are true and they are completely intertwined. Myrdal captured the reality of this dilemma, observing that "America is continually struggling for its soul."[14]

America is, in fact, a great nation striving to live up to the high ideals of freedom and self-governance. Sadly, it is also a nation with a sordid history of racism and legalized discrimination. Right from the beginning, "American political culture acquired a contradictory quality that it has never entirely shed." As Professors Marc Landy and Sidney Milkis put it, "An exemplary democratic politics . . . came to coexist with toleration for the most thoroughgoing dehumanizing oppression and victimization of a large minority of the population."[15]

The contrast between these competing narratives is so stark that it boggles the mind.

The core contradiction was captured on the nation's 76th birthday by an eloquent man who had escaped the bondage of slavery. "What, to the American slave, is your Fourth of July?" In 1852, Frederick Douglass described it as "a day that reveals to him, more than all the other days in the year, the gross injustice and cruelty to which he is the constant victim." While millions of white Americans celebrated the signing of the Declaration of Independence, Douglass called the celebration a "sham" filled with "fraud, deception, impiety and hypocrisy."[16]

Those are tough words, especially for people who love America and see it as a force for good in the world. But, as Landy and Milkis remind us, they reflect a fundamental truth we must never forget. "Like Abraham Lincoln and Martin Luther King, Douglass made clear that slavery robbed the Revolution of its true meaning."[17]

Sadly, that disconnect between an American celebration and the experience of black Americans was not left behind in the 19th century.

In 1963, the United States Civil Rights Commission held a celebration to commemorate the 100th anniversary of the date when Lincoln signed the Emancipation Proclamation. But the ongoing legalized discrimination of the Jim Crow era convinced many black Americans that there was little to celebrate.

"Second class citizenship, a form of up-date slavery is still rampant,"[18] observed *The Birmingham World*. Julius Hobson, a leader for the Congress of Racial Equality, declined an invitation to participate in the official celebration. He could not, "in good conscience, join a celebration of freedom in the United States which I and no other Negro have ever enjoyed."[19]

Even the then-Vice President of the United States, Lyndon B. Johnson, had to admit that "Emancipation was a Proclamation but not a fact."[20] Longtime *Wall Street Journal* Bureau Chief Douglas A. Blackmon expressed the underlying problem like this: "We are tainted by the failures of our fathers to fulfill our national credos when their courage was most needed."[21]

Blackmon's Pulitzer Prize-winning book, *Slavery by Another Name*, documented how the hypocrisy continued long after the Civil War supposedly brought an end to slavery. In a practice that lasted until 1945, black men in the South were routinely rounded up for petty crimes, imprisoned, and sold to work for anyone who would pay, including some of America's largest corporations.[22]

The black "convicts" did the work, but it was the jailers who got paid. For example, in 1929 "two Mississippi sheriffs reported making between $20,000 and $30,000 each ... for procuring black laborers and selling them to local planters."[23] That was an awful lot of money back in 1929. More significantly, it was an unconscionable offense against both the black workers and the high ideals of our nation.

What makes everything about this history even worse is that the development of American slavery was a conscious choice made by democratically elected governments.

CRONY CAPITALISM

When British pirates brought the first Africans to Jamestown, the laws that eventually made American slavery so horrific didn't yet exist. "Evidence suggests many of these early Africans were treated much like white-indentured servants," according to Holy Cross Professor Edward T. O'Donnell. "That is, they were held as laborers for a term of service, then granted freedom."[24] Initially, their skin color wasn't a decisive issue. "In less than two decades after arriving, many of this skilled and intelligent first generation of Jamestown Africans were free and had established their own farms and communities in Tidewater Virginia."[25]

Unfortunately, the representative assembly in Jamestown saw no limits to its power over individual lives. The very first legislators in America believed everyone should go to church and therefore "made Sabbath observance mandatory." Even though the first legislative session lasted just six days, they also found time to pass "prohibitions against gambling, drunkenness, and idleness."[26] That sense of an all-powerful legislature opened the door for another practice that still troubles us today— crony capitalism.

Starting in the 1660s, wealthy planters and colonial legislatures teamed up to create a captive labor force by making slavery "permanent and hereditary." New laws were passed that applied only to persons of color and made slavery "a good investment."[27] Colonial legislatures even overturned British common law and decreed that children born to enslaved women were slaves at birth. Most sickening of all, a Virginia law passed in 1669 declared that killing your own slave was not considered murder.[28]

Think about that for a moment. A duly elected colonial legislature believed it had the authority to declare that killing another human being was not murder. That's what happens when business and political elites use government power for their own selfish gain. They trample the freedoms of others.

We have, of course, made substantial progress since the days of slavery. But the contradictory strands of American history are still competing for the soul of our nation. It is a competition that cannot last forever. As Lincoln eloquently observed, "A house divided against itself cannot stand," Sooner or later, "it will cease to be divided. It will become all one thing or all the other."[29]

Fortunately, when the time comes that we cease to be divided, there is good reason to believe it is the noble strand that will prevail. The idealism of the Declaration "cannot be long ignored or repudiated, for sooner or later it returns to plague the council of practical politics," according to Pulitzer Prize-winning historian Vernon L. Parrington. He adds that such idealism "is constantly breaking out in fresh revolt."[30]

Today, that fresh revolt of idealism is poised to "lift our nation from the quicksands of racial injustice to the solid rock of brotherhood."[31] The millennial generation will lead the way by building on the powerful legacy of the civil rights movement and utilizing the tools of the digital revolution.

But the road ahead will not be easy. The shameful part of our heritage is deeply embedded in our system of politics and government.

THE FEDERAL GOVERNMENT VS. BILLIE HOLIDAY

In the 1920s, Harry Anslinger worked for an agency in the Treasury Department charged with enforcing Prohibition. He got the job the old-fashioned way—or at least the political way—by marrying into the family of the Treasury Secretary. When Congress created an independent Bureau of Narcotics, the well-connected bureaucrat was put in charge.[32]

At that time, marijuana was legal and the nation's first drug czar was OK with it. He claimed it was an "absurd fallacy"[33] to believe that marijuana caused violent crime. But when it served his desire for power, the bureaucrat changed his tune and claimed, "Marijuana is a lethal weapon, a killer weed." It is "the worst of all narcotics—far worse than the use of morphine or cocaine."[34]

What caused this change of heart? It was certainly not based upon new medical research. In fact, the drug warrior had to attack and suppress a substantial volume of medical research that challenged his claims. At one point, he received written opinions from 29 experts saying marijuana was not a threat and one saying that it was.[35] Naturally, the bureaucrat only accepted the one that backed his view.

Why? His sudden desire to outlaw pot came from a belief that black Americans used the drug more than white people. While serving a nation founded on the belief that all of us are created equal, Anslinger led an explicitly racist crusade to criminalize marijuana.

The bureaucrat had a special hatred of black entertainers and jazz music. He claimed that "it sounded like the jungles in the dead of night" and involved "unbelievably ancient indecent rites of the East Indies."[36] He dreamed of bringing down black jazz legends like Charlie Parker, Louis Armstrong, and Thelonious Monk. "Please prepare all cases in your jurisdiction involving musicians in violation of the marijuana laws. We will have a great national round-up arrest of all such persons on a single day. I will let you know what day."[37] Fortunately, that day never came.

As this hateful mix was brewing, Billie Holiday was coming to the nation's attention. The life of the woman known as Lady Day should have been celebrated as an all-American success story. Growing up alone in unimaginable poverty, she rose to the pinnacle of her profession and became one of the greatest jazz vocalists of all time.

But that wasn't what Anslinger saw. He "wanted to bring the full thump of the federal government down upon that scourge of modern society, his Public Enemy #1: Billie Holiday."[38]

The trouble grew partially out of the fact that Holiday used her voice and celebrity to protest the ongoing practice of lynching black men in the American South (in the 1930s, there were more than 100 lynchings).[39] One night, the performer asked the audience at an integrated club in New York to be quiet and listen carefully. The waiters stopped serving and the lights were turned down.[40] Holiday then sang "Strange Fruit" in public for the first time, emerging as "a black woman expressing grief and fury at the mass murder of her brothers in the South—their battered bodies hanging from the trees."[41]

Today, "Strange Fruit" is considered one of the greatest jazz songs of all time.[42] The Recording Industry Association has officially recognized it as one of the top songs of the 20th century—from any genre.[43] Jazz itself has been recognized by Congress as "a rare and valuable national treasure."[44] But that's not the way it was in Anslinger's America. Fearing retribution, Holiday's record label refused to release the protest song and she had to go elsewhere.[45]

Government harassment of the singer began the day after she first sang "Strange Fruit" in public.[46] The agent assigned to Holiday had a "long history of planting drugs on women" and other questionable behavior.[47] Following one arrest by the dubious agent, the star "immediately offered to go into a clinic to be monitored." By showing that "she would experience no withdrawal symptoms" Holiday hoped to "prove she was clean and being framed."[48] A jury sided with the singer.

To be clear, Holiday was no saint and had real challenges with addiction. However, Judy Garland and other white performers had similar issues. For them, the drug czar took an entirely different approach. He had a "friendly chat" with Garland and "advised her to take longer vacations between pictures." He also took the extraordinary step of writing to the white star's movie studio and fraudulently "assuring them she didn't have a drug problem at all."[49]

While lying to protect Garland, Anslinger ordered Holiday to stop singing "Strange Fruit." Not only did she refuse, the singer made that powerful song a special performance to end every show.[50] The bureaucratic bully then stepped up his crusade and banned her from singing in any venue where alcohol was sold.[51] Since every jazz club served drinks, there were few legitimate job opportunities left for the performer, and Holiday's life spun out of control.

Today, it's hard to imagine a world where the federal government decides who could sing in a nightclub. Such authority was part of the legal hangover resulting from America's ill-fated experiment with Prohibition. Unfortunately, it was precisely the kind of arbitrary power that a bureaucrat like Anslinger could abuse for his own personal agenda.

That personal agenda included silencing Holiday. As a final insult, while the legendary performer was lying on her death bed at the age of 44, federal agents arrested her one last time. They fingerprinted her, took a mug shot, interrogated her, and refused to let her talk to an attorney.[52]

This is what happens when federal bureaucrats are given too much discretionary authority and too little oversight. It helps explain why many "poor black communities [thought] the War on Drugs was part of a genocidal plan by the government to destroy black people in the United States."[53] The lingering impact of Anslinger's racist war on drugs is also seen in the fact that black Americans today are four times more likely than whites to be arrested on charges of marijuana possession.[54]

PROGRESS, BUT STILL A LONG WAY TO GO

Sadly, Anslinger's abuses were not a solitary exception to an otherwise sterling record.

For 300 years, from the 1660s to the 1960s, our nation literally had one set of laws for white people and another set of laws for black people. Four of our first five presidents owned slaves while proclaiming freedom. Those presidents administered our government for 32 of its first 36 years. Racism was not an aberration in a country firmly committed to liberty and justice to all. It was not a side story. It was and is an integral part of America's story, competing with the American Creed to define our national character.

America's history of legalized discrimination was finally brought down by the heroic civil rights movement of the 1950s and '60s. Since then, our nation has made significant progress toward racial equality, including the election of our first black president. But we still have a long way to go before our nation lives up to its rhetoric as a land filled with liberty and justice for all.

Today, 50 years after the civil rights movement made its mark, our nation remains deeply divided over racial issues. "Nearly 9-in-10 voters nationwide (87%) consider racial and ethnic discrimination to be a problem in the United States, including 68% who describe this as a big problem," according to the Monmouth University Polling Institute.[55]

The Pew Research Center reports an especially discouraging fact: 43 percent of black Americans don't think their country will ever make the changes needed to bring about true equality.[56]

The ongoing polarization can even be seen in the holiday celebrating Martin Luther King's birthday. King famously bemoaned the fact that Sunday mornings at church were the most segregated hour in America.[57] Sadly, observance of Martin Luther King Day is just as segregated.[58]

Adding to the challenge, many Americans believe race relations are getting worse. The *New York Times* reported that President Barack Obama's time in office produced a "sharp deterioration in the country's optimistic racial attitudes."[59] The election of Donald Trump is not expected to reverse that trend. Just 25 percent of voters expect the new president's efforts will lead to improved race relations. Nearly half (46 percent) expect it will make things worse. Among African Americans, 74 percent expect things to get worse.[60]

Fortunately, most Americans—including most white Americans—recognize that we have more work to do before black Americans obtain the full blessings of liberty and equality promised in the Declaration of Independence.[61] And, in a country where the culture leads and the politicians lag behind, the public recognition of the problem matters more than the failures of our political system.

THE HARMFUL LEGACY OF STATES' RIGHTS IDEOLOGY

Like just about every other problem facing our nation, the solutions to our racial divide cannot be found through politics as usual. Community problem solving is the only viable path forward.

Pragmatic community problem solving builds upon the "Putting People First" model of governance described earlier in Chapter 5. It empowers individuals and communities by shifting decision-making power and authority closer to home. In practical terms, that means taking power away from the federal government and the regulatory state.

Throughout this book, I have made the case that this approach is consistent with America's highest ideals and deepest traditions. But, I also recognize that many African Americans and other persons of color get nervous about any call to reduce federal power. That skepticism is an understandable response to the noxious legacy of the states' rights theory of government.

"States' rights," notes Yale University Law Professor Heather K. Gerken, "have been invoked to defend some of the most despicable institutions in American history, most notably slavery and Jim Crow."[62] Developed by men like Calhoun and other defenders of slavery, the states' rights theory was used for more than a century to justify the denial of rights to black Americans. It became the legal rationale for letting Southern states inflict violence and abuse on their black populations without federal interference.

Those of us who believe in community problem solving and are committed to our nation's highest ideals must directly confront this legacy. We need to recognize why so many black Americans instinctively believe that taking power away from the federal government will lead to a restoration of segregation and abuse. Then, we need to show why community problem solving will lead to a much brighter future.

A good place to start is with the presidential election of 1876.

That election took place a decade after the conclusion of America's Civil War. "Congressional Republicans had sought to build a biracial coalition that could control state and local governments in the former Confederacy."[63] Military force was required to protect the rights of newly freed black residents and the authority of those newly imposed governments. During Reconstruction, over 600 black men were elected to state legislatures, 16 to the U.S. Congress, and two to the U.S. Senate.[64]

Congress had passed the Ku Klux Klan Act of 1871, which designated certain crimes committed by individuals as federal offenses. Those crimes included "conspiracies to deprive citizens of the right to hold office, serve on juries and enjoy the equal protection of the law." President Ulysses S. Grant used this authority to send in more troops "to crush Klan activity in South Carolina and other areas of the South."[65] Needless to say, those developments were not welcomed by Southern leaders who had just fought a war to defend slavery. Many living in the former Confederate states felt as if they were an occupied country.

That's where the presidential election came into play.

The Republicans nominated Rutherford B. Hayes to run against Democrat Samuel Tilden. Hayes was a reformer who alienated many of what we would today call the Republican establishment in Washington. The final result was close and controversial. Tilden was leading by 12 Electoral College votes but there were disputed results in three Southern states. Those states had 13 Electoral College votes. All Tilden needed to do was win one of the disputed votes and he would become president.

The races in those states were close and the results disputed because of "force, intimidation, and fraud used by Democrats to keep blacks from the polls."[66] In those days, black voters were part of the Republican coalition. "Had blacks been allowed to vote freely, Hayes easily would have carried all three states in dispute" and one or two others.[67]

A long and contentious process unfolded in Congress over many months to determine the winner. The crisis created by the suppression of the black vote gave Southerners leverage to gain concessions from the man who would succeed Grant as president.

At a decisive moment, a Democratic Congressman from Louisiana announced that he had received assurances that Hayes would "be guided by a policy of conciliation toward the southern states." More specifically, he was told that a President Hayes would not "use the Federal authority or the Army" against those states. Southern opposition to Hayes ended almost immediately and he was awarded all 13 disputed delegates.[68] With that decision, Hayes won the presidency by the narrowest of margins, 185 Electoral College votes to 184.

In other words, Southern Democrats helped Republican Hayes be elected president. In exchange, within a month of taking office, Hayes withdrew the troops that were protecting the rights of black Americans and America's highest ideals.[69] The South was then free to impose slavery by another name. "At least 10 percent of the black legislators elected during the 1867-1868 constitutional conventions became victims of violence . . . including seven who were killed."[70] That was just the beginning.

Adding special insult to this corrupt bargain, it occurred during the Centennial Celebration of the document that spelled out our founding ideals—the Declaration of Independence. The torch-bearing arm of the Statue of Liberty had already been created and was on display in Philadelphia and New York. Now "recognized as a universal symbol of freedom and democracy"[71] it was constructed and dedicated during a time when freedom and democracy were being systematically taken away from black Americans in the South.

THE FEDERAL GOVERNMENT EMERGES AS AN OCCASIONAL ALLY

More than 140 years have passed since that bargain was struck. In all that time, the Southern states have sent just one black U.S. senator to Washington. South Carolina's Tim Scott was elected in 2012.

During those years, it would be wrong to say that the federal government was a friend to its African-American citizens. There were plenty of Harry Anslingers in the federal bureaucracy. However, it was sometimes less hostile to black Americans than southern state governments and occasionally did the right thing.

- In 1948, President Harry S. Truman issued an executive order to integrate the U.S. military.

- In 1957, President Dwight D. Eisenhower sent the Army's 101st Airborne Division to enforce a court order and protect the "Little Rock Nine" so that they could enter Central High School without harm.

- In 1961, federal marshals were belatedly sent in to protect the Freedom Riders trying to desegregate interstate buses. But those marshals were sent after significant violence had already been inflicted by local authorities and mobs.

- In 1962, federal troops were sent in by President John F. Kennedy to protect the first African-American admitted to the University of Mississippi—James Meredith. By then, the need for federal protection from state and local government thugs had already become a regular feature of the civil rights era.

Much of this federal protection was offered reluctantly. At one point, Attorney General Robert Kennedy did "not feel that the Department of Justice can side with one group or the other in disputes over Constitutional rights."[72] When the Kennedys called for a cooling-off period, activist James Farmer Jr. said, "We have been cooling off for 350 years, and if we cooled off any more, we'd be in a deep freeze."[73]

Still, while the federal government was often an unreliable ally to the civil rights movement, it was frequently the only government ally Southern blacks could find. Freedom fighters generally felt "it was a great relief to be in a federal court." There was no chance of justice for black Americans in Southern state courts. But, in federal courts, many came to believe that they had "an honest chance of justice before the law."[74]

With this history, it's no wonder that many people instantly assume that shifting power away from the federal government will prove dangerous for people of color. Remember, only 40 percent of what we see comes from what we observe and the other 60 percent is filled in with what we expect to see. What civil rights activists expect is defined by the negative strand of American history.

This helps explain the sheer panic that many people of color experienced when Trump was elected president. For those who believe that the federal government is the only thing protecting minorities from racism and discrimination, the character and beliefs of the person running that government are vitally important.

TIMES REALLY HAVE CHANGED

Those of us who believe in community problem solving recognize that politicians are not nearly as important as they think they are. Presidents matter, but not as much as those who idolize the federal government would like us to believe. The good news is that the United States remains a nation where the culture leads and the politicians lag behind.

Fortunately, cultural attitudes on racial issues have changed dramatically since the civil rights era. One example of this change can be seen in opinions concerning Martin Luther King Jr. Back in the 1960s, he was one of "the most disliked American political figures." At one point, 68 percent of Americans had a negative opinion of the civil rights leader.[75] Today, he has become one of the most revered figures in American history. In fact, more than 80 percent of Americans have a favorable opinion of him.[76]

Back in 1963, the March on Washington was viewed positively by just 23 percent of Americans.[77] That was the event where King delivered his "I Have a Dream" speech. Today, King's speech is rightly recognized alongside the Declaration of Independence and the Gettysburg Address as one of the clearest expressions of the American Creed.

The changing attitudes can be seen across a whole range of events from the Civil Rights era. My review of survey data from the 1960s found that actions like the Freedom Rides and lunch counter sit-ins were consistently and deeply unpopular at the time. Most believed that the protests did more harm than good. The motives were also suspect: 75 percent of Americans believed that communist agitators were involved.[78]

Today, those same events are seen as part of a historic freedom movement that challenged our nation to live up to its stated ideals.

The brilliant strategy of nonviolent protests was an expression of faith that, given a choice, most Americans would embrace the noble strand of our history. Black leaders counted on the fact that if white Americans saw the reality of segregation, the vast majority would reject it. And they were right. The movement produced a "wholesale attitudinal change that occurred between the late 1960s and early 1970s."[79]

Many believe the turning point came in 1963 by events in Birmingham. When Bull Connor unleashed fire hoses and attack dogs on peaceful black citizens, millions of Americans were shocked and horrified by the televised images. Two years later, during the protests and battles in Selma, a Harris poll found that Americans were far more sympathetic to the protesters than in earlier efforts. "By a 48% to 21% margin" Americans "sided more with the civil rights groups involved than with the state of Alabama."[80]

It was this cultural change, not political leadership, that led to the passage of the Voting Rights Act of 1965. Before Congress did anything, 76 percent of Americans were "in favor of a then-proposed equal rights voting law."[81]

MORE THAN ATTITUDES HAVE CHANGED

That cultural change brought on by the nonviolent protest movement led the nation forward. One often overlooked impact is that it changed the dynamics of what it means to restore local control to communities. More than two dozen large U.S. cities now have a majority black population. These include Atlanta, Detroit, Birmingham, Baltimore, New Orleans, and Cleveland. In fact, even Richmond, Virginia—the capitol of the old Confederacy—had a majority black population as of the 2010 census.[82]

"In each of those cases, minority rule—where national minorities constitute local majorities—allows minorities to protect themselves rather than look to courts as their source of solace." Yale University's Gerken notes that this new dynamic "empowers racial minorities and dissenters." What's different now is that empowerment comes "not by shielding them from the majority, but by turning them into one."[83]

Because local governments are more responsive to community control than state or federal governments, this new reality opens up the possibility of creative approaches for the nation's racial dialogue to continue in a healthy manner.

After learning that some of its predecessor companies had owned slaves, Wachovia Bank issued a formal apology to "all Americans, and especially to African-Americans and people of African descent."[84] Ken Thompson, Wachovia's CEO, "was overwhelmed by the emotional impact our apology had . . . for African-American employees." The end result was "cathartic" and led to "a deeper trust."[85]

This apology leading to a deeper trust came about solely because of actions taken by a city with a substantial black population. A Chicago law required any company wanting to do business with the city to first disclose whether they had ever profited from slavery. Wachovia took this request seriously and hired "a team of historians . . . to investigate the past record of Wachovia, all the banks it had acquired, and all their corporate predecessors."[86] The historians found that the Georgia Railroad and Banking Company owned at least 162 slaves. Additionally, the Bank of Charleston accepted at least 529 slaves as collateral and took ownership of some when customers defaulted.[87]

It was the serious research effort, not just the formal words of apology, that helped bring about the positive response to this distasteful news. Wachovia is to be commended for taking the task seriously, but the North Carolina bank would never have acted on its own. It acted only because the city of Chicago felt it was important to demand such disclosure. It took a local government, responsive to community control, to do something the federal government would never have accomplished.

STATES DON'T HAVE RIGHTS

Saying that things have changed does not mean we can rest on our laurels and pretend we have done enough. We must affirm in word and deed that racism is a cancer that must be removed before it destroys all that is worth loving in the United States. It is as much a threat to freedom, equality, and self-governance as the regulatory state.

But, no matter how often we say it—and no matter how pure our motives—those who have been victimized by racial discrimination will remain skeptical. Who could blame them? They've heard it all before. Far too many others have come along mouthing noble words to mask evil intentions.

What can we do to overcome the skepticism?

We need to make clear that a massive campaign of community problem solving is the polar opposite of the hateful states' rights ideology. Community problem solving is based upon reaching for the nation's highest ideals of freedom, equality, and self-governance. The states' rights ideology was developed to reject those founding ideals and defend slavery.

A good starting point is to emphasize that states don't have rights, people have rights. In fact, our country was founded on the belief that all of us are created equal and have certain unalienable rights. That's the foundation of all community problem-solving efforts and the "Putting People First" model of governance.

A few years back, I wrote a column making this argument and it drew an apoplectic response from a few Washington-based conservatives. I was told that it was a "nutty" idea and that states' rights are guaranteed by the 10th Amendment to the Constitution. That's a common refrain, but it's a distortion of what the Constitution really says.

The 10th Amendment is about limiting the power of the federal government. It says that the federal government can do only what is authorized by the Constitution, a limit many people believe has long been ignored. But the amendment says absolutely nothing about granting rights to states. People have rights, and the Constitution does not give states the right to take them away.

Our nation's founding document—the Declaration of Independence—makes it clear that no legitimate government—local, state, or federal—can rule without the consent of the governed. It is equally clear that no legitimate government—local, state, or federal—can deny citizens their right to life, liberty, and the pursuit of happiness. Governments are created to protect those rights, not take them away.

This perspective implies that no one level of government is inherently better than another. All governments are subject to corruption simply because human beings run them.

Sometimes local governments or state governments will be more committed to defending freedom and equality than the federal government. Sometimes the reverse will be true. That's why the concept of separation of powers is so important. It is the only way to ensure that no one level of government—or one group of politicians—is all powerful. The only way to protect freedom for all is to broadly disperse power and encourage competition between governments.

This is the argument we must make to those who fear that more local control means a return to segregation. We need to show that all Americans—specifically including people of color—will be better off when we place more power in the hands of the local community rather than the federal government.

A MORE COMPLETE HISTORY OF CIVIL RIGHTS

Fortunately, we don't need to rely on theory to make this point. The history of the United States makes it for us. The civil rights movement would never have succeeded by waiting for the federal government to act. Its efforts were the culmination of a centuries-long community problem-solving effort to overcome the negative strand of American history.

In 1781, six years before the Constitution was written, the Chief Justice of the Massachusetts Supreme Court issued a ruling that effectively banned slavery in the Bay State.[88] He based that ruling on the rhetoric of the Declaration of Independence. Slavery was inconsistent with our nation's high ideals.

This is an especially interesting example because a Virginia slaveholder wrote the words of the Declaration. Yet, within a few years those words were used by a Massachusetts judge to rule against slavery. It is hard to find a better example of the power of an idea.

Over several decades, many northern governments took additional steps to abolish slavery and many private groups aggressively agitated for abolition. Equally important, the national culture adopted freedom and liberty as our defining ideals. This made it possible for heroes like Harriet

Tubman to help countless slaves escape through an informal network of meeting places and safe houses known as the Underground Railroad.

Tubman was the best known of many "conductors" who guided escaping slaves along the "railroad" to freedom. A remarkable woman, Tubman was born into slavery and managed to escape. But she was committed to going back and leading more people to freedom, a commitment that earned her the nickname Moses. She repeatedly risked her freedom and her life by going back into the slave state of Maryland 13 times over 11 years. She later worked behind enemy lines for the Union Army during the Civil War.[89]

Tubman is credited with directly rescuing about 70 people from slavery and giving specific instructions to nearly as many others.[90] It's impossible to estimate how many more were inspired to escape by her well-publicized successes. All told, as many as 100,000 slaves may have found freedom through the Underground Railroad.[91]

This was community problem solving on a grand scale. It involved free people like Harriet Tubman working together in innovative ways, private associations providing support, and state governments offering an alternative. It was seen in the South as a dire threat to slavery. Recognizing that these efforts would eventually force the federal government to protect the rights of its black citizens, Southern states chose to provoke a deadly war rather than letting the community problem solving continue.

Later, a cultural phenomenon known as the Great Migration provided a valuable platform for future progress. Starting early in the 20th century, 6 million black Americans exercised the power to walk away from the South. When the migration began, 92 percent of blacks lived in the South. When it was over, nearly half lived outside the South.[92]

This migration created a vital network of black businesses, churches, clubs, and families who were free of the Jim Crow laws. This network showed that another way of life was possible for black Americans. Racism and discrimination existed in the North, of course, but there were also more opportunities than could be found in the South. Those opportunities later provided financial and other support for the civil rights movement.

One example of the impact was the Harlem Renaissance. This was a "cultural, social, and artistic explosion" that took place in the 1920s and

'30s. Harlem attracted "black writers, artists, musicians, photographers, poets, and scholars" who were fleeing the South.[93]

Harry Belafonte personified the connection between this renaissance and the civil rights movement. Born in Harlem during the renaissance, he became an enormously successful pop star. Like Holiday, he used his celebrity to draw attention to civil rights abuses. Unlike Holiday, he was financially successful. During the battle in Birmingham, he bailed King out of jail and raised money to do the same for other protesters. He also provided funding for the Freedom Rides, the Student Nonviolent Coordinating Committee (SNCC), voter registration drives, and the March on Washington.[94]

There were plenty of other cultural influences advancing the cause of black Americans during this era. Jesse Owens was a gold medal winner in the 1936 Olympics held in Adolf Hitler's Germany. A year later, Joe Louis became heavyweight champion of the boxing world and a national hero. In 1947, Jackie Robinson began his Hall of Fame career by breaking the Major League color barrier.[95]

Technology also played a role, specifically the then-new technology of television. Throughout the movement's great triumphs in Montgomery, Little Rock, Birmingham, Selma and beyond, it was television that helped the nation see and grasp the true essence of segregation. It was the response to televised events that changed the culture and finally forced the federal government to provide at least modest support.

In short, the civil rights movement would never have succeeded by simply relying upon our political system. An all-hands-on-board approach was needed involving abolitionists, churches, businesses, northern state governments, nonviolent protestors, private associations, and more. That is the only way to move the culture.

TWO STRANDS—ONE HISTORY

Since 1619, two competing strands of history have defined America. Now is the time for the shameful strand to die and the noble strand to flourish.

Looking back on it from the perspective of the 21st century, it seems clear that America's War of Independence and the civil rights movement were part of the same revolution, a revolution for liberty, equality, and self-governance. Unfortunately, too many Americans still look at them as entirely separate events.

Those who see only the noble strand in our history tend to downplay the civil rights movement as little more than the end of an embarrassing oversight in our national heritage. Those who see only the shameful strand downplay the Founding Fathers as hypocrites who used the rhetoric of freedom and equality while practicing oppression and discrimination.

To move forward, we need to incorporate both struggles into our national storyline. We must see that Montgomery, Birmingham, and Selma are as much a part of the American Revolution as Bunker Hill, Valley Forge, and Yorktown. And we need to recognize that in both struggles, the real victories came in the "minds and hearts of the people." As John Adams put it, "This radical change in the principles, opinions, sentiments, and affections of the people, was the real American Revolution."[96]

To fully eliminate the negative strand of our nation's history, we must be totally committed to shaping the culture by building a society worthy of our highest ideals. That requires embedding equality and inclusiveness into our community problem-solving approaches as deeply as legalized discrimination was embedded in the foundations of our government. In a world where the culture leads and the politicians lag behind, this is the only way to cleanse our government from its original sin. Sooner or later, the politicians will catch up.

That's what community problem solving is all about. An inclusive culture will insure that all Americans—including African-Americans—benefit from the coming improvements in banking, transportation, education, and health care. I don't know what the specific solutions will look like, any more than I know what the new schools or health care centers will look like. But I do know that American culture has turned the corner and will reject any solutions that exclude minorities or the poor.

CHAPTER 12

POVERTY, INEQUALITY, AND OPPORTUNITY

AMERICA HAS LONG BEEN KNOWN as the land of opportunity. It's a key part of our national identity that naturally goes hand in hand with a commitment to freedom, equality, and self-governance. "When one starts poor," Abraham Lincoln observed, a "free society is such that he knows he can better his condition."[1]

More recently, Secretary of State Condoleezza Rice put it like this: "The essence of America—that which really unites us—is not ethnicity, or nationality or religion." Instead, we are united by the idea "that you can come from humble circumstances and do great things."[2]

That's the American Dream. The man who coined that phrase, James Truslow Adams, described it as "a dream of social order in which each man and each woman shall be able to attain to the fullest stature of which they are innately capable." Everyone should "be recognized by others for what they are, regardless of the fortuitous circumstances of birth or position."[3]

Adams believed that this concept is the "greatest contribution we have made to the thought and welfare of the world."[4] It's a dream of a profoundly moral and just society. The land of opportunity is a place where all who are able accept the responsibility to provide for themselves and their family. And, because everyone can get ahead by working hard and making good decisions, it's a land where poverty does not exist. Even those with temporarily low incomes have a viable path to a better life.

The dream envisions a society where people use their freedom to work together in community and create a better world. Like our founding ideals, it is a noble vision worth striving for even if it can never be fully and perfectly realized. Reaching for those ideals and creating a land of opportunity is America at its best. It's a vision that makes our nation a worthy city on the hill with the power to reshape the world.

Over the past couple of centuries, the message of freedom and opportunity has attracted countless millions to leave their homeland and come to America. It's also encouraged millions already here to strike out on their own and launch a new business. Not only do these efforts fuel our economic growth, they represent the way our nation is supposed to work. It's a theme constantly celebrated in popular culture.

In the 19th century, countless Horatio Alger tales told of poor boys working hard and reaching middle-class respectability. Today, the biggest hit on Broadway tells how an orphaned immigrant with no money and no name rose to become a key leader in the American Revolution and our nation's first treasury secretary. *Hamilton* is an inspiring tale of opportunity, ambition, and hard work presented as a tale of the young nation itself.

AN AMAZING WOMAN

Sometimes, true stories are even more amazing than myths. Consider, for example, a Seattle woman born in 1929 just as the Depression was getting started. In the 1950s, Mary spent a few years teaching junior high school before becoming a full-time mom.

As her children grew, the talented volunteer got involved with civic groups including the Junior League, Children's Orthopedic Hospital, and many others. Some of her efforts "opened doors of corporate boardrooms and executive suites to women." In 1975, Mary was named president of United Way of King County. She was the first woman in that role and later became the first woman to chair the national United Way's executive committee.[5]

In a fortuitous coincidence, John Opel served with Mary on the United Way Board. At that time, he was the president of IBM and his company needed someone to develop an operating system for its first PC.

When Microsoft was mentioned as a possibility, Opel responded, "Oh, that's run by Bill Gates, Mary Gates' son."[6]

IBM, of course, ended up making a deal with the young entrepreneur. That contract launched Mary's son down the path to becoming the world's richest man with a net worth of over $80 billion.[7] But, as her son built his business, Mary continued to do philanthropic work. Among other things, she ran a project urging people to give 5 percent of their income and five hours a week of their time to civic causes. Sadly, Mary Gates succumbed to cancer at the age of 64.[8] But her legacy lives on.

Following his mother's example, Bill Gates eventually left Microsoft to become a philanthropist. He has already given away tens of billions of dollars and created an enormous charitable foundation. "My full-time work for the rest of my life is this foundation."[9] Its U.S. projects seek "to ensure that all people—especially those with the fewest resources—have access to the opportunities they need to succeed in school and life."[10]

In 2010, the tech billionaire teamed up with Warren Buffett to launch "The Giving Pledge," a public campaign encouraging rich people to give away at least half of their wealth. "We live in an exciting time for philanthropy," they declared. It's a time "where innovative approaches and advances in technology have redefined what's possible."[11]

Their message was so enticing that "most of America's wealthiest people have signed on,"[12] including Michael Bloomberg, Mark Zuckerberg, and Elon Musk. "The Giving Pledge" has generated hundreds of billions of dollars for charity, but its success is built on a simple reality. As the foundation makes clear, "Grassroots movements are proving every day how a single individual, regardless of wealth, can make a lasting impact on the lives of others."[13]

Bill and Melinda Gates did more than just encourage others to give away money. They led the way with a pledge to give away 95 percent of their wealth. Why? Because since childhood both had been taught "the values of volunteerism and civic engagement. Our families believed that if life happens to bless you, you should use those gifts as well and as wisely as you can."[14]

That's the legacy of Mary Gates. She helped her son generate fabulous wealth, and her example encouraged him to give that wealth away. It all began with the simple act of stepping forward to serve others. That's a step all of us can take to help create a better world.

MORE THAN MONEY

As Mary Gates understood, the American Dream has always been about more than money. It is "deeply rooted in the concept of a journey." Rather than fantasies about striking it rich, it's "about finding success and fulfillment along the way."[15] One revealing survey found that just 27 percent of Americans admire those who are rich. However, 88 percent admire those who work hard and get rich.[16]

It's not the money that matters. It's the hard work that draws rave reviews.

This broader understanding is bound up in our unalienable right to "life, liberty, and the pursuit of happiness." The freedom to pursue happiness is the force that creates a land of opportunity. It works because we get to choose our own dreams and define success for ourselves.

"For some people," Arthur Brooks points out, "success means business success, while for others, it means helping the poor, raising good kids, building a nonprofit, or making beautiful art — whatever allows people to create value in their lives and in the lives of others."[17] Brooks, president of the American Enterprise Institute, has written extensively about the tremendously gratifying sense of accomplishment that comes from creating value in "our lives or in the lives of others."

> Earned success is the stuff of entrepreneurs who seek value through innovation, hard work and passion. Earned success is what parents feel when their children do wonderful things, what social innovators feel when they change lives, what artists feel when they create something of beauty.[18]

Volumes of research back up this commonsense notion that happiness does not come solely from a bigger bank account. Americans are a lot wealthier than we were 40 years ago. In fact, our average income has doubled (even after adjusting for inflation).[19] But survey results consistently show year after year that we aren't any happier.[20]

Other data convey the same sense. The most admired professions in 21st-century America are not necessarily those with the biggest paychecks. Doctors top the list, but firefighters make the cut as well. Kathy Steinberg of the Harris Poll reports that admired jobs "are typically those that are important to civilization [and] society in general."[21] Despite relatively low paychecks, Americans strongly encourage today's children to pursue jobs as teachers, nurses, and police officers.[22]

Happiness and personal satisfaction don't come from money alone; they come from earned success. Such success is based upon creating value in the lives of others, and it is the reality that drives the community problem-solving process.

THE LAND OF OPPORTUNITY VS. THE REGULATORY STATE

The vision of a land where people can work hard and earn their success remains extraordinarily powerful in the 21st century. But many Americans fear it's a vision that describes our nation's past more than its future. Some worry that today's children simply won't have the opportunities that their parents had. Others are concerned that the desire for an opportunity to succeed has been replaced by an entitlement mindset.

The declining sense of opportunity in 21st-century America is directly related to growth of the regulatory state. That's because opportunity thrives only in an environment of freedom, equality, and self-governance.

- The land of opportunity is a land where the people are in charge. Everyone is empowered to pursue their own success.

- The regulatory state is a land where unelected panels of government experts are in charge. Everyone else must ask permission first.

The conflict between the regulatory state and a land of opportunity is at the heart of 21st-century concerns about America's future. As the bureaucracy increases, opportunity decreases.

Rejecting America's founding ideals, the regulatory state is celebrated by those who place more faith in government and bureaucrats than they do in everyday Americans and community organizations. The foolhardiness of such faith was highlighted by a couple of ambitious young economists who thought ski lift operators weren't very smart.

Every skier knows that busy days on the slopes lead to longer lift lines. How this became a lesson in the value of street smarts is told in David Warsh's history of the economics profession: *Knowledge and the Wealth of Nations*. In the 1980s, Robert Barro and Paul Romer saw the long lines as "prima facie evidence of market failure." They assumed that the business owners were missing an opportunity to make more money by charging higher prices on busy days.[23]

What makes this example so important is that Barro and Romer are not fools or fringe economists. Quite the opposite. They are both brilliant men, highly respected in their field. Barro has PhDs in both economics and physics. Romer is chief economist at the World Bank. Both have taught at prestigious universities, published widely, and are affiliated with the National Bureau of Economic Research.[24]

But when it came to pricing lift tickets at a ski resort, Barro and Romer were no match for those with more pragmatic street smarts that come from running a business. The researchers eventually figured out that longer lines on crowded days meant that skiers enjoyed fewer runs down the mountain for their money. In the language of economists, this meant that the customers were paying more per ride even though the daily fee was the same. The business owners probably didn't think of it that way, but they didn't need expert economists to tell them that charging more would have chased away customers and profits.

Barro and Romer deserve credit for publicly acknowledging that they were wrong. But imagine if they had been federal bureaucrats in charge of pricing ski lift tickets. Elaborate models would have been developed and detailed rules put in place. Prices would have been set and penalties imposed for those who tried to get around them.

The ski lift operators would have complained about how impractical the rules were, but their concerns would have been dismissed. After all, the regulators would reason, how could a mere ski lift operator know more than a brilliant expert on the government payroll? The regulatory actions would have led to higher prices, lower profits, and fewer people enjoying the thrill of a great day on the slopes. But have no fear: As the business declined and fewer people skied, the experts would be on hand to offer even more "help."

The ski slope saga is not an isolated example of experts misunderstanding the nuances of a situation. It's the norm. No expert in any field can possibly account for all the variables that arise when free people pursue their own success. And no one person, no matter how smart, can possibly figure out all the possible ways to get around the problems and challenges of everyday life.

Unfortunately, the political world is filled with people who ignore the evidence and believe that they know what's best for the rest of us. Over the past four decades, this elitist view has fueled the growth of the regulatory state and reduced the opportunities available to everyday Americans.

It is time to reverse that trend. The most straightforward way to increase opportunity for all Americans is to reduce the size and strength of the federal bureaucracy. That's also the only way to ensure that our children and grandchildren will live in a land of opportunity.

A MORAL CHALLENGE

Reducing the federal bureaucracy will address the pragmatic concerns about generating economic growth and increasing opportunities. That's a goal we can accomplish using the strategy of Radical Incrementalism discussed in Chapter 9.

But simply rolling back the influence of burdensome bureaucrats is not enough. Those who lift up America's highest ideals must also address a moral challenge raised in recent years.

"America likes to think of itself as a land of opportunity, and others view it in much the same light," says Nobel Prize-winning economist Joseph Stiglitz. After analyzing the numbers, however, he concluded that "the American dream is a myth. ... There is less equality of opportunity in the United States today than there is in Europe—or, indeed, in any advanced industrial country for which there are data."[25]

Other economists look at the same data and reach the opposite conclusion. However, the central challenge raised by critics such as Stiglitz can never be answered by dueling economic statistics. They see America as a class-based society where a birth lottery determines each person's future. Those born into affluent families will remain affluent and those born into poverty will remain stuck in poverty. They believe the occasional exceptions—either up or down—are determined primarily by luck rather than hard work and individual choices.

This is a stinging critique of our national heritage and it raises a troubling question: If it's all just a matter of luck, how can we justify condemning some to live in poverty while others bask in dazzling affluence?

Most Americans are appropriately skeptical of these overstated claims. Two out of three (64 percent) believe that their own financial well-being depends primarily upon their own actions.[26] This is the traditional American view that hard work, doing a good job, and making good choices will lead to a good life. Luck may be a factor, but it's just one of many issues we must deal with on the journey through life.

At the same time, however, most Americans also recognize that there is work to be done. There remains an enormous gap between the rhetoric and reality of opportunity. Fewer than half of us believe that children from all races have access to opportunity. Only 40 percent believe that opportunity is available to children at all income levels.[27]

It is an uncomfortable truth that some Americans have virtually no credible opportunities before them. No matter how hard they are willing to work, there are no jobs available. Others have such limited opportunities that getting ahead in life is roughly equivalent to pulling an inside straight.

WE DON'T HAVE THE DATA WE NEED

The obvious answer to addressing the needs of lower-income Americans is to ensure that every American who is willing to work has a realistic chance of getting ahead. The tools of the digital revolution combined with the idealism of the millennial generation will unlock new ways to make this happen.

It's exciting to realize that the seismic changes coming to the fields of education and health care have the potential to benefit the poor more than anyone else. It's exhilarating to think of how smartphones can develop entirely new ways of mentoring and supporting people who need a bit of guidance and reassurance along the way.

Unfortunately, while we have the tools to address the challenge, we have little reliable data on how many people are excluded from opportunity and who they are. That's true despite the reams of poverty statistics generated by the federal bureaucracy. In fact, those statistics generate more confusion than clarity.

When President Lyndon Johnson launched his War on Poverty, a Social Security Administration economist developed America's official poverty measurements. Mollie Orshansky estimated the minimal costs needed for food, shelter, and other necessities. If someone didn't earn enough to pay for such basics, they were officially classified as poor.[28]

That formula could have served as a reasonable starting point for discussions about measuring poverty. Unfortunately, the data quickly became a source of political rhetoric rather than serious analysis. Making matters even worse, it contained a foundational flaw that continues to bedevil us a half century later.

Back in the mid-'60s, many experts "assumed that most who experienced poverty did so for extended periods of time." If that were true, Orshansky's model would have been a reliable measure of progress in the fight to reduce poverty. But, "it turns out that this image was incorrect."[29] Other government data collected over the years shows that about half of those "in poverty" get out within four months or less."[30]

This means that the official poverty statistics include a lot of people who experience a temporary loss of income but are far from living in poverty. Today, if a high-priced executive leaves her job and is weighing other offers, she is officially said to be living in poverty. The same is true of a manufacturing worker suffering through a temporary layoff or anybody else searching for a job. There have even been times while writing this book that I would have been classified as living in poverty.

This explains why "the typical American defined as poor by the Census Bureau has a car, air conditioning, and cable or satellite TV." The official data also show that "half of the poor have computers, 43 percent have Internet, and 40 percent have a wide-screen plasma or LCD TV."[31]

The truth is that people living in poverty don't have such items. But most people the government classifies as living in poverty aren't really poor, at least not by any commonsense definition of the term.

The statistical impact of this one faulty assumption is astounding. Government figures claim that in a four-year presidential term, more than a third of Americans experience poverty.[32] Analysts have drawn upon those numbers to estimate that approximately four-fifths of the U.S. population is at a significant risk of economic vulnerability during their lifetimes.[33]

Those estimates are consistent with a worldview suggesting that the luck of the draw determines our financial fate. We are all just one unfortunate event away from living in horrible poverty. No matter how hard we work, we should remember the old saying, "There but for the grace of God go I."

But when you drill down a little deeper, an entirely different picture emerges. Rather than poverty being a realistic threat for nearly four out of five Americans, real poverty affects a much smaller and more narrowly defined segment of the population. Approximately 3 percent of Americans live in what is called "chronic poverty."[34]

Chronic poverty means living for years and years without enough income to provide for the basic necessities of life. It's living without the hope of a better life or the dignity that comes from earned success. Government assistance provides some support, but those living in chronic poverty have a difficult time seeing a land of opportunity anywhere on the horizon.

To extend opportunities to all Americans, we need a better understanding of the challenge before us. We need to distinguish between those living in poverty, those with limited opportunities, and those facing temporary financial hardships.

NO EXCUSES

As we gain more knowledge about those who lack opportunities, the American people will use the power of community to produce solutions.

Research consistently shows strong public support for meeting the needs of the poor. At the same time, however, "about 7 in 10 Americans said that even if the government were 'willing to spend whatever is necessary to eliminate poverty,' officials do not know enough to accomplish that goal."[35]

Partly because it is an ineffective approach, most Americans do not believe that the government should be primarily responsible for addressing poverty. Instead, many look to family, churches, and charities to take the lead.[36] This is consistent with the all-hands-on-board community problem-solving approach.

It works because concern for the poor has extraordinarily deep roots in the Judeo-Christian culture that shaped our nation. From the Law of Moses onward, the need to provide for widows, orphans, and outsiders is found throughout the Bible. The very first thing Jesus did when launching his public ministry was to declare that he had been anointed "to proclaim good news to the poor."[37]

During colonial America's formative years, the Methodist movement swept through the nation with a message of service. "Do all the good you can. By all the means you can. In all the ways you can,"[38] urged John Wesley, the movement's founder. The Methodist influence remained strong in the decades following independence, and service to others became firmly embedded in the American Dream.

In the 20th century, Rabbi Abraham Joshua Heschel taught that "there is no limit to the concern one must feel for the suffering of human beings."[39] In our time, Redeemer Presbyterian's pastor Tim Keller considers it "offensive to God" and "evil" if the "church does not care for the poor."[40] Faith-based organizations like the Salvation Army continue to provide tremendous support for those in need. Countless local congregations of all faiths provide food banks, shelter, and assistance.

Of course, concern for the poor is not restricted to those with religious beliefs. A tech-driven, micro-lending nonprofit called Kiva has no faith-based ties. But it fights poverty as well. Their mission is to "connect people through lending to alleviate poverty." Kiva aims to "celebrate and support people looking to create a better future for themselves, their families and their communities."[41]

Through Kiva, anybody can lend as little as $25 to "help a borrower start or grow a business, go to school, access clean energy or realize their potential. For some, it's a matter of survival, for others it's the fuel for a life-long ambition." So far, Kiva has lent nearly a billion dollars to 2.2 million people around the globe and enjoyed a 97.1 percent repayment rate.[42]

Kiva wants to create a "world where all people hold the power to create opportunity for themselves and others."[43] Their innovative approach recognizes that expecting people to provide for themselves is not a burden; it is an opportunity to gain the satisfaction that comes from earned success. Like Pope Francis, the folks at Kiva recognize that "work is fundamental to the dignity of the person."[44]

WHY DOES POVERTY STILL EXIST?

Given the strong cultural commitment to help those in need and the tremendous affluence of our nation, perhaps the most surprising thing about chronic poverty is that it continues to exist at all.

The simplest explanation for our failure to eradicate poverty may have been given by the anti-poverty activist Richard Cornuelle back when the War on Poverty was just getting started. The problem is not "apathy or indifference"; it's "a lack of savvy about what to do." He believed that we will find more help than needed if the situation is made "visible, and the way to help is obvious."[45]

This brings us back to the damage done by the official government data on poverty.

Roughly 80 percent of those officially described as living in poverty at any time are not really living in poverty (while 15 percent are officially in poverty, only 3 percent are in chronic poverty). They are going through a tough stretch, but are not poverty-stricken. Rather than making the chronically poor visible so that we can figure out how to help, the official figures bury the real poor beneath an avalanche of other data.

In a healthy political system, it would make sense to fix the official measure of poverty. Most experts from across the ideological spectrum recognize that the official numbers are deeply flawed.

But we don't have a healthy system, and the poverty statistics have become thoroughly enmeshed in the bureaucratic process. In fact, they are now used to determine which people and communities get large amounts of federal funding. So if a better measure of poverty were developed, it would create political winners and losers. Some areas and people would receive more federal funding, others less. Politicians and lobbyists from the areas at risk of losing funding would thwart any effort to bring about meaningful change.

This is not just a theoretical concern. A second major flaw in the official poverty numbers is that they are calculated on a one-size-fits-all basis. There is no recognition of the fact that the cost of living is much higher in some parts of the country than others. So, as I write this, a family of four in rural Mississippi earning $24,000 a year would be defined as living in poverty. But a family of four living in New York City that earns $25,000 a year would not.

In reality, of course, $24,000 in Mississippi goes a lot farther than $25,000 in Manhattan. The difference is so dramatic that the same income in some parts of Mississippi would go roughly twice as far as it would in New York City.[46] Despite what the official figures show, the urban New York family is far more likely to be in poverty than the rural Mississippi family.

That's a fairly typical example of the distortion created by the official data. The government figures consistently *overestimate* the reality of poverty in rural southern states and *underestimate* poverty in urban areas throughout the rest of the nation. In fact, nine of the top ten states with the highest levels of official poverty also happen to be states with below average cost-of-living. At the other end of the scale, the reverse is true.[47]

In a very real sense, the official poverty statistics tell us more about the comparable cost of living in various states than they do about poverty. The failure to adjust for differing costs of living and the inclusion of non-poor in the poverty data are far from the only problems associated with the official data. Collectively, these flaws have hidden the reality of poverty in America.

A COMMUNITY PROBLEM-SOLVING RESPONSE

The American people are extraordinarily generous, and our culture has a deep commitment to helping those in need. The problem is not a lack of caring about those who are stuck in poverty, it is a failure of leadership.

From the day the War on Poverty was launched in Johnson's first State-of-the-Union Address,[48] the federal bureaucracy has been in charge. It is time for a change. New leadership is needed that can realistically define the problem and encourage everyone to get involved in the hunt for solutions.

Groups outside of Washington should provide a better public understanding about the reality of poverty in the United States. That means learning what we can from the existing federal data and then starting from scratch to develop better tools. This could be done by independent research groups, large charity organizations, state governments, local governments and others.

Step-by step, leadership will flow away from the federal bureaucracy and be taken over by those who provide the most useful information. This will move us closer to eliminating poverty in America because improved leadership will put community-based resources to better use. It's a phenomenon we see in sports all the time. A talented football team with the wrong coach can't get out of its own way. But provide the right leadership and the players end up with Super Bowl rings.

It's impossible to know precisely what the new measurement tools will teach us, but digging into the existing data provides a few hints. We are likely to see that existing safety net programs do a decent job meeting the needs of those experiencing temporary financial hardship, but fail to help those who need it most.

That's not really a surprise since those in need are just a small fraction of the people officially defined as living in poverty. The political process will naturally serve the 80 percent whose needs are easier to fulfill than the 20 percent whose needs are far more difficult.

Better data is also likely to show that real poverty is much more prevalent in urban settings rather than rural areas. There will probably be decimated geographic areas with virtually no jobs available or social networks connecting residents to the land of opportunity. Special efforts will be required to bring opportunity to anyone living in such troubled areas. And, due to the competing strands of our history, the chronically poor are more likely to be minorities rather than white.

The problems created by the lack of opportunity will never be solved until leadership in the War on Poverty is taken away from the federal bureaucracy. The new leadership will make visible the reality of poverty in America. And once that reality is made visible, the power of community will find ways to address it.

Peter Cove was one of the young men drawn to Washington to fight Johnson's War on Poverty in the 1960s. By 1984, he had become disillusioned with the lack of progress. However, he retained a passion for fighting poverty and searched to find a better way of addressing the problem.[49] He started a for-profit company, America Works, that "has placed over 500,000 people in jobs." Cove proudly notes that this includes "ex-offenders, veterans, the homeless, people with disabilities on SSI, children aging out of foster care, food stamp recipients and non-custodial parents who are unemployed and cannot pay child support."[50]

Cove based his company on the belief that "people on welfare can and want to go to work." Additionally, work combined with on-the-job training curriculum, designed by employers, not training in isolation, is central to that effort." He dismisses training unconnected to a specific job. Perhaps most important, Cove says "getting a job is easy, but keeping the job is hard." So his company works with the new hires for "six months to provide counseling, on-the-job coaching, interventions to navigate workplace issues," and more.[51]

Cove is not alone in his passion to fight poverty or his disappointment with the bureaucracy's approach. New leadership will encourage new ideas and effective solutions that no one has thought of yet. The best solutions will focus on providing the dignity that comes from earned success. They will bring to life Lincoln's view that anyone born poor in a free society has a chance to improve their circumstances. And they will build upon the service motive of people like Mary Gates and others who step forward to serve others and become role models for us all.

Community leaders will seek out the best practices from across the land and adapt them to their neighborhood situation. The resulting programs in Idaho will look different than those in Michigan. They will look different in California's central valley than in LA or San Francisco. That's the way it should be. America is a diverse nation in need of diverse solutions.

PROVIDING OPPORTUNITY FOR ALL

Most Americans today live in a land of opportunity. In fact, 63 percent believe they are living the American Dream.[52]

It's hard for anyone living in a world filled with opportunities to notice that others are on the outside looking in. Our challenge, then, is to recognize both the power of the dream and the need to extend it to every corner of American life. It's good for middle-class Americans to have opportunities but it's not enough unless poor children have them too.

We should recognize that rolling back the burden of the regulatory state will open new opportunities for working class Americans and millions of low-income workers. But just getting the bureaucrats out of the way is not enough. Those who believe in America's founding ideals—and the land of opportunity those ideals make possible—must be committed to ensuring that opportunity is available to all.

Ultimately, that means community problem solvers must go into the most economically depressed neighborhoods and do whatever it takes to empower those living in poverty. We need to develop an all-hands-on-board approach so that everyone in those communities can get ahead if they are willing to work. It will be a lot tougher than paying taxes and letting government deal with the problem, but providing opportunities for all will make our nation a worthy city on a hill. We will have created a moral and just society with the power to reshape the world.

CHAPTER 13

LEADERSHIP
AND CULTURAL VALUES

I T'S BEEN WELL OVER A DECADE since I lost faith in the political process and began the long personal journey that led me to a renewed sense of optimism about America's future. It's been seven years since the house fire helped me recognize that the answer I was seeking—and the answer that America needs—can be found only through community problem solving.

As I've shared the experience of my journey with others, I've been constantly reminded of the core challenge facing every speaker and writer—what we say and write is often not the same as what our audience hears and reads. That's because all of us bring our own filters and experiences into every conversation. Remember, only 40 percent of what we see comes in through our eyes. We fill in the rest with what we expect to see.

Knowing the back stories of American history, I was not surprised to hear legitimate concerns about the impact of community problem solving on minorities, working class Americans, and those living in poverty. Those concerns and questions deserve honest and thoughtful answers. That's why I directly addressed them in the preceding chapters. It's also why I believe so strongly in launching a massive campaign of community problem solving. The best way to overcome a skeptical audience is with deeds, not words. As an old teacher of mine used to say, "Show, don't tell."

I was, however, caught completely off guard by one topic that popped up repeatedly. Every time I spoke about putting power in the hands of everyday Americans and local communities, the question of leadership came up. Doesn't *somebody* have to be in charge? Don't we need leaders to help make everything work?

In my mind, those questions made no sense. Of course, we need leaders! It seemed self-evident to me that the all-hands-on-board approach required more leaders and stronger leadership than the all-politics, all-the-time model of the regulatory state. I thought that's what I had been saying, but it's not what people were hearing.

FINDING THE LEADERS WE NEED

The disconnect probably stemmed from my repeated comments about the culture leading and the politicians lagging behind. While that's true, the culture is not a leader in the same sense as a person can be a leader. What I had failed to emphasize enough was the role community leaders played in driving the culture and eventually forcing the politicians to catch up.

So, I modified my pitch a bit and started talking about the need for millions of local leaders to guide the country. To my surprise, this led some listeners to even deeper despair. After all, we can't even find enough good leaders to elect and send to Washington. And, there's only 537 of them—the president, vice-president, 100 senators and 435 members of Congress. If we can't find 537 leaders for the federal government, where on earth will we find millions more?

The good news is that we don't need to find them. The leaders we need are already in place. The problem is the same as the one I experienced when my family helped empty an 18-wheeler filled with yams. If we looked in the wrong direction, it was depressing. But when we found the right perspective, it was exhilarating.

We will never see the leaders America needs if we look for them in official Washington. While politics has a role to play, it's not the lead role. Only when you look away from the world of politics can you see those who really lead the nation.

One of the first things to see is that there are nearly 1,000 state and local elected officials for every federal office holder. All told, there are at least 519,000 elected officials including more than a quarter of a million city, town, and township office holders; over 150,000 county officials and school board members; and more than 80,000 elected to serve in all kinds of special districts.[1]

It's impossible to get an accurate count both because the numbers are so big and because they are constantly changing. Every year, "some towns and townships go out of business while other local government associations are added." Ballotpedia CEO Leslie Graves notes that "throughout the country, school districts, cities, counties and other local jurisdictions change how many elected representatives they have,"[2] which adds to the confusion.

Even a casual observer is aware that most of these local elected officials don't behave like members of Congress. Rather than obsessing about power and money and using one to get the other, local officials generally focus on service. The vast majority tirelessly do all kinds of thankless tasks to keep their communities going in exchange for little compensation or recognition.

After our house fire, we were anxious to quickly rebuild our home. Randy Bishop, a local council member, assured us the township would do everything possible to move the approval process along quickly. He did more than just talk a good game. When one of the approval boards suggested they might not find the time to even consider our application, Randy showed up at the meeting himself and didn't leave until our plans were approved. He had to stay all night, but he was true to his word.

Like Randy, most of the nation's half-million local elected officials are part of the community problem-solving world rather than the political class. Most have day jobs and many routinely rotate in and out of elected positions. One year, they're an elected official, the next they head a nonprofit, and the next they take some time with family. The end result is that we have millions of former elected officials who are no longer in office but continue to serve as community problem solvers.

Since we live in a land where every institution and relationship has a role to play in governing society, the leadership pool is much deeper than just elected officials. The nation has roughly 350,000 religious congregations[3] providing services to both the faithful and the community at large. In addition to having a pastor, priest, rabbi or imam, each of these congregations relies upon many volunteer leaders to accomplish their tasks.

Even that's just the tip of the iceberg. Lions Club International was created to "do whatever is needed to help their local communities." They boast that "whenever a Lions club gets together, problems get smaller. And communities get better."[4] The secular, non-political organization has 46,000 chapters and 1.4 million members worldwide. Each of those 46,000 chapters requires many leaders. The same is true for Rotary Clubs, Kiwanis Clubs and other service clubs.

Overall, tens of millions of Americans are involved in "charitable or volunteer organizations such as Habitat for Humanity or the Humane Society." Similar numbers are "active in community groups or neighborhood associations" while others are involved with "support groups for people with a particular illness or personal situation."[5] These projects offer all kinds of leadership opportunities big and small.

Not everyone who gets involved in such projects takes a leadership role, but millions do step forward and lead where they can. Sometimes it's just helping with the logistics of a dinner or social event. Other times, community leadership roles become almost a full-time job. Most people, though, are happy to serve so long as they see an opportunity to make a difference.

These leaders drive the culture by serving as vehicles through which power can be returned to the people. They are held to a much higher level of accountability than federal officials. Regardless of whether they lead through a local government, religious organization, service group, or in some other way, those they serve all have the power to walk away. If a leader or group fails to meet their needs, their followers will look elsewhere to find someone who does.

This form of servant leadership doesn't draw the attention showered upon the political elite, but it's the leadership that helps create a better world. Collectively, the efforts of these local leaders shape and define what we see as the culture.

BONDING AND BRIDGING ORGANIZATIONS

Community leaders work through a variety of local groups formed to meet a specific need. Most groups also produce an important side benefit that is even more valuable than their formal mission. "Social capital can have what economists call 'positive externalities,'" according to sociologist Robert Putnam. "Quite apart from their utility in solving the immediate problem (improving wages at Harvard or test scores in Philly), interpersonal ties are useful for many other purposes."[6]

Putnam suggests that there are distinct "bonding" and "bridging" forms of social capital.[7] Both are vital to the functioning of a healthy community.

Bonding groups strengthen social ties among similar people. The similarities could be based upon whatever identity bonds people together—age, ethnicity, faith, gender, marital status, shared interests, common history, geography, or something else entirely. These groups provide the people who help you move into a new apartment and bring meals when you're sick. They accept you because of who you are despite your eccentricities and imperfections. You're part of the family (or tribe).

Bonding groups also play an important role in facilitating social change. It is easier to discuss hopes and fears with people who share your values than with the public at large. That makes bonding groups an important space to process the implications of whatever is shaking up your world.

Bridging groups, on the other hand, "link people together with others across a cleavage that typically divides society (like race, or class, or religion)."[8] They enable people from different backgrounds, perspectives, and tribes to build trust and learn from each other. It's hard to overstate the importance of such groups in a nation as diverse as the United States.

Not surprisingly, Putnam notes that bridging social capital "is harder to create than bonding social capital—after all, birds of a feather flock together."[9] One common way to build important bridges is by tapping into the almost universal human desire to work together and create a better world. Many civic organizations bridge racial, ethnic, and religious divides by focusing on projects that strengthen the community at large.

Bridging can also be accomplished by groups that get together just for fun. I am familiar with a gaming community in Texas that includes a PhD candidate, an electrician, MDs, a high school student, an Air Force engineer, and a man delivering pizza while looking for his next job. It includes white, black, Hispanic, and Asian members. The group bonds through weekly competitions at a local gaming store in ways that earlier generations met in bowling leagues. It's a weekly boys night out. The guys periodically travel to other cities for larger competitions and do so wearing a team t-shirt sponsored by their local store.

In a digital and virtual reality world, it's especially important to create social groups that bring people together for in-person conversation and camaraderie. Whenever such friendships form across traditional cultural and demographic lines, the fabric of the community is strengthened. Such strong relationships create an interlocking web of groups and individuals that connect each of us with the larger world. These networks increase the problem-solving capacity of individual communities and the nation at large.

LEARNING FROM THE WORLD OF SPORTS

Most of the time, the various groups in our society move together in harmony because they are free to pursue their own interests. Gamers can have their fun because they're not interfering with the rights of anyone else to do the same. They don't need to seek anyone's approval (other than their spouse) and they don't have to worry about approving anybody else's plans.

Occasionally, however, the interests of some groups clash over important and competing objectives. Every now and then, these clashes can escalate in a way that threatens to completely tear apart a community. Those are the times when social capital resources are most needed. Leaders must draw upon that capital to build appropriate bridges between the competing groups.

I live in an area that is home to fans of both the New York Giants and their bitter rivals, the Philadelphia Eagles. Obviously, we have competing interests when it comes to football. But we also have other interests that keep our football rivalries to the level of friendly banter. I go to church with Eagles fans, played in a band with a couple, and have worked with several over the years. They're great people, despite their poor choice of a football team.

Still, if community leaders want to build stronger ties between the competing fans, a little bit of care is required. Inviting both sets of fans to a sports bar when their teams are playing would not be a good idea.

In fact, the likely result would be even bigger barriers to friendship between Eagles and Giants fans. That's especially true if a fair amount of beer is involved.

However, even among groups with competing goals, it is possible to find common ground. If Eagles and Giants fans met at a sports bar when the Dallas Cowboys are playing, we would join forces to root against our common enemy.

In this example, wise leadership can build bridges by simply understanding the group dynamics and picking the right game to watch.

GAYS AND CHRISTIANS

"Social capital," according to Putnam, "represents not a comfortable alternative to social conflict but a way of making controversy productive."[10]

In the 21st century, there are many social conflicts that need more productive means of resolution. That's certainly true of the contentious disputes between the LGBT community and Evangelical Christians. As is always the case, the problem is made worse by the fact that only 40 percent of what we see comes in through our eyes. The other 60 percent comes from what we expect to see.

Brookings scholar Jonathan Rauch has addressed these competing perspectives perhaps more directly than anyone else in the nation. A married gay man, he is fervently committed to America's founding ideals including freedom of speech and religion. In a remarkable 2016 speech, Rauch noted how people on both sides of the divide assume an absolutist view of their own righteousness while denying any legitimate basis to the claims of the other side. Those self-serving views define what they expect to see.

When church-goers raise genuine, faith-based concerns about same-sex marriage or related issues, many of Rauch's gay friends see nothing more than "a desire to discriminate in the name of religion." They believe it is a hypocritical effort "to deny LGBT people legal protections and social equality which religious people already enjoy and take for granted."[11]

On the other hand, Rauch notes that many Christians don't believe LGBT activists are interested in equality but rather "will not be satisfied until people of faith ... are made to be in fear of speaking their minds, of living up to their deeply held religious beliefs. They want us driven out."[12] A Catholic friend of Rauch's is worried that someone will "make it impossible for me to raise my kids in my faith."[13]

These wildly different perceptions present real obstacles to be overcome.

They can, however, be overcome by building upon existing social capital and finding common ground. This is not just theory, it's already happened in a number of places. One widely noted and successful compromise took place between church leaders, the LGBT community, and others in Utah. It came about when all involved began "focusing on our commonalities. ... What are the things that we share in common?"[14]

The specifics of the Utah solution won't work everywhere because one-size-fits-all solutions don't work in a diverse society. But just about every community has the social capital and the desire to find appropriate common ground and solutions.

FINDING COMMON GROUND

Just as Giants and Eagles fans have relationships beyond their football rivalry, the same is true for gays and evangelicals. Members of the competing groups come together daily in the ordinary routines of life and community. And, it's important to recognize that they don't come together primarily as members of competing groups. Instead, they are co-workers, customers, relatives, and often members of the same clubs.

That reality has brought about a stunning change during my lifetime. As mentioned earlier, I never met an openly gay man until 1975. When Tony and I became friends, I was already 19 years old! He stood out because very few gay men at the time were open about their sexuality.

Today, it's hard to imagine any 19-year-olds without several openly gay friends. In fact, just about all Americans now "know someone who is gay or lesbian." That includes 85 percent of evangelicals.[15] And, by the way, just about everyone knows churchgoing evangelicals. Whether it's through school, work, social activities, service projects or cheering for the same football team, friendships and social capital are being developed daily.

These friendships build bridges and highlight everyone's shared interest in maintaining a healthy community. As Rauch puts it, "It is possible to believe that you're morally in the right, though, and still want to get along with your friends and neighbors in a pluralistic society." That's true for both gays and evangelicals. While a few on each side prefer scorched earth tactics and a fight to the death, the vast majority "both desire and manage to get along with many people we disagree with." We value community enough that we want to get along with others even when the disagreements are "on moral issues."[16]

Fortunately, we live in a nation that allows us the freedom to be together without forcing us to be the same. That's the beauty of the American Creed, the deeply embedded belief that each of us has the right to live our own lives as we see fit so long as we don't deny the right of others to do the same. That Creed has the power to unite gays, evangelicals, and every American. All that is needed is a willingness to acknowledge that everyone—especially those with whom we disagree—are equally worthy of the right to life, liberty, and the pursuit of happiness.

Once this common ground is recognized, something else becomes clear about the conflicts between gays and evangelicals. Not only do both sides embrace the American Creed, both also believe they are simply trying to live their lives as they see fit. As both gays and evangelicals see it, their side is the one that wants nothing more than to live and let live. Both sides believe that they want only the freedom that is their birthright as an American.

Neither side sees the other in that manner. In fact, both gay and evangelical activists believe that the other side is actively working to deny them their rights.

The question, then, is how can we build upon the common ground and overcome the common misunderstandings to create a solution where everyone benefits? How, for example, can we protect the rights of same-sex couples who believe they have the right to hire any wedding photographer with the rights of photographers whose sincere religious beliefs prevent them from participating in a same sex-marriage?

Rauch believes the answer can be found in avoiding what he calls "over-deterrence." Such a "zero-tolerance" approach is "blind to diversity of community preferences and precludes geographic variation." As a result, "Texas and Massachusetts must have the same rules, virtually guaranteeing a bad fit for one place or the other, or both."[17]

If anything, the scholar is understating the problem. The regulatory state today operates a system of selective over-deterrence. Bureaucrats preach and enforce zero-tolerance on some things while completely ignoring other violations. The really scary part is that the bureaucratic priorities can change overnight. That's what happened when Harry Ainslinger launched his crusade to bring down black jazz musicians and hound Billie Holiday to her deathbed.

In such a regulatory world, nobody is safe from the whims of the bureaucracy.

Rather than accepting a one-size-fits-all solution determined by courts and bureaucrats, Rauch believes it's important to consider context. In general, he assumes that most caterers, bakers, florists, and others will serve whoever is willing to pay. That's a reasonable assumption, and it's the strongest pragmatic assurance of equal treatment for same-sex couples.

But he also encourages a safety valve to protect those whose sincere religious beliefs prevent them from participating in a same-sex wedding. And the safety valve should be developed in context. In a city where 99 bakers are willing to cater to whomever is willing to pay, there is no need to force another baker to do anything that might violate his or her beliefs. Different and more creative solutions might be needed in a rural community with only one baker.

Rauch highlighted several practical solutions as a starting point, some of them drawn from the history of the civil rights movement. They build upon a recognition that there are legitimate concerns all around and also upon the need to avoid unnecessary conflict. But the specifics of the policy solutions aren't nearly as important as the larger point he is making.

Rauch wants to elevate the dialogue by encouraging the nation to live up to its highest ideals. He wants gays and evangelicals and others to search together for a circumstance where everybody involved gets to live their own life as they see fit. That's a pragmatic approach building upon our nation's commitment to freedom, equality, and self-governance.

Ultimately, the Brookings scholar recognizes that "this is not a decision only about gay people or religious people. It's a decision about . . .

whether we can interpret America's core principles in ways that honor and celebrate America's characteristic pragmatism and diversity."[18]

WHO DECIDES?

In practical terms, that decision will be made by the actions of America's community leaders.

Obviously, with millions and millions of community leaders, there will be no agreed-upon and unified approach. Most of the time, local leaders aren't thinking about resolving great issues or interpreting "America's core principles in ways that honor and celebrate America's characteristic pragmatism and diversity." Instead, they are too busy trying to find enough hours in the day and searching for pragmatic solutions to the immediate problem in front of them.

But their leadership style will be heavily influenced by whether they view the world through the perspective of the regulatory state or are committed to America's founding ideals of freedom, equality, and self-governance.

Those who hold the regulatory-state worldview tend to focus their energies on what happens in official Washington rather than the local community. They buy into the false notion that every problem must have a political solution and that the solution must eventually be handed down in Supreme Court rulings and bureaucratic rules.

Whether working with gays, evangelicals, or anybody else, leaders obsessed with official Washington have a very negative impact on local communities. Believing that their needs can be met only through political debate, local believers in the regulatory state treat their community group's members as an army that must be whipped into shape. It's an approach that requires constant reminders about the moral righteousness of their cause and a concerted effort to demonize the opposition.

Following the regulatory state model requires local leaders to value ideology and politics over pragmatism and community. It destroys social capital by emphasizing conflict and a win-at-all-costs attitude. This approach is the political equivalent of bringing Giants' and Eagles' fans to a sports bar when their teams are competing to go to the Super Bowl.

In stark contrast, leaders who instinctively embrace America's highest ideals recognize that every relationship requires hard work and maintaining the fabric of a community is no different. They encourage cooperation and rely upon social capital resources to develop win-win situations for all involved.

Rather than seeing competing groups in a fight to the death, they see friends and colleagues working together through a challenging situation. Despite the difficulties, good leaders value the effort because it strengthens the fabric of community. They bring competing groups together by finding forums to highlight common ground; the political equivalent of bringing Giants and Eagles fans together to root against the Cowboys.

Bridging efforts can help provide the foundation and understanding needed to develop win-win resolutions. But the biggest changes often come from within close bonding groups, rather than between groups. That's because they provide a setting where people can freely discuss their concerns and questions without fear of being targeted. It's a place where members of the tribe can explore ways of remaining true to their beliefs while also allowing those with different beliefs to do the same.

For example, it is easier for Christians to explore questions about same-sex marriage with others who share their belief than with outside activists who view them as hypocrites. Good leaders can take advantage of this by encouraging their flock to explore the issue in terms of their own core beliefs. Those beliefs include the fact that God's love is available to everyone and we are to be representatives of Christ on earth. How should those beliefs be reflected in the daily behavior of individuals and their church?

The LGBT community has the same opportunity for reflection. Rauch, for example, offers this point for consideration: "Given our own historical role as victims of majoritarian repression—repression which was cultural as well as legal—LGBT people should be wary of joining or abetting campaigns to enforce moral conformity."[19] How should that perspective be reflected in the daily behavior of individuals and LGBT organizations?

I certainly don't mean to suggest that the answers are easy to find. It's often very difficult to understand people with a fundamentally different worldview. Sometimes, we have to be comfortable with the idea of being uncomfortable. And we must always keep in mind that even those with whom we disagree are deserving of the right to life, liberty, and the pursuit of happiness.

But, while difficult, changes within bonding groups can change the world. Once again, the world of sports provides a great example.

JACKIE ROBINSON

On April 15, 1947, Jackie Robinson made history by breaking the Major League color barrier. MVP awards, All-Star selections, and championships recognized his skills as a player. His larger legacy was honored when all of Major League Baseball retired his number. Nobody else on any team will ever wear number 42 again. The sole exception is on April 15 each year, Jackie Robinson Day. On that day, every player, coach, and manager on every team wears his number in celebration of his life. No other player has ever received such an honor.

Robinson deserves all the accolades he has received. The courage and class he displayed in the face of hatred and vicious personal attacks are almost beyond belief. He and his wife demonstrated the power of non-violent resistance years before the world ever heard of Martin Luther King Jr.

It takes nothing away from Robinson to note he would not have had the chance to achieve such legendary stature without the efforts of Dodgers President Branch Rickey. In a world where every institution and relationship has a role to play in governing society, the baseball executive provided a great example of how a business can play a positive role in governing society.

Rickey was a Christian who believed it was his calling to integrate Major League Baseball and saw "an opportunity to intervene in the moral history of the nation."[20] He was also a wise leader who understood both the difficulties involved and the importance of doing it right, one step at a time. In 1943, four years before Robinson made history, Rickey took the first formal step in the process by seeking approval for his plan from the Dodgers board of directors.[21]

Anybody who's ever served on a committee or a board can imagine the reaction when Rickey first floated the idea. He probably got sick of hearing, "It's never been done before." After recovering from the initial shock, board members almost certainly wondered about whether the league would allow it. Some might have raised business questions about the impact on ticket sales. And, of course, Rickey probably heard the old standby of those who oppose change, "It's a good idea, but maybe we should wait until somebody else goes first."

After getting board approval, Rickey began searching for the right man. That meant so much more than just finding a good ballplayer. Rickey "felt strongly that if the person he chose for this extraordinary task could be goaded into saying the wrong thing or appearing in any way as less than noble and dignified, the press would have a field day," wrote biographer Eric Metaxas. Even worse, "the whole idea of integrating baseball would likely be set back another ten or fifteen years."[22]

Two years after getting board approval, Rickey first met Robinson. The baseball exec made clear the level of hate and abuse that Robinson would have to endure. Obviously, Robinson knew firsthand the reality of American racism, but Rickey wanted the ballplayer to carefully consider how much harder it would be when he took such a visible and historic step to oppose segregation.

The Dodgers leader also made clear that the whole world would be watching Robinson's every move. He built upon the common ground of their shared faith, pointed Robinson to Jesus's Sermon on the Mount, and said he was looking for a man "with guts enough not to fight back."[23] Rickey also provided assurance that he would do all he could to support the ballplayer, a commitment he honored. Robinson then committed himself to non-retaliation, and the rest is history.

GREAT LEADERS MAKE IT EASIER FOR OTHERS TO FOLLOW

Few leaders have the wisdom and courage of Jackie Robinson and Branch Rickey. They are so rare, in fact, that we can't afford to limit our leadership search to the dysfunctional world of official Washington. The all-hands-on-board community problem-solving approach enables leaders to emerge where they are needed rather than where we are looking for them.

Fortunately, we don't need such transformational leaders every step of the way. Their impact percolates through society, making it easier for other leaders to follow. Just as gay and evangelical leaders can learn from the agreements in Utah, other baseball teams learned from the Dodgers.

Within three months after Robinson broke the color barrier, two other teams added black players to their roster. All it took was for somebody else to go first. Two years later, Don Newcombe became the first black man to pitch in the World Series. Within 12 years, every single Major League team had black players on their rosters. During that 12-year stretch, black ballplayers won the National League MVP award eight times.[24]

Pee Wee Reese, the Dodgers' shortstop in those days, provided his own form of individual leadership. During Robinson's second season, the merciless taunting from bigoted fans was particularly difficult one day. The man with the guts not to fight back was unable to respond, so Reese responded for him with a wonderfully appropriate gesture. He simply walked over and put an arm around his double-play partner. The sight of a Southern white man taking this step quieted the crowd and is now commemorated with a statue in Brooklyn.[25]

It's important to note that Rickey changed all of baseball simply by changing his own organization. That's because of the tremendous overlapping network of people and relationships that holds our society together. When a visible organization like the Dodgers dramatically changed its standards, it sent shockwaves throughout the entire network, forcing others to adapt. It generated untold millions of conversations among baseball fans who carried those discussions into other areas of life.

As a result, the impact of Rickey's calling was felt far beyond the world of baseball. PBS reports that it "was a major blow to segregation everywhere."[26] One year after Jackie Robinson joined the Dodgers, President Harry Truman integrated the U.S. military. The culture leads and politicians lag behind.

Dealing with the Dodgers decision led to the integration of many hotels and restaurants where the Dodgers' stayed. Other organizations changed as well. *The Sporting News,* a paper that opposed integration of baseball, ended up naming Robinson its Rookie of the Year in 1947.[27]

Nearly nine years after Robinson's first Major League at-bat, Rosa Parks refused to give up her seat on a bus in Montgomery. That's when Martin Luther King Jr. emerged as a leader and applied the lessons of nonviolent resistance on an even broader scale. Acknowledging the debt his movement owed to the ballplayer, King called Robinson "a pilgrim that walked in the lonesome byways toward the high road of Freedom. He was a sit-inner before sit-ins, a freedom rider before freedom rides."[28]

Still, it took 17 years before Congress caught up to the Brooklyn Dodgers and passed major civil rights legislation. In fact, by the time Congress got around to acting, the Dodgers weren't even in Brooklyn anymore. Once again, the culture leads and politicians lag behind.

And the culture is shaped by community leaders who move the nation forward.

Most of the time, those leaders bring about change by first changing the actions of their own organizations.

PASSING ON THE CULTURE OF FREEDOM

America needs strong leadership to "interpret America's core principles in ways that honor and celebrate America's characteristic pragmatism and diversity."[29] But it's a different kind of leadership than most people are looking to find. Pragmatic community problem solvers are already working to resolve the social conflicts of our time. They are doing so by encouraging each other to live up to their own beliefs and the highest ideals of our nation. There is a lot of work to be done, and these are the people we should come alongside or line up behind to do it.

This perspective on leadership explains why I can be so pessimistic about our nation's political system yet optimistic about the future. Even though politics has failed, community leaders are ensuring that America will not.

These leaders provide hope for the future because they are passing on core cultural beliefs to future generations. Most of all, they pass on the belief that has irritated political elites for more than two centuries: every American has the right to live our own life as we see fit, so long as we do not interfere with the right of others to do the same.

It's important to recognize that this attitude did not begin with nobles and royals, or even colonial political legends. "The Revolution began quietly in homes and schoolrooms across the colonies in the reading lessons women gave to children." Utah Professor of English Gillian Brown has described a dynamic colonial conversation conducted through "primers, readers, fables, fairy tales, political rhetoric, and novels through which Americans developed a sense of themselves as a sovereign people distinct from England."[30]

Brown added, "Long before Revolutionary sermons and speeches, the ideal of self-determination resided intimately in the colonial imagination."[31] The ideals that we now cherish as the American Creed were nurtured and passed on by unknown leaders in households and communities throughout colonial America.

This distinct culture came about because colonial Americans had more pragmatic experience with freedom and self-governance "than any part of mankind in the eighteenth century." Pulitzer Prize winning historian Gordon Wood put it like this: "While the speculative philosophers of Europe were laboriously searching their minds in an effort to decide the first principles of liberty, the Americans had come to experience vividly that liberty in their everyday lives."[32]

Sometimes, experiencing liberty in that way generated seemingly small changes in practice that revealed enormous differences in understanding. For example, English citizens had long claimed the right to petition their government. The colonists did too, but they took it one step further and started giving formal and binding instructions to their representatives. More than a semantic difference, the new approach reflected a fundamentally different perception of who is in charge. As George Washington put it, petitioning is "asking a favour" rather than "claiming a right."[33] You petition a superior, you instruct a subordinate.

In early 1776, Thomas Paine's publication of *Common Sense* tapped into this rich cultural heritage and quickly became "the most incendiary and popular pamphlet of the entire revolutionary era." Declaring government to be a "necessary evil" and calling for independence, the provocative document crystallized the public mood. Paine envisioned lofty goals for the new nation, believing that the colonial fight for freedom and self-governance was "in a great measure the cause of mankind. . . . We have it in our power to begin the world over again."[34]

This ongoing cultural dialogue did more than create a new nation. It created an entirely new way of looking at the relationship between a free people and their government.

No longer accepting the idea that kings had a divine right to rule over others, the colonial dialogue gave birth to the game-changing ideal that governments derive their only "just authority from the consent of the governed." The basic idea was simple—the people should be in charge. Figuring out what it looks like in the day-to-day operation of a government and a society has proven to be far more difficult. Much of American history has been devoted to working out that question.

Over the past two centuries or so, the ongoing discussion helped create the checks and balances in the U.S. Constitution while extending the vote to women, black Americans, and those without property. It was a driving force to have voters (rather than state legislators) elect U.S. senators and to expand the protections provided by the Bill of Rights. And it is still working to extend the promise of freedom and equality to all citizens.

Now, it's our turn.

Fortunately, the leaders we need are already in place.

CHAPTER 14

A ONE-SIZE-FITS-ALL GOVERNMENT CANNOT SURVIVE IN THE IPAD ERA

ONE OF THE GREAT EVENTS IN HISTORY was the creation of the United States Constitution. Both George Washington and James Madison called it "the miracle at Philadelphia."[1] So much attention has been focused on the details of how it was created that it's easy to lose sight of the bigger picture.

The accomplishments of the Constitutional Convention were significant. But the rights and freedoms we enjoy as Americans were not invented by a bunch of guys in powdered wigs during that long-ago summer. Instead, they grew out of more than five centuries of pragmatic experimentation.

The experimentation began with the sealing of Magna Carta at Runnymede on June 15, 1215. That document began to carve out freedoms that no king could take away and required the ruler to get permission for tax hikes and other actions. It was the first step on the road to a parliamentary system of government and quickly became an important symbol of liberty.

Daniel Hannan, a British Member of the European Parliament, correctly points out that there is a direct line of thought from Runnymede to Philadelphia, from Magna Carta to the Declaration of Independence. Hannan, whose district includes the site where the historic charter was sealed, notes that the colonists in 1776 did not see themselves as creating "a new privilege," but confirming "an ancient one."[2]

This strong connection came about because the colonies were settled during a period of fierce debate about Magna Carta and freedom. Actually, to call it a fierce debate is a bit of an understatement. Shortly after seven of the original 13 colonies were established, an English Civil War broke out in 1642. King Charles I was executed in 1649. Things didn't settle down until the overthrow of another king decades later. That 1688 event became known as England's Glorious Revolution.

The impact on colonial thought was so strong that noted author Kevin Phillips believes the English Civil War can be seen as "almost an American Pre-Revolution." The "words and aspects" we associate with 1776 "echoed the old-country cleavages of the 1640s."[3] And, Hannan adds, those words from the 1640s "looked back to Magna Carta."[4]

AN AMERICAN TWIST

While building upon centuries of experimentation from England, the American colonies quickly added their own unique twists. One, mentioned earlier, was to simply start Harvard College without bothering to get permission from the king. This pragmatic first step toward an expansion of freedom eventually created thousands upon thousands of voluntary associations that played a vital role in governing colonial society.

The colonists consistently pushed the boundaries of freedom faster and further than the old country. That's largely because most who left for the New World were seeking more freedom and opportunity than they had at home.

This tendency to expand freedom was highlighted at the expense of New York's colonial governor, William Cosby, during the 1730s. The unpopular ruler inspired the creation of America's first alternative newspaper—the *New York Weekly Journal*. John Peter Zenger printed the newspaper, which included several editorials attacking the governor. Without knowing it, the printer was about to play a key role in developing freedom of the press.

Cosby tried to shut down the paper by bringing charges of "seditious libel" against Zenger. Seditious libel, under British law, meant knowingly printing anything against the Crown or officials of the government. Even if what was printed turned out to be true, it was illegal to print it! The governor was so unpopular, however, that two grand juries refused to indict Zenger. Other officials refused to act against him as well. Finally, the governor took the unusual step of having the attorney general issue a special ruling leading to Zenger's arrest.

Zenger spent eight months in prison, but his wife kept printing the paper. When the trial finally arrived, Zenger's attorney shocked the prosecution by freely admitting that his client had published the documents that upset the governor. In terms of the law at the time, that was a clear admission of guilt.

But Zenger's attorney went further. He argued that the ability to criticize the government was essential to freedom. The question, he said, "is not the cause of one poor printer ... No! It may in its consequence affect every free man that lives under a British Government on the main of America. It is the best cause. It is the cause of liberty."[5]

The jury took less than 10 minutes to find Zenger "not guilty." He was released from prison the next day, promptly printed an account of his trial, and freedom of the press was on its way to becoming established in the colonial culture. Events like this blazed new trails in the path to freedom. They also contributed to a growing cultural and legal divide between London and the colonies.[6]

The Historical Society of the New York Courts points out that "the Zenger case did not establish legal precedent in seditious libel or freedom of the press." However, it did something even more important. "It influenced how people thought about these subjects and led, many decades later, to the protections embodied in the ... Bill of Rights."[7]

This was the culture that created the Constitution of the United States. Catherine Drinker Bowen, author of a classic book on how it all came about, noted the long history of pragmatic experimentation. "Since the beginning, the country had moved toward this moment, toward self-government, toward union." It was a process of "trial, error, success, retreat" going back at least to 1639.[8]

Most important of all, the Constitutional Convention was conducted in the shadow of a document that had given voice to America's founding ideals a decade earlier. The Declaration of Independence and the Constitution were intimately and naturally connected because they emerged from the same culture. As Hillsdale College President Larry

Arnn observed, the Constitution was a blueprint for government directly addressing the concerns that the Declaration had raised against the king of England.[9]

It takes nothing away from those who drafted the Constitution to note that they were simply building upon centuries of experimentation with the concept of freedom. Quite the opposite, in fact. The key to their success was creating a governing structure broadly consistent with the culture and the Spirit of 1776. That's the reason the Constitution survived and is still relevant today.

The ideals they built upon, developed over centuries, became what we now revere as the American Creed: the belief that all of us have the right to live our lives as we see fit so long as we don't interfere with the rights of others to do the same.

A CHILLING PERSPECTIVE

America's founding ideals of freedom, equality, and self-governance developed over centuries, but opponents of those ideals have been pushing back just as long. Eight centuries ago, King John I had no intention of honoring Magna Carta, but he died before he could do anything about it. The idea that even a king should be subject to the rule of law proved too powerful for his successors to overcome.

From the very beginning in our own country, there have always been some political leaders and others who rejected its founding ideals. Defenders of slavery and Jim Crow laws fundamentally rejected the founding ideal of equality. Convinced of their own superiority, they were willing to sacrifice freedom and self-governance to perpetuate inequality. For most of our history, these activists were the primary threat to those founding ideals.

Today, the primary challenge comes from advocates of the regulatory state who reject the founding commitment to self-governance. Despite the historical evidence, they believe the nation will be better off if we let bureaucrats make the important decisions for the rest of us. Convinced of their own superiority, they are willing to sacrifice the founding ideals of freedom and equality to empower the bureaucracy.

This narrow ideological perspective was clearly articulated in one of the most chilling books I have ever read, *The Executive Unbound: After the Madisonian Republic.* In it, a pair of respected law professors from Chicago and Harvard urge us to turn back the clock and reject all the lessons learned during 800 years of pragmatic experimentation with freedom.

Eric A. Posner and Adrian Vermeule think it is well past time to replace the "Madisonian Republic," or constitutional government. The reference in the title comes from the fact that James Madison was the primary drafter of the Constitution and one of its leading advocates.

While most of us celebrate the Madisonian system of checks and balances, Posner and Vermeule see it as nothing more than an outdated "historical curiosity."[10] They say our Constitutional approach "overestimates the need for the separation of powers and even the rule of law."[11] It's more than a little discomforting when law professors dismiss the rule of law!

About the only thing I could agree with in the entire book was Posner and Vermeule's admission that it is impossible to "reconcile the administrative state" with America's founding ideals.[12] For me, the obvious way to solve that disconnect is to reach for the high ideals and find a better system of formal governance.

Posner and Vermeule instead believe "the technological problems in the modern era . . . require continuous monitoring and adjustment, tasks that only an executive bureaucracy can handle."[13] Starting with such faith in the bureaucracy, they are not at all troubled by the fact that the regulatory state violates our founding ideals.

What does deeply trouble the scholars is something they call "tyrannophobia." They define this condition as an irrational "fear of dictatorship" and trace its roots back to the beginnings of our nation. These teachers of the law claim that tyrannophobic views were "reflected in the Declaration of Independence and founding debates."[14] To be clear, what they call tyrannophobia is what the rest of us call a commitment to freedom, equality, and self-governance.

Posner and Vermeule think it's time for the American people to give up on those founding ideals and accept the fact that the "administrative state is inevitable." They argue "that law cannot hope to constrain the

232 THE SUN IS STILL RISING

modern executive," so everyone should simply "make their peace with the new political order."[15] The scholars are especially concerned that tyrannophobia is preventing us from turning over enough power to presidents and bureaucrats.

In a world where Presidents Barack Obama and Donald Trump have proven the ability to shake up millions of lives with the stroke of a pen, it's hard to believe anybody thinks presidents should have even more unconstrained power. But that's the perspective of regulatory zealots.

Rather than a system of carefully thought out checks and balances, the law professors claim that public opinion is enough to control the bureaucracy. "The executive," they assert, "can operate effectively only by proving over and over that it deserves the public's trust."[16] The problem with this theory is that it's already been proven wrong. As noted earlier in Chapter 8, during the entire four decades of the regulatory state, there has never been a time when most Americans trusted the federal government. If public opinion were really sufficient to control the bureaucrats, we wouldn't have the regulatory state today.

One of Posner and Vermeule's most stunning assertions is that even a loss of freedom might not be as bad as we think. "It is not even clear whether authoritarian governments systematically offer different public policies than democracies do." As a result, "democratic institutions should not assume that the loss of well-being caused by a transition from democracy to dictatorship is higher than it in fact is."[17]

It is beyond horrifying that law professors at prestigious schools believe there's not much difference between democracy and dictatorship. On the bright side, I am grateful that professors Posner and Vermeule have so clearly highlighted the choice between America's founding ideals and the regulatory state.

HOW DID IT HAPPEN?

Posner and Vermeule are far from the first to reject America's commitment to self-governance and they won't be the last. It is a recurring problem that can be traced all the way back to the Constitutional Convention.

Connecticut delegate Roger Sherman thought the people should have "as little to do as may be about the government."[18] Alexander Hamilton even proposed that the United States should have an elected monarch who would rule until death or impeachment and have extensive powers.[19] Fortunately, that idea didn't sit too well with other delegates who had just finished a war against a king with too much power.

In practical terms, however, it was George Washington who brought an end to the idea of electing a monarch or a president for life. His decision to step down after two terms set a precedent that lasted for more than a century and a half. The timing was fortuitous because the revered leader died just three years after leaving office. Had he stayed for one more term, America would have been saddled with a troubling precedent of the president serving until death.

Over time, of course, new technologies made it possible to communicate over long distances and the nation became more centralized. Not surprisingly, the functions of government followed the cultural trends. The Interstate Commerce Commission became the first federal regulatory agency in 1887.[20]

In that same year, a young scholar complained that our cultural heritage had "successfully studied the art of curbing executive power to the constant neglect of the art of perfecting executive methods." In other words, "it has exercised itself much more in controlling than in energizing government." He suggested it was time to look elsewhere for ideas, specifically to "French and German professors."[21]

The article expressed frustration with the fact that "nowadays the bulk of mankind votes" and described voters as "selfish, ignorant, timid, stubborn, or foolish." The author dreamed of a nation led by "a corps of civil servants prepared by a special schooling and drilled, after appointment, into a perfected organization, with appropriate hierarchy and characteristic discipline."[22]

These attitudes grew stronger among political elites of the 19th century. They wanted a more powerful central government. Many who expressed these views naturally assumed that they would have leadership roles in such a government. In fact, the young scholar quoted above eventually became president of the United States. As president, Woodrow Wilson oversaw a tremendous increase in federal authority.

SELF-INTEREST OF THE BUREAUCRACY

During that same era, the emerging bureaucracy demonstrated just how far it would go to protect its own interests. *The Wright Brothers,* a wonderful book by historian David McCullough, tells the tale of one of the great successes in American history and how it provoked an *Empire Strikes Back* response from the bureaucrats.

When two brothers from Dayton, Ohio, built and piloted the world's first airplane, it was an embarrassment for official Washington. The federal government had spent years and $50,000 of taxpayer money trying to accomplish that feat. That doesn't sound like much in the 21st century, but at the time it was "the largest appropriation yet granted by the U.S. War Department."[23]

The Smithsonian Institution, under the direction of Samuel Langley, used those funds to build a Great Aerodrome. Unfortunately, in two public trials, the Langley contraption failed spectacularly and plunged into the Potomac River.[24]

Just a few months later, Orville and Wilbur Wright accomplished what the bureaucracy could not. And they did so despite spending only $1,000. Not only that, they had "no college education, no formal technical training, no experience working with anyone other than themselves, no friends in high places, no financial backers, no government subsidies, and little money of their own."[25]

One key to their success was pragmatic experimentation. Where the Smithsonian and others focused on developing theories of flight, the Wrights spent a lot of time flying gliders and learning from their mistakes. "It wasn't luck that made them fly; it was hard work and common sense; they put their whole heart and soul and all their energy into an idea."[26]

The success of the boys from Dayton was unwelcome news to the Smithsonian. Their initial reaction was to deny the truth about the Wright brothers' success. Disparaging rumors were spread.

Later, they went even further and tried to rewrite history.

Eleven years after the first flight at Kitty Hawk, government officials came up with a story blaming Langley's failure on "the launching device for his aerodrome, not the machine itself."[27] So, they built a new launching device, got the aerodrome to fly, and claimed victory. Then, in a truly breathtaking example of bureaucratic chutzpah, the Smithsonian endorsed a claim that Langley had "designed and built the first man-carrying flying machine capable of sustained flight."

What made this fraud even worse is that Langley's plane never actually worked—not even with the new launcher. Before its first and only flight, the Smithsonian modified the craft based on knowledge gained since the Wright brothers' first flight. Then, they put Langley's "Great Aerodrome," on display calling it "the first man-carrying flying machine capable of sustained flight."[28] But, the modifications that made it fly were removed before the machine was put on display in the museum.

Generations of visitors were intentionally deceived.

"It was a lie pure and simple," noted another biographer of the Wright brothers, Fred Howard. "But it bore the imprimatur of the venerable Smithsonian and over the years would find its way into magazines, history books, and encyclopedias, much to the annoyance of those familiar with the facts."[29]

The Smithsonian continued the deception for years by refusing to display the Wright brothers' plane. Finally, in 1928, "Orville sent the 1903 Flyer to England on loan to the Science Museum in London." Only then did the Smithsonian finally admit the truth.[30] It wasn't until 1948— 45 years after the historic first flight—that the world's first working plane was finally brought back and displayed in the Smithsonian.

By then, however, both Orville and Wilbur Wright had died. The bureaucracy had outlasted them.

THE HISTORICAL ABERRATION

As elite support for centralized power grew and the bureaucracy learned to defend its own interests, the Great Depression of the 1930s spurred another round of increased centralization known as the New Deal. Still, despite the efforts of many who thought they should rule over the rest of us, the public commitment to freedom and self-governance generally prevented things from getting too far out of hand.

That all changed on the morning of December 7, 1941. "Never before or since has America been so unified," according to historian Craig Shirley. "There were virtually no Americans against their country getting into World War II after the unprovoked attack by the Japanese at Pearl Harbor."[31] In that unity, and in a desire to preserve the nation, Americans trusted their government as never before or since.

Shirley's book, *December 1941: 31 Days That Changed America and Saved the World,* recounts how President Franklin D. Roosevelt was swiftly authorized to do much more than expand the military and fight other armies. He was given more power than any president ever. In fairness to FDR, authorized is too tame a word. The president was expected to put all of the country's resources, private or public, to use in the war effort.

Before it was over, Roosevelt and his team ran all aspects of the American economy and life. That included banning the sale of private automobiles so that factories could build military aircraft, commandeering all raw materials needed for the war effort, censoring the media, imposing wage and price controls, imprisoning citizens of Japanese origin, and much more.

But he won the war.

His successor, Harry Truman, began the process of winning the peace. After World War II, the U.S. enjoyed an economic boom unrivaled in history.

In short, the response to Pearl Harbor gave the federal government a fair amount of credibility and a large dose of goodwill.

Politicians of the time, sincerely convinced that a larger government would be good for the economy and the nation, seized the moment. In a clean break from America's history, Congress quickly declared that the federal government was now in charge of managing the economy.[32] A decade and a half later, President John F. Kennedy claimed that this law had played a big role in creating the postwar economic boom.[33]

It was this historical aberration—a brief moment in history when Americans placed enormous trust in the federal government—that allowed the regulatory state to firmly take root in American society.

The moment didn't last.

During the 1960s and early 1970s, the next generation of politicians squandered whatever good will and credibility the federal government had earned. But it wasn't just the mistakes of politicians that created the distrust. It was simply a return to the natural order of things.

Unfortunately, before America's natural and healthy skepticism about centralized power returned, the Nixon administration put in place the foundations of the regulatory state. Since then, regulatory zealots have acted as what sociologist Robert Nisbet called "secular missionaries." The self-interest of their agencies became a top priority, just as it had been in response to the Wright brothers' success. The true believers were "inwardly driven to expand [the bureaucracy] into every corner of social life."[34] And they've been doing it for more than four decades.

The success of the regulatory state at getting around the constitutional system of checks and balances is the force that broke our system of politics and government. It was designed to reduce what Wilson considered the "meddlesome" influence of voters, and it has done just that.

AMERICA'S BEST DAYS ARE STILL TO COME

The challenge before us today is figuring out what we can do about it.

That's been the central question driving my long personal journey from pessimism about America's dysfunctional political system to optimism about America's future.

The most important step on that journey was losing faith in the political process. That eventually freed me to recognize that the solutions we need will never be found in official Washington. Instead, we needed to look to the rest of the nation for leadership. Community problem solving, fueled by the digital revolution and inspired by the millennial generation, is poised to overcome our failed system of politics and government. We may not be able to make government work better, but that won't stop us from making society work better.

As I developed that message and shared it with various audiences, I was always impressed that so many people wanted to be part of the solution. They wanted to know what kind of reforms would really make a difference and what they could do about it. But I was haunted by the fact that they were exclusively focused on seeking political solutions.

Sometimes, for example, I would be asked if passing term limits was the answer. Having worked for years as a leader in the term limits movement, I naturally believe such limits would be a good idea.

However, there were two practical problems with that approach. The first is that term limits are not a silver-bullet solution. They might make Congress work a bit better, but they are not enough to fix a broken and corrupt system. That's especially true when Congress has so little control over the regulators. The second is that there is no way to make it happen. The Supreme Court has ruled that only Congress can initiate the effort to impose limits on itself. Expecting that to happen is a bit like expecting toddlers to set a reasonable bedtime for themselves. Forget about it.

Everywhere I went, I encountered people who wanted to do what they could to help the country. It broke my heart to tell them the political system was so badly broken that there was nothing for them to do. It took me more than a decade to finally figure out an answer, and it involves five steps we can all take.

Losing faith in our dysfunctional system of politics and government is the essential first step for anyone who wants America to create a bright future for our children and grandchildren.

To be clear, this does not mean avoiding politics like the plague. You should vote, even if it's only to choose between the lesser of two evils. And you should get involved on issues near and dear to your heart. Sometimes, political involvement is needed just for damage control. But you should never fall into the trap of believing that political solutions alone will address the problems facing the nation.

For those who love this country, losing faith in our political system is a hard step to take. It certainly was for me. I really wanted to believe that the system works the way I was brought up to think it did. It hurts to recognize that our current form of government—the regulatory state—"is not merely unconstitutional; it is anti-constitutional." As Boston University Law Professor Gary Lawson pointed out, "The Constitution was designed specifically to prevent the emergence of [these] kinds of institutions."

Only by recognizing this reality and losing faith can we be freed to explore other ways of working together in community. That leads directly to the second step each of us can take. We can all get involved and take part in a massive campaign of community problem solving. If your only civic engagement is through the political process, you're not doing enough.

Problem-solving approaches come in all shapes and sizes. Sometimes it's as simple as helping a friend in need or serving meals at a community food bank. It might also mean getting people together for a bit of community building fun or launching a small business that provides a needed service.

But there are also much larger efforts like Uber's service to consumers that completely revamped the ride-sharing world. Other potentially game-changing projects were described in Chapter 10—Change is Good, Transitions are Hard. Things like parents and teachers coming together to create a new school or health care providers experimenting with new technologies and ways of delivering service.

Most efforts are either driven by entrepreneurs or community groups seeing a specific need. Some are even consciously intended to provide an alternative to government programs. Richard Cornuelle, the anti-poverty activist mentioned earlier, "decided to pick a problem and prove, by competing directly with the government, that the independent sector could outperform the government sector."[35] The result was a program to help low-income students afford college.

Every one of us has different skills, passions, opportunities, and communities to serve. We must all find our own most effective way to get involved. The key is getting involved where we are and doing all that we can. We should focus on problem solving first and have confidence that the policy changes will eventually catch up.

To some people, this doesn't seem to be enough. They want to gear up the forces to fight a single climactic political battle that will determine our nation's future. I understand the adrenaline rush that comes from getting caught up in such political bouts, but I also know they won't get us where we want to go. We don't live in a *Star Wars* movie where a single miraculous shot can destroy the Death Star.

That's why the more mundane and realistic approach of community problem solving and Radical Incrementalism is a better approach. Just as Goliath would have crushed David in hand-to-hand combat, the regulatory state will destroy any serious political opponents. But when we change the game and focus on pragmatic community problem solving, there's no way the bureaucracy can win.

Using our freedom to work together in community is the most effective way to defeat the regulatory state and move the nation forward. But it is not the easy path. A massive campaign of community problem solving requires far more work than simply voting and assuming the politicians will take care of it. And any effort to work around the regulatory state will encounter serious pushback from the political class.

So, the third step each of us can take is to be optimistic. Maintaining hope is the only thing that will keep us going during the tough times.

I am not suggesting that we should simply keep a smile on our face when times are tough and pretend that everything will be all right. Instead, we need to develop an optimism solidly grounded in the understanding that those who believe in America's founding ideals have a stronger position than those who believe in the regulatory state. The fundamentals favor the good guys.

Such a belief comes from fully appreciating the reality that the culture leads and politicians lag behind. Like a man who built his house on a solid foundation, the Declaration of Independence and United States Constitution were grounded on the solid foundation of centuries of pragmatic experimentation. They embraced and reflected the culture that was leading the nation. That culture continues to lead the nation today.

The tools of the digital revolution reinforce and strengthen this cultural commitment to freedom, equality, and self-governance. As Harvard's Nicco Mele puts it, "The devices and connectivity so essential to modern life put unprecedented power in the hands of every individual."[36] The 200 million smartphones in the nation today are the greatest force for change in the history of the world because they bring power to the people.

Those who dream of centralized power in the hands of a ruling elite are like the man who built a castle on the sand. Lacking any foundation in American culture and grounded only in a temporary historical aberration, the regulatory state is ill prepared to withstand the storm of a decentralizing society. As Mele observed, "Radical connectivity is toxic to traditional power structures."[37] A one-size-fits-all central government cannot survive in the iPad era.

It is hard work to gain the confidence that comes from knowing the culture leads. It's taken me a decade to get there and I still have to work at it every day. It often requires focusing on a particular item in the news that is presented as a political issue and then intentionally looking for a different angle. Sometimes, talking it through with others and hearing new perspectives helps. That leads to the fourth step: Sharing the experience.

Like problem solving itself, sharing the experience can take many forms. One is to create and/or participate in small groups dedicated to community problem solving like those mentioned in Chapter 9. It might also mean bringing some of the ideas about the culture leading into your daily social media experience or chats with friends. You might even share this book or ideas from it with interested friends and family.

At its core, sharing the experience is important because that's what community is all about. As the shared experience grows, it becomes easier to deal with the loss of faith in our dysfunctional political system, get directly involved in creating a better world, and have confidence in America's future.

Remember, "Beach bodies are made in winter." In the world of sports, championships are won on the practice field long before they are realized in the big game. Sharing the experience is also a way of preparing ourselves to be more effective advocates of community problem solving.

The fifth step is foundational. While doing the grinding, tireless, and often thankless work of community problem solving, we must never lose sight of the fact that we're doing it to lift up America's high ideals. We must cherish and remain true to our nation's commitment to freedom, equality, and self-governance.

These are five steps we can all take to create a bright future for our nation: (1) Lose faith in our dysfunctional system of politics and government; (2) get directly involved in a massive campaign of community problem solving; (3) be optimistic because we realize the culture leads and politicians lag behind; (4) share the experience with others; and (5) remain true to America's highest ideals.

If we do all of that, we will be what Martin Luther King Jr. called "creative dissenters." We "will call our beloved nation to a higher destiny, to a new plateau of compassion, to a more noble expression of humanness."[38] Guided by millions of local leaders and the millennial generation, we will show how much free people working together in community can accomplish.

The nation's 63 million volunteers and 27 million entrepreneurs will solve the challenges of our health care and education systems while creating a better world for our children and grandchildren. By encouraging every institution and relationship to fulfill its role in governing society, we will dramatically reduce poverty, heal racial divides, and expand freedom. We will draw our nation ever closer to becoming a land filled with opportunity, liberty, and justice for all.

Lose faith, get involved, be optimistic, share the experience, and remain true to our nation's highest ideals. If we do that, we will show that while politics has failed, America will not.

ACKNOWLEDGMENTS

A BOOK LIKE THIS can come together only with the support and assistance of many people.

For me, that list starts with my wife, Laura. Not only was she patient and supportive during the seemingly never-ending process that stretched from 2015 to 2017, she was also the frontline editor for every page. Most of the time, she just offered suggestions to make things easier to follow. Sometimes, though, Laura made it clear that I had to start a section or a chapter all over again. And she was always right! Her willingness to provide blunt feedback early in the process made this a better book. Her belief that I had something worth writing about gave me the strength to keep going.

Josiah Peterson was my research assistant for this book. At least that's the way he started. This bright young man was brought on to verify all my citations and make sure I was accurately presenting my data and arguments. But, as we worked together over time, Josiah also grew comfortable suggesting additional perspectives and challenging some of my comments. There are anecdotes included only because of Josiah's probing and some great stories left out because they just didn't fit.

Greg Thornbury, president of The King's College in New York, provided great encouragement as I was being worn down by the grind of a long project. The enthusiasm he voiced was backed by a commitment to launch an Institute for Community Driven Solutions at his school.

And, of course, I must thank previous president Boyd Matheson and current CEO Rick Larsen, along with the entire team at Sutherland Institute, for publishing this work. Special thanks to Pamela Whitmore, Stan Rasmussen, and Kelsey Witt, who handled final editing, logistics, and promotion.

Much of the journey described in this book was driven by audiences for speeches I've given over the past decade. Every time I speak, I learn something from the audience, a process that is exhilarating and refreshing. Thanks to everyone who asked questions and provided feedback. Speeches before countless business, civic, political, and campus groups were arranged by the Premiere Speakers Bureau. Shawn Hanks, Jordan Smallwood, and the entire Premiere Team are top-tier professionals who make the speaking circuit easy to navigate.

Many others reviewed sections of the book and offered feedback or constructive criticism. Others provided data for specific topics. This list includes David Boaz, Ann Buck, Raj Chetty, Elisabeth Clemens, Lucas Dayton, Chris Edwards, Leslie Graves, Brittany Gunkler, Daniel Hannan, Charles Hughes, Kathy Shea Keefe, Mario Kranjac, Guy Maisnik, Eric O'Keefe, Jonathan James, Casey Patterson, Roger Pilon, Elissa Prichep, Andy Rasmussen, Jonathan Rauch, Ryan Rupe, Larry Sanger, Mike Tanner, Kristin Tate, Mari Will, and Juan Williams. I am sure there are others, and I apologize to anybody whose contributions I neglected to mention.

Volkswagen Group's Audi luxury brand made an invaluable contribution by giving me the opportunity to ride in a self-driving car for the first time. That experience clarified for me just how much we underestimate the magnitude of change coming over the next generation. Special thanks to Brad Stertz and Anna Schneider for making it happen. Also, thanks to Mitch Bainwol from the Alliance of Automobile Manufacturers for putting me in touch with the Audi team.

Ralph del Campo is a good friend who helped me think more strategically about the issues described in this book. Sid Milkis, PhD, who now teaches at the University of Virginia, long ago helped me understand politics from a broader perspective.

My agent, Frank Breeden of Premiere Authors, prodded me to more concisely state my case (and he also kept pushing until it was concise enough to be an intriguing title).

And, of course, I am grateful to Amity Shlaes for writing the Foreword to this book.

This entire effort is the result of a lifetime of learning, and it's been an amazing journey. I remember first getting caught up in the national political scene and later coming to the crushing realization that our political system is broken. Then there was a new burst of optimism as I recognized all the progress that is being made outside of political circles.

As I came to the conclusion of the book, I realized that the journey and the learning will continue. I want to thank, in advance, everyone who will respond to this book and provide further understanding of how the culture leads and politicians lag behind.

SCOTT RASMUSSEN
August 2018

NOTES

CHAPTER 1

1. Nicco Mele, *The End of Big: How the Internet Makes David the New Goliath* (New York: St. Martin's Press, 2013), 2.

2. Ron Fournier, "The Outsiders: How Can Millennials Change Washington If They Hate It?," *The Atlantic*, August 26, 2013. http://www.theatlantic.com/politics/archive/2013/08/the-outsiders-how-can-millennials-change-washington-if-they-hate-it/278920/

3. "The Greensboro Sit-In," History.com, 2010, accessed February 3, 2017. http://www.history.com/topics/black-history/the-greensboro-sit-in

4. Marc Landy and Sidney M. Milkis, *American Government: Enduring Principles, Critical Choices*, 3rd Edition, (New York: Cambridge University Press, 2014), 55.

5. Kevin Phillips, *1775: A Good Year for Revolution*, (New York: Penguin Group, 2012), 17-18.

6. David Hackett Fischer, *Liberty and Freedom: A Visual History of America's Founding Ideas* (New York, Oxford University Press, 2004), 1-2.

7. Oscar Handlin and Mary Handlin, *Dimensions of Liberty*, (New York: Macmillan Pub Co, 1966), 5.

8. Landy and Milkis, *American Government: Enduring Principles, Critical Choices*, 41.

9. Thomas Jefferson, "May 8, 1825 Letter to Henry Lee," *The American Soul: The Contested Legacy of the Declaration of Independence*, ed. Justin Buckley Dyer, (Lanham, Maryland: Rowman and Littlefield, 2012), 19.

10. Martin Luther King, Jr., *Where Do We Go From Here: Chaos or Community?*, (Boston: Beacon Press, 2010), 18.

11. Ibid., 59.

12. Meghan Barr, "Friends, Kin Key to Sandy Survival," AP, June 24, 2013. http://www.apnorc.org/news-media/Pages/News+Media/friends-kin-key-to-sandy-survival.aspx

13. Ibid.

14. Danika Fears, "'Lunch angel' pays kids' overdue accounts at elementary school," Today, February 6, 2014. http://www.today.com/parents/lunch-angel-pays-kids-overdue-accounts-elementary-school-2D12062213

15. "Coke, Pepsi dropping controversial 'BVO' from all drinks," USA Today, May 5, 2014. http://www.usatoday.com/story/news/nation/2014/05/05/coke-pepsi-dropping-bvo-from-all-drinks/8736657/

16. Mallory Simon, "Island DIY: Kauai residents don't wait for state to repair road," CNN, April 9, 2009. http://www.cnn.com/2009/US/04/09/hawaii.volunteers.repair/index.html?iref=topnews

17. Deborah Ward, "Official statement from Hawaii DLNR regarding re-opening of Polihale on 4-25-09," Hawaii Explorer, April 24, 2009. http://www.kauaiexplorer.com/Polihale_Open4-09.pdf

18. Ibid.

CHAPTER 2

1. Aaron Wildavsky, The Revolt Against the Masses, (New Jersey: Transaction Publishers, 2002), 52.

2. "Table 1.1—Summary of Receipts, Outlays, and Surpluses or Deficits (-): 1789-2021," Historical Tables, White House Office of Management and Budget. https://www.whitehouse.gov/omb/budget/Historicals

3. Michael Tanner, "Trump on 'Waste, Fraud, and Abuse," National Review, February 17, 2016. http://www.nationalreview.com/article/431446/trump-waste-fraud-and-abuse

4. William G. Gale, Melissa S. Kearney, and Peter R. Orszag, "Would a significant increase in the top income tax rate substantially alter income inequality?," Brookings, September 28, 2015. http://www.brookings.edu/research/papers/2015/09/28-increase-in-top-income-tax-rate-not-substantially-alter-income-inequality-gale-kearney-orszag

5. Wildavsky, The Revolt, 53.

6. Philip Rucker and Robert Costa, "Time for a GOP panic? Establishment worried Carson or Trump might win," Washington Post, November 13, 2015.

7. Wildavsky, The Revolt, 53.

8. Jon Rauch, Government's End: Why Washington Stopped Working, (New York: Public Affairs, 1999), 231.

9. Ibid., 260.

10. W. E. Channing, People's Edition of the Entire Works of W.E. Channing, D.D., Volume 1, (Belfast: Simms and M'intyre, 1843), 146.

11. Arthur M. Schlesinger Sr., "Biography of a Nation of Joiners," The American Historical Review, Vol L, No. 1, October 1944, 4.

12. Constance Smith and Anne Freedman, *Voluntary Associations: Perspectives on the Literature*, (Cambridge: Harvard University Press, 1972), 33.

13. Elisabeth S. Clemens and Doug Guthrie, *Politics and Partnerships: The Role of Voluntary Associations in America's Political Past and Present*, (Chicago: University of Chicago Press, 2011), 32.

14. "1973 Report from N.O.W. Task Force on Volunteerism," found in *Teaching Feminist Activism: Strategies from the Field*, eds. Nancy A Naples and Karen Bojar, (New York: Routledge, 2002), 64.

15. Kelley Holland, "For millions, 401(k) plans have fallen short," CNBC, March 23, 2015. http://www.cnbc.com/2015/03/20/l-it-the-401k-is-a-failure.html

16. Public Law 95-600, "An Act: To amend the Internal Revenue Code of 1954 to reduce income taxes, and for other purposes," November 6, 1978. http://www.scribd.com/doc/62002113/Revenue-Act-of-1978-PL-95-600

17. Originally accessed through "Ted Benna: Bio," on ExpertPlan.com in November 2015, https://www.expertplan.com/experts/tedbio.jsp. Site has since been taken down but quotes were reconfirmed via e-mail with Ted Benna, "RE: Quote for Book," sent to jpeterson@tkc.edu, on January 31, 2017.

18. Fred Williams, "R. Theodore Benna," *Pensions&Investments*, October 27, 2003.

19. "401(k) fast facts," American Benefits Council, April 2014. http://www.americanbenefitscouncil.org/pub/e613e1b6-f57b-1368-c1fb-966598903769

20. Donna J. Kelley, Abdul Ali, Candida Brush, Andrew C. Corbett, Caroline Daniels, Phillip H. Kim, Thomas S. Lyons, Mahdi Majbrouri, and Edward G. Rogoff, "2014 United States Report – National Entrepreneurial Assessment for the United States of America," *Global Entrepreneurship Monitor*, Babson College and Baruch College Zicklin School of Business, 2015, 7. http://www.babson.edu/Academics/centers/blank-center/global-research/gem/Documents/GEM%20USA%202014.pdf

21. Robert Jesse Willhide, "Annual Survey of Public Employment & Payroll Summary Report: 2013, Economy-Wide Statistics Briefs: Public Sector," United States Census Bureau, December 19, 2014. http://www2.census.gov/govs/apes/2013_summary_report.pdf

22. "National Center for Charitable Statistics: Number of Nonprofit Organization in the United States, 2003-2013," Urban Institute, accessed June 7, 2016. http://nccsweb.urban.org/PubApps/profile1.php?state=US

23. Clifford Grammich, Kirk Hadaway, Richard Houseal, Dale E. Jones, Alexei Krindatch, Richie Stanley, and Richard H. Taylor, "U.S. Religion Census 2010: Summary Findings," Association of Statisticians of American Religious Bodies, May 1, 2012, 10. http://www.rcms2010.org/press_release/ACP%2020120501.pdf

24. Timothy Sandoval, "Donations Grow 4% to $373 Billion, Says 'Giving USA,'" The Chronicle of Philanthropy, June 14, 2016. https://www.philanthropy.com/article/Donations-Grow-4-to-373/236790

25. "World Economic Outlook Database – Report for Selected Countries and Subjects," International Monetary Fund, October 2016. http://www.imf.org/external/pubs/ft/weo/2016/02/

26. Arthur Brooks, *Who Really Cares*, (New York: Basic Books, 2007), 120.

27. Quote from: Jeremy Beer, *The Philanthropic Revolution: An Alternative History of American Charity*, (Philadelphia: University of Pennsylvania Press, 2015), 5. Original data from: Lester Salamon, S. Wojciech Sokolowski, Megan Haddock, and Helen Tice, *The State of Global Civil Society and Volunteering: Latest findings from the implementation of the UN Nonprofit Handbook*, John Hopkins University Center for Civil Society Studies, March 2013, pg. 4. http://ccss.jhu.edu/wp-content/uploads/downloads/2013/04/JHU_ Global-Civil-Society-Volunteering_FINAL_3.2013.pdf

28. "Volunteering in the United States, 2015: News Release," Bureau of Labor Statistics, United States Department of Labor, February 25, 2016. http://www.bls.gov/news.release/pdf/volun.pdf

29. "Volunteering and Civic Life in America," Corporation for National & Community Service, accessed May 1, 2017. https://www.nationalservice.gov/vcla

30. "Food and Fund Partners," Feeding America, June 2016. http://www.feedingamerica.org/about-us/about-feeding-america/partners/food-and-fund-partners/?referrer=https://www.google.com/

31. "Habitat for Humanity surpasses 1 million families served worldwide," Habitat for Humanity, November 18, 2014. http://www.habitat.org/newsroom/2014archive/11-18-2014-habitat-surpasses-1-million-families-served-worldwide

32. "Scope of the Nonprofit Sector," Independent Sector, accessed June 8, 2016. https://www.independentsector.org/scope_of_the_sector

33. "Summary Memorandum transmitting results from Heartland Monitor Survey XX," FTI Consulting, April 28, 2014. http://heartlandmonitor.com/wp-content/uploads/2015/03/Heartland-XX-Key-Findings-Memo-04-28-14-5pm-CT.pdf

34. Ibid.

35. Ibid.

36. Ibid.

37. "Volunteering in the United States, 2015: News Release."

38. "Scope of the Nonprofit Sector."

39. Donna Kelley, Slavica Singer, Mike Herrington, "2015/16 Global Report," *Global Entrepreneurship Monitor*, 2016. http://www.gemconsortium.org/report

40. Adam Putnam, "Bowling Alone: About the Book," BowlingAlone.com, accessed June 8, 2016. http://bowlingalone.com/

41. Adam Putnam, "Social Capital Primer," BowlingAlone.com, accessed June 8, 2016. http://bowlingalone.com/?page_id=13

42. Putnam, "Social Capital Primer."

43. William Schambra, "Most Americans aren't 'efficient' philanthropists. That's a good thing." *Washington Post*, September 9, 2015.

44. Oscar Handlin and Mary Handlin, *Dimensions of Liberty*, (New York: Macmillan Pub Co 1966), 111.

45. Jeremy Beer, "The Philanthropic Revolution: An Alternative History of American Charity" (Philadelphia: University of Pennsylvania Press, 2015). 46.

46. "Philanthropy Timeline: Giving in the 1700s," National Philanthropic Trust, accessed June 8, 2016. http://www.nptrust.org/history-of-giving/timeline/1700s/

47. Marc Landy and Sidney M. Milkis, *American Government: Balancing Democracy and Rights*, (New York: Cambridge University Press, 2008), 93.

48. "America's First Direct Mail Campaign," Pushing the Envelope, Smithsonian's National Postal Museum Blog, July 29, 2010. http://postalmuseumblog.si.edu/2010/07/americas-first-direct-mail-campaign.html

49. Landy and Milkis, 123.

50. "America's First Direct Mail Campaign," Pushing the Envelope, Smithsonian's National Postal Museum Blog, July 29, 2010. http://postalmuseumblog.si.edu/2010/07/americas-first-direct-mail-campaign.html

51. Edward T. O'Donnell, *Turning Points in American History – Lecture 11, The Great Courses*, July 8, 2013.

52. Ibid.

53. "Population from 1790 to 1990," Census.gov, Department of Commerce, September 27, 1993. https://www.census.gov/population/censusdata/table-4.pdf

54. O'Donnell, *Turning Points*.

55. Thomas Jefferson, *Notes on the State of Virginia* (Richmond: J. W. Randolph, 1853). Originally written in 1781 and first published in 1784.

56. Handlin and Handlin, *Dimensions of Liberty*, 5.

57. David Boaz, "The Man Who Would Not Be King," Commentary, February 20, 2006. http://www.cato.org/publications/commentary/man-who-would-not-be-king

CHAPTER 3

1. "Voting & Elections," Votes PA, Pennsylvania.Gov, accessed June 23, 2016. http://www.votespa.com/portal/server.pt/community/about_voting_and_elections/13508/importance_of_voting/585276

2. Nancy Duarte, *Resonate: Present Visual Stories that Transform Audiences*, (New Jersey: John Wiley & Sons, 2010), 4.

3. James Q. Wilson, *Political Organizations*, (New Jersey: Princeton University Press, 1995), 22.

4. Barack Obama, "Remarks by the President in Town Hall on Middle-Class Economics," Ivy Tech Community College, Indianapolis, Indiana, February 6, 2015, WhiteHouse.Gov, https://www.whitehouse.gov/the-press-office/2015/02/06/remarks-president-town-hall-middle-class-economics

5. Albert A. Hirschmann, *Exit, Voice, and Loyalty: Responses to Decline in Firms, Organizations, and States*, (Cambridge: Harvard University Press, 1970), 17.

6. Ibid., 106.

7. "Minimum Salary," Baseball-Reference.com, November 19, 2015. http://www.baseball-reference.com/bullpen/Minimum_salary

8. Ibid.

9. Wilson, *Political Organizations*, 27.

10. Ibid., 261.

11. Charles M. Tiebout, "A Pure Theory of Local Expenditures," *Journal of Political Economy*, Vol. 64, No. 5 (October 1956).

12. "Migration/Geographic Mobility: Calculating Migration Expectancy Using ACS Data," United States Census Bureau, accessed June 23, 2016, https://www.census.gov/hhes/migration/about/cal-mig-exp.html

13. "Lifetime Mobility in the United States: 2010 – American Community Survey Briefs," United States Census Bureau, November 2011, https://www.census.gov/content/dam/Census/library/publications/2011/acs/acsbr10-07.pdf

14. "Geographical Mobility: 2008 to 2009 – Population Characteristics," United States Census Bureau, November 2011, https://www.census.gov/content/dam/Census/library/publications/2011/demo/p20-565.pdf

15. Manuela Tobias, "The States of Our Union . . . Are Not All Strong," Politico.com, January 12, 2016. http://www.politico.com/magazine/story/2016/01/state-of-the-union-2016-state-ranking-213521

16. "State-to-State Migration Flows: 2014," United States Census Bureau, February 26, 2016. https://www.census.gov/data/tables/time-series/demo/geographic-mobility/state-to-state-migration.html

17. Tobias, "The States of Our Union."

18. Ibid.

19. Fareed Zakaria, *The Future of Freedom: Illiberal Democracy at Home and Abroad*, (New York: W.W. Norton & Company, 2007), 32.

20. Ibid., 31.

21. Ibid.

22. "Dec 10, 1869: Wyoming grants women the vote," This Day in History, History.com, accessed June 23, 2016, http://www.history.com/this-day-in-history/wyoming-grants-women-the-vote

23. "Women Suffrage Timeline (1840-1920)," National Women's History Museum, accessed June 23, 2016, https://www.nwhm.org/education-resources/history/woman-suffrage-timeline

24. Gretchen Woelfle, *Jeannette Rankin: Political Pioneer*, (Honesdale, PA: Calkins Creek, 2007) 75, 80.

25. Martin Luther King, Jr., *Stride Toward Freedom: The Montgomery Story*, (Boston: Beacon Press, 2010), 31.

26. Ibid., 52.

27. Ibid., 39.

28. Juan Williams, *Eyes on the Prize: America's Civil Rights Years, 1954-1965*, (New York: Penguin Books, 2013), 72.

29. King, *Stride Toward Freedom*, 61.

30. Williams, *Eyes on the Prize*, 88.

31. King, *Stride Toward Freedom*, 97.

32. Williams, *Eyes on the Prize*, 89.

33. "Philanthropy Timeline: Giving in the 1600s," National Philanthropic Trust, accessed June 23, 2016, http://www.nptrust.org/history-of-giving/timeline/1600s/.

34. John Winthrop, "A Modell of Christian Charity," 1630 on board the Arbella in the Atlantic Ocean, Collections of the Massachusetts Historical Society, (Boston 1838, 3rd series, 7:31-48), http://history.hanover.edu/texts/winthmod.html

35. Frederick Rudolph, *The American Colleges and Universities: A History*, (Athens, GA: University of Georgia Press, 1990), 6.

36. Ibid., 4.

37. William L Kingsley, *Yale College: A Sketch of Its History, Volume 1*, (New York: Harry Holt and Company, 1879), 21.

38. John Brubacher and Willis Rudy, *Higher Education in Transition: A History of American Colleges and Universities*, (New Brunswick: Transaction Publishers, 1997), 31.

39. Kingsley, *Yale College*, 21.

40. Oscar Handlin and Mary Handlin, *Dimensions of Liberty*, (New York: Macmillan Pub Co, 1966), 92.

41. "Philanthropy Timeline: Giving in the 1700s," National Philanthropic Trust, accessed June 23, 2016, http://www.nptrust.org/history-of-giving/timeline/1700s/

42. Ibid.

43. Ibid.

44. Ibid.

45. Ibid.

46. Arthur Schlesinger, "Biography of a Nation of Joiners," *The American Historical Review*, Vol L, No. 1, October 1944, 4.

47. "Philanthropy Timeline."

48. Handlin and Handlin, *Dimensions of Liberty*, 111.

49. Schlesinger, "Biography of a Nation of Joiners," 3.

50. Robert A Dahl, *How Democratic is the American Constitution?*, (New Haven: Yale University Press, 2003), 9.

51. Alexis de Tocqueville, translated by Harvey Mansfield and Delba Winthrop, *Democracy in America*, (Chicago: University of Chicago Press, 2000), 489.

52. Ibid.

53. Elisabeth S. Clemens and Doug Guthrie, *Politics and Partnerships: The Role of Voluntary Associations in Americas Political Past and Present*, (Chicago: University of Chicago Press, 2010), 36.

54. Ibid., 33.

55. *Trustees of Dartmouth College v. Woodward*, 17-518, The United States Supreme Court, February 2, 1819.

56. Clemens and Guthrie, *Politics and Partnerships*, 31.

57. Ibid., 35.

58. Robert Nisbet, *The Quest for Community: A Study in the Ethics of Order and Freedom*, (Wilmington, DE: Intercollegiate Studies Institute, 2010), 244.

59. Larry Arnn, *The Founders' Key: The Divine and Natural Connection Between the Declaration and the Constitution and What We Risk by Losing It*, (Nashville: Thomas Nelson, 2013), 30.

60. Constance Smith and Anne Freedman, *Voluntary Associations: Perspectives on the Literature*, (Cambridge: Harvard University Press, 1972), 22.

61. Clemens and Guthrie, *Politics and Partnerships*, 2.

62. Ibid., 3.

CHAPTER 4

1. Ed Catmull and Amy Wallace, *Creativity, Inc.: Overcoming the Unseen Forces that Stand in the Way of True Inspiration*, (New York: Random House, 2014), 209.

2. Committee on Scientific Approaches to Understanding and Maximizing the Validity and Reliability of Eyewitness Identification in Law Enforcement and the Courts, et al., *Identifying the Culprit: Assessing Eyewitness Identification*, (National Academies Press, 2015), 11.

3. Candice Millard, *Destiny of the Republic: A Tale of Madness, Medicine and the Murder of a President*, (New York: Anchor Books, 2012), 157.

4. Ibid., 152.

5. Lolita D Gray, "Are the Best and Brightest Attracted to Public Service?," *PA Times*, American Society for Public Administration, May 31, 2013,http://patimes.org/brightest-attracted-public-service/

6. Karen Hughes and Victoria Reggie Kennedy, "Public service, a noble calling," philly.com, July 24, 2013, http://articles.philly.com/2013-07-24/news/40750800_1_public-service-community-service-americans

7. "Profit," Thesaurus.com, accessed June 24, 2016. http://www.thesaurus.com/browse/profit

8. Arthur Delaney and Sam Stein, "Another Mass Shooting, Another Deluge Of Tweeted Prayers," *The Huffington Post*, December 2, 2015. http://www.huffingtonpost.com/entry/shootings-thoughts-prayers_565f57d5e4b08e945fedd2ad

9. "Summary Memorandum transmitting results from Heartland Monitor Survey XX," FTI Consulting, April 28, 2014.http://heartlandmonitor.com/wp-content/uploads/2015/03/Heartland-XX-Key-Findings-Memo-04-28-14-5pm-CT.pdf

10. Ibid.

11. "Mark Twain's Brand of American Humor," *The Los Angeles Times*, May 14, 2015. http://www.latimes.com/la-et-mark-twain-quotes-20150513-htmlstory.html

12. "The History of the City of Muscle Shoals," CityofMuscleShoals.com, accessed June 24, 2016. http://www.cityofmuscleshoals.com/?ID=11

13. Ibid.

14. "More about . . . Senator George Norris State Historic Site," State Historical Society, Official Nebraska Government Website, accessed June 24, 2016. http://www.nebraskahistory.org/sites/norris/moreinfo.htm

15. Amity Shlaes, *The Forgotten Man*, (New York: Harper Perennial, 2008), 8.

16. Mike Isaac, "Uber Extends an Olive Branch to Local Governments: Its Data," *The New York Times*, January 2017. https://www.nytimes.com/2017/01/08/technology/uber-movement-traffic-data.html

17. Richard Waters (moderator), Meghan Joyce, Mario Kranjac, Jon Ziglar, "Panel: Governments, Smart Cities and the Next Wave of Innovation," FT Innovate Conference, New York, New York, Financial Times, December 9, 2015. https://live.ft.com/Events/2015/FT-Innovate-20152?=&v=4663481601001

18. "Govern," Dictionary.com, accessed June 24, 2016. http://dictionary.reference.com/browse/govern?s=t

19. "Govern," MerriamWebster.Com, accessed June 24, 2016. http://www.merriam-webster.com/dictionary/govern

20. Robert Putnam and Kristin Goss, *Democracies in Flux: The Evolution of Social Capital in Contemporary Society*, (New York: Oxford University Press, 2004), 6.

21. Ibid.

22. Associated Press, "Friends, neighbors were more helpful than government after Sandy, poll finds," NJ.com, June 24, 2013.

23. John Sides, "Do Americans Want to Govern Themselves?," *Washington Post*, August 23, 2010. http://voices.washingtonpost.com/ezra-klein/2010/08/do_americans_want_to_govern_th.html

24. John Hibbing and Elizabeth Theiss-Morse, *Stealth Democracy: Americans' Beliefs About How Government Should Work*, (Cambridge: Cambridge University Press, 2002), 3.

25. "Minnesota State Highway Investment Plan: 2014-2033," Minnesota Department of Transportation, accessed June 24, 2016. http://www.dot.state.mn.us/planning/mnship/

26. Joe Loveland, "In planning for highways of 2033 MnDOT should consider driverless cars," MINNPOST, January 6, 2014. https://www.minnpost.com/minnesota-blog-cabin/2014/01/planning-highways-2033-mndot-should-consider-driverless-cars

27. Patcharinee Tientrakool, "Reliable Neighborcast Protocol for Vehicular ad hoc Networks," Columbia University Academic Commons, 2011. http://academiccommons.columbia.edu/catalog/ac:134198

28. Ezra Klein and Alvin Chang, "'Political identity is fair game for hatred': how Republicans and Democrats discriminate," Vox.com, December 7, 2015. http://www.vox.com/2015/12/7/9790764/partisan-discrimination

29. Adam Waytz, Liane Young, and Jeremy Ginges, "Motive attribution asymmetry for love vs. hate drives intractable conflict," Proceedings of the National Academy of Sciences of the United States of America, July 25, 2014. http://www.pnas.org/content/111/44/15687.abstract

30. Daniel Hannan, *Inventing Freedom: How the English-Speaking Peoples Made the Modern World*, (New York: Broadside Books, 2014), 120.

31. Robert Nisbet, *The Quest for Community: A Study in the Ethics of Order and Freedom*, (Wilmington, DE: Intercollegiate Studies Institute, 2010), 269.

32. Aaron Wildavsky, *The Revolt Against the Masses*, (New Jersey: Transaction Publishers, 2002), 52.

CHAPTER 5

1. William Kornhauser, *Politics of Mass Society*, (New York: Routledge, 2010), 74.

2. John R Hibbing and Elizabeth Theiss-Morse, *Stealth Democracy: Americans' Beliefs about How Government Should Work*, (Cambridge: Cambridge University Press, 2002), 211.

3. Robert Nisbet, *The Quest for Community: A study in the Ethics of Order and Freedom*, (Wilmington, DE: Intercollegiate Studies Institute, 2010), 244, 249.

4. Ibid., 246.

5. Ibid., 245.

6. Ron Miller, "BlackBerry Goes Shopping Again, Buys Good Technology," Tech Crunch, September 4, 2015. http://techcrunch.com/2015/09/04/blackberry-goes-shopping-again-buys-good-technology/#.3agcspl:EARh

7. Thomas Sowell, *Intellectuals and Society*, (New York: Basic Books, 2012), 164-5.

8. John Kenneth Galbraith, *The New Industrial State*, (New Jersey: Princeton University Press, 2007), 36.

9. "U.S. Vehicle Sales Market Share by Company, 1961-2015," WardsAuto, Jan 22, 2016. http://wardsauto.com/datasheet/us-vehicle-sales-market-share-company-1961-2014

10. Ibid.

11. Yuri Kageyama, "Toyota beats Volkswagen and GM in global vehicle sales after first 9 months of this year," *U.S. News & World Report*, October 26, 2015. http://www.usnews.com/news/business/articles/2015/10/26/toyota-at-top-in-global-vehicle-sales-for-first-9-months

12. Martin Luther King, Jr., *Stride Toward Freedom: The Montgomery Story*, (Boston: Beacon Press, 2010), 80.

13. Ben White, "Big business on sequester: Zzzz," Politico, February 28, 2013. http://www.politico.com/story/2013/02/big-business-on-sequestration-been-there-done-that-088211?o=1

14. "General Dynamics (NYSE:GD)," Forecast International – AeroWeb, accessed January 30, 2017. http://www.fi-aeroweb.com/firms/Customers/Customers-General-Dynamics.html

15. "Combined Financial Statements and Reports of Independent Certified Public Accountants," Corporation for Public Broadcasting and Affiliate, September 20, 2015. http://www.cpb.org/files/aboutcpb/financials/audited/cpb_combinedstatements_fy15.pdf

16. Chris Matthews, "American taxpayers give an $18 billion gift to the post office every year," Fortune, Mary 27, 2015, http://fortune.com/2015/03/27/us-postal-service/, and "National Park Foundation 2015 Annual Report" National Parks Foundation, Accessed January 30, 2017, https://prod.nationalparks.org/sites/default/files/Annual_Report_FY15.pdf

17. "Where Does TVA Get the Money It Needs?," TVAkids.com, accessed July 13, 2016. https://www.tvakids.com/whatistva/money.htm

18. White, "Big business on sequester: Zzzz."

19. Ibid.

20. "More than 3500 Organizations Demand End to Sequestration Cuts," NDDUnited, TFAI, & AIA, February 11, 2013. https://www.aau.edu/WorkArea/DownloadAsset.aspx?id=14190

21. Ibid.

22. Alison LaCroix, *The Ideological Origins of American Federalism*, (Cambridge: Harvard University Press, 2011), 68-69.

23. Ibid.

24. Matthew 6:24, *Holy Bible – New International Version*, (Grand Rapids: Zondervan, 2011)

25. Anne Stauffer and Justin Theal, "Federal Funds Supply 30.8 Cents of Each State Revenue Dollar," The Pew Charitable Trusts, July 28, 2016. http://www.pewtrusts.org/en/research-and-analysis/analysis/2016/07/28/federal-funds-supply-308-cents-of-each-state-revenue-dollar

26. LaCroix, *The Ideological Origins of American Federalism*, 51.

27. Oscar Handlin and Mary Handlin, *Dimensions of Liberty*, (New York: Macmillan Pub Co, 1966), 66.

28. Amir Nasr and Fawn Johnson, "Voters Aren't Ready for Driverless Cars, Poll Shows," *Morning Consult*, February 8, 2016. https://morningconsult. com/2016/02/08/voters-arent-ready-for-driverless-cars-poll-shows/

29. Andy Seehan, "Uber Self-Driving Cars Hit The Streets Of Pittsburgh," CBS Pittsburgh, September 14, 2016. http://pittsburgh.cbslocal.com/2016/09/14/ uber-driverless-cars-hit-the-streets-of-pittsburgh/

30. Mitch Bainwol, "Disrupter Series: Self-Driving Cars," House Subcommittee on Commerce, Manufacturing, and Trade, November 15, 2016. https://democrats-energycommerce.house.gov/committee-activity/hearings/hearing-on-disrupter-series-self-driving-cars-subcommittee-on-commerce

31. Ibid.

32. "Autonomous | Self-Driving Vehicles Legislation," National Conference of State Legislatures, December 12, 2016. http://www.ncsl.org/research/transportation/ autonomous-vehicles-legislation.aspx#

33. Douglas MacMillan and Rolfe Winkler, "Google's Prototype for Autonomous Driving Has No Steering Wheel," *The Wall Street Journal*, May 27, 2014. http:// blogs.wsj.com/digits/2014/05/27/googles-prototype-for-autonomous-driving-has-no-steering-wheel/

34. Google created a workaround by adding a temporary steering wheel and pedal system to keep testing in California.

35. Alex Davies, "California's New Self-Driving Car Rules Are Great for Texas," Wired.com, December 17, 2015. https://www.wired.com/2015/12/californias-new-self-driving-car-rules-are-great-for-texas/

36. Reuters, "New California Law Allows Test of Autonomous Shuttle With No Driver," *Fortune*, September 29, 2016. http://fortune.com/2016/09/29/ california-law-test-autonomous-shuttle/

37. "NEMA Reiterates that Light Bulb Efficiency Standards Remain, Consumers Retain Diverse Options for Efficient Light Bulbs," National Electrical Manufacturers Association, December 16, 2011. http://www.nema.org/News/ Pages/NEMA-Reiterates-that-Light-Bulb-Efficiency-Standards-Remain-Consumers-Retain-Diverse-Options-for-Efficient-Light-Bulbs.aspx

38. Ryan Tracy and Stephanie Gleason, "New Flare-Up in Light Bulb Wars," *The Wall Street Journal*, July 9, 2011. http://www.wsj.com/articles/SB100014240527 02304793504576434122693094168

39. Nick Gillespie and Todd Krainin, "The Dumbest New Ban in 2014: Incandescent Light Bulbs," Reason.com, January 9, 2014. https://reason.com/ reasontv/2014/01/09/the-dumbest-new-ban-in-2014-incandescent

40. Jon Rauch, *Government's End: Why Washington Stopped Working*, (New York: Public Affairs, 1999), 74.

41. Mike Ramsey and Alistair Barr, "California Proposes Driverless-Car Rules," *The Wall Street Journal*, December 16, 2015. http://www.wsj.com/articles/california-proposes-rules-for-autonomous-cars-1450293308

42. Ibid.

43. Jon Ziglar, "Panel 09: Governments, Smart Cities and the Next Wave of Innovation," FT Innovate US 2015. https://live.ft.com/Events/2015/FT-Innovate-20152=&v=4663481601001

44. Cass Sunstein, "Beyond Marbury: The Executive's Power to Say What the Law Is," *The Yale Law Journal*, Vol CXV, No. 9, September 2006. http://www.yalelawjournal.org/essay/beyond-ligmarburylig-the-executives-power-to-say-what-the-law-is

45. Cass Sunstein, "Why Paternalism Is Your Friend," *New Republic*, April 8, 2013. https://newrepublic.com/article/112817/cass-sunstein-simpler-book-excerpt-why-paternalism-your-friend

46. Cass Sunstein, *Simpler: The Future of Government*, (New York: Simon & Schuster, 2014), 197.

47. Marc Landy and Sidney M. Milkis, *American Government: Enduring Principles, Critical Choices, 3rd Edition*, (New York: Cambridge University Press, 2014), 55.

48. Sowell, *Intellectuals and Society*, 46.

49. Ibid., 46-47.

CHAPTER 6

1. Samuel Kernell and Laurie Rice, "Cable and the Partisan Polarization of the President's Audience," *Presidential Studies Quarterly*, VOL 41, No. 4, 25 September 2011, p 695.

2. Gary Edgerton and Jeffrey Jones, *The Essential HBO Reader*, (Lexington: University Press of Kentucky, 2009), 4.

3. "The IBM Punched Card," IBM 100: Icons of Progress, accessed August 1, 2016. http://www-03.ibm.com/ibm/history/ibm100/us/en/icons/punchcard/

4. Dan Knight, "Personal Computer History: The First 25 Years," LowEndMac.com, April 26, 2014. http://lowendmac.com/2014/personal-computer-history-the-first-25-years/

5. "Changing Channels: Americans View Just 17 Channels Despite Record Number to Choose From," Nielson: Media and Entertainment, May 6, 2014. http://www.nielsen.com/us/en/insights/news/2014/changing-channels-americans-view-just-17-channels-despite-record-number-to-choose-from.html

6. Jack Schofield, "Ken Olsen Obituary," *The Guardian*, February 9, 2011. https://www.theguardian.com/technology/2011/feb/09/ken-olsen-obituary

7. "Number of Breweries," Brewers Association, 2016, accessed February 9, 2017. https://www.brewersassociation.org/statistics/number-of-breweries/

8. "Homebrewing Stats," American Homebrewers Association, 2013, accessed February 16, 2017. https://www.homebrewersassociation.org/membership/homebrewing-stats/

9. Nicco Mele, *The End of Big: How the Digital Revolution Makes David the New Goliath*, (New York: St. Martin's Press, 2014), 6.

10. Allen Kent and James Williams, "Computing and Spaceflight: An Introduction," Computers and Spaceflight: The NASA Experience, Nasa.gov, accessed August 1, 2016. http://history.nasa.gov/computers/Computing.html

11. John Kenneth Galbraith, *The New Industrial State*, (Princeton: Princeton University Press, 2007), 40.

12. Arthur C. Clarke, *Childhood's End*, (San Diego: Harcourt, Brace & World, 1953).

13. Dennis Feltham Jones, *Colossus*, (London: Rupert Hart-Davis Ltd., 1966), *Colossus*, by Dennis Feltham Jones (1966), and the subsequent film, *Colossus: The Forbin Project*, Universal Pictures, 1970.

14. Robert Vance Presthus, *The Organizational Society: An Analysis and a Theory*, (Whitefish, MT: Literary Licensing , 2012).

15. Steven Lubar, "'Do Not Fold, Spindle or Mutilate': A Cultural History of the Punch Card," *The Journal of American Culture*, VOL 15, NO. 4, p. 44, December 1992. http://design.osu.edu/carlson/history/PDFs/lubar-hollerith.pdf

16. Michael Otten, *University Authority and the Student: Berkeley Experience*, (Oakland: University of California Press, 1971), 6.

17. Lubar, "'Do Not Fold, Spindle or Mutilate': A Cultural History of the Punch Card."

18. Ibid.

19. "Mario Savio on the operation of the machine," at the University of California, December 2, 1964, cherumaz, August 9, 2010, accessed February 9, 2017. https://www.youtube.com/watch?v=PhFvZRT7Ds0

20. Seth Rosenfeld, "60s Free Speech leader got caught in FBI web," SFGate, October 10, 2004. http://www.sfgate.com/politics/article/60s-Free-Speech-leader-got-caught-in-FBI-web-2718540.php

21. Ryan Neal, "PRISM-Proof Your Smartphone: 10 Apps To Keep The NSA Out Of Your Phone," *International Business Times*, June 24, 2013. http://www.ibtimes.com/prism-proof-your-smartphone-10-apps-keep-nsa-out-your-phone-1321085

22. Craig Timberg and Greg Miller, "FBI blasts Apple, Google for locking police out of phones," *The Washington Post*, September 25, 2014. https://www.washingtonpost.com/business/technology/2014/09/25/68c4e08e-4344-11e4-9a15-137aa0153527_story.html

23. James B. Comey, "Going Dark: Are Technology, Privacy, and Public Safety on a Collision Course?," remarks at the Brookings Institute, Washington D.C., October 16, 2014. https://www.fbi.gov/news/speeches/going-dark-are-technology-privacy-and-public-safety-on-a-collision-course

24. Ibid.

25. Andrea Peterson, "LOVEINT: When NSA officers use their spying power on love interests," *The Washington Post*, August 24, 2013. https://www.washingtonpost.com/news/the-switch/wp/2013/08/24/loveint-when-nsa-officers-use-their-spying-power-on-love-interests/

26. "J. Edgar Hoover," *Encyclopedia Britanica*, accessed August 1, 2016. http://www.britannica.com/biography/J-Edgar-Hoover

27. "Announcing a new era of integrated electronics – advertisement for the Intel 4004," *Artifact Details*, Computer History Museum, accessed August 1, 2016. http://www.computerhistory.org/collections/catalog/102635150

28. Suzanne Deffree, "Intell 4004 is announced, November 15, 1971," EDN Network, November 15, 2015. http://www.edn.com/electronics-blogs/edn-moments/4401541/Intel-4004-is-announced—November-15—1971

29. "Satcom-I" Lockheed Martin, 2017, accessed February 9, 2017. http://www.lockheedmartin.com/us/100years/stories/satcom.html

30. Gary Edgerton and Jeffrey Jones, *The Essential HBO Reader*, (Lexington: University Press of Kentucky, 2009), 5.

31. Matt Mitovich, "Midseason Ratings Report: What Are Each Network's Best & Worst Shows?," TVLine.com, December 23, 2016. http://tvline.com/2016/12/23/ratings-2016-2017-tv-season-winners-losers/

32. Charles L. Ponce de Leon, "The Most Trusted Man in America," *Dissent Magazine*, February 1, 2013. https://www.dissentmagazine.org/online_articles/the-most-trusted-man-in-america

33. Brian Stelter, "Debate breaks record as most-watched in U.S. history," Money.cnn.com, September 27, 2016. http://money.cnn.com/2016/09/27/media/debate-ratings-record-viewership/

34. "Computer Ownership Up Sharply in the 1990s," Issues in Labor Statistics, U.S. Department of Labor: Bureau of Labor Statistics, March 1999. http://www.bls.gov/opub/btn/archive/computer-ownership-up-sharply-in-the-1990s-pdf.pdf

35. Eric C. Newburger, "Home Computers and Internet Use in the United States: August 2000," Current Population Reports, U.S. Census Bureau, September 2001, 1. https://www.census.gov/prod/2001pubs/p23-207.pdf, and Thom File, "Computer and Internet Use in the United States," Population Characteristics, United States Census Bureau, May 2013, 1. https://www.census.gov/prod/2013pubs/p20-569.pdf

36. "Statistics," YouTube: Press, accessed August 1, 2016. https://www.youtube.com/yt/press/statistics.html

37. Madhumita Murgia, "Marc Andreessen: 'In 20 years, every physical item will have a chip implanted in it,'" *The Telegraph*, December 23, 2015. http://www.telegraph.co.uk/technology/internet/12050185/Marc-Andreessen-In-20-years-every-physical-item-will-have-a-chip-implanted-in-it.html

38. "A Snapshot of Diabetes in the United States," Center for Disease Control and Prevention, June 17, 2014. http://www.cdc.gov/features/diabetesfactsheet/

39. "BD Diabetes Learning Center," *BD Medical Technology*, accessed August 1, 2016. http://www.bd.com/us/diabetes/page.aspx?cat=7001&id=31662

40. "Android: Friends Furever," *Android*, February 5, 2015, accessed February 9, 2017. https://www.youtube.com/watch?v=vnVuqfXohxc

41. Darren Waters, "What Happened to Dungeons and Dragons?," BBC News, April 26, 2004. http://news.bbc.co.uk/2/hi/uk_news/magazine/3655627.stm

42. Ana Douglas, "Here Are The 10 Highest Grossing Video Games Ever*," *Business Insider: Entertainment*, June 13, 2012. http://www.businessinsider.com/here-are-the-top-10-highest-grossing-video-games-of-all-time-2012-6?op=1

43. Samit Sarkar, "Blizzard reaches 100M lifetime World of Warcraft accounts," Polygon.com, January 28, 2014. http://www.polygon.com/2014/1/28/5354856/world-of-warcraft-100m-accounts-lifetime

44. "RPG – Video Game," Kickstarter.com, accessed February 10, 2017. https://www.kickstarter.com/discover/advanced?term=rpg&category_id=35&sort=magic&seed=2477891&page=1

45. Mary Meeker, "Internet Trends Report-2015," KPCB, May 27, 2015. http://www.kpcb.com/blog/2015-internet-trends

46. Martin Luther King, Jr., *Stride Toward Freedom: The Montgomery Story*, (Boston: Beacon Press, 2010), 101.

47. Ibid., 118.

48. Ibid., 141.

49. Ibid., 178.

50. Ibid., 177.

CHAPTER 7

1. Nicco Mele, *The End of Big: How the Internet Makes David the New Goliath* (New York: St. Martin's Press, 2013), 250.

2. "The top 500 sites on the web," Alexa, accessed January 23, 2016. http://www.alexa.com/topsites/category/Top/News

3. Howard Kurtz, "After Blogs Got Hits, CBS Got a Black Eye," *The Washington Post*, September 20, 2004. http://www.washingtonpost.com/wp-dyn/articles/A34153-2004Sep19.html

4. Mele, *The End of Big: How the Internet Makes David the New Goliath*, 64.

5. Haley Draznin, "Rare footage shows FDR walking at 1937 Major League Baseball All Star Game," CNN, May 16, 2014. http://www.cnn.com/2014/05/16/us/franklin-delano-roosevelt-walking-video/

6. Samuel Kernell and Laurie Rice, "Cable and the Partisan Polarization of the President's Audience," *Presidential Studies Quarterly*, Vol. 41, No. 4, 25 September 2011, 710.

7. Richard Nixon, "Address to the Nation Announcing Decision To Resign the Office of President of the United States," August 8, 1974. Online by Gerhard Peters and John T. Woolley, The American Presidency Project. http://www. presidency.ucsb.edu/ws/?pid=4324.

8. Kernell and Rice, "Cable and the Partisan Polarization of the President's Audience," 710.

9. "31.7 Million Viewers Tune In To Watch President Obama's State of the Union Address," *Nielsen: Media and Entertainment*, January 21, 2015. http://www. nielsen.com/us/en/insights/news/2015/31-7-million-viewers-tune-in-to-watch-pres-obamas-state-of-the-union-adress.html

10. Kernell and Rice, "Cable and the Partisan Polarization of the President's Audience," 693.

11. *President's Commission for a National Agenda for the Eighties, A National Agenda for the Eighties: Report*, (Washington D.C.: 1980), 9, 11.

12. Ibid., 3.

13. Ibid., 10.

14. Ibid., 52-56.

15. E.g., Arthur Schlesinger Jr., *The Imperial Presidency*, (New York: Houghton Mifflin, 1973).

16. Mele, *The End of Big: How the Internet Makes David the New Goliath*, 21.

17. John Schachter, "'When the President Does It That Means It Is Not Illegal.' Where in Article II Is That Line?," American Constitution Society for Law and Policy, June 11, 2012. http://www.acslaw.org/acsblog/%E2%80%98when-the-president-does-it-that-means-it-is-not-illegal%E2%80%99-where-in-article-ii-is-that-line

18. Amy Goodman, "WikiLeaks' 'Kissinger Cables' underline the world's debt to Bradley Manning," *The Guardian*, April 11, 2013, https://www.theguardian. com/commentisfree/2013/apr/11/wikileaks-kissinger-cables-bradley-manning. Referencing Henry Kissinger discussing "Aid Cut-off; Cyprus," with Melih Esenbel, the Turkish Minister of Foreign Affairs, in the Minister's Office, Ankara Turkey, May 10, 1975. "Memorandum of Conversation May 10, 1975," meeting between Melih Esenbel, Sukru Elekdag, Nacdet Tezel, Ercument Yavazalp, Ecmel Barutcu, Henry Kissinger, William Macomber, Joseph Sisco, Arthur Hartman, and Peter Rodman. Accessed August 2, 2016. https://wikileaks.org/plusd/cables/P860114-1573_MC_b.html#efmCS3CUB

19. Jonathan Rauch, "What Nixon Wrought: The Worst Presidency of the Century," originally published in *The New Republic*, May 16, 1994, accessed through Articles by Jonathan Rauch on August 2, 2016. http://www.jonathanrauch.com/jrauch_articles/2005/01/what_nixon_wrou.html

20. Ibid.

21. Jonathan Turley, "The rise of the fourth branch of government," *The Washington Post*, May 24, 2013. https://www.washingtonpost.com/opinions/the-rise-of-the-fourth-branch-of-government/2013/05/24/c7faaad0-c2ed-11e2-9fe2-6ee52d0eb7c1_story.html

22. Christopher Demuth, "The Regulatory State," *National Affairs*, No. 12, Summer 2012. http://www.nationalaffairs.com/publications/detail/the-regulatory-state

23. Jonathan Turley, "A Tale of Two Circuits: Obamacare Is Either On Life Support Or In Robust Health," JonathanTurley.org, July 23, 2014. http://jonathanturley.org/2014/07/23/a-tale-of-two-circuits-obamacare-is-either-on-life-support-or-in-robust-health/

24. Chevron U.S.A., Inc. v. Natural Resources Defense Council, Inc., 476 U.S. 837, (1984). Accessed February 10, 2017, through Oyez, https://www.oyez.org/cases/1983/82-1005

25. John Roberts, "Dissent," City of Arlington, Tex. v. FCC, 11-1545, The United States Supreme Court, May 20, 2013. https://www.supremecourt.gov/opinions/12pdf/11-1545_1b7d.pdf

26. Clyde Wayne Crews, "Ten Thousand Commandments 2015," Competitive Enterprise Institute, May 8, 2015. https://cei.org/10kc2015

27. Turley, "The rise of the fourth branch of government."

28. Jonathan Koppell, *The Politics of Quasi-Government: Hybrid Organizations and the Dynamics of Bureaucratic Control*, (Cambridge: Cambridge University Press, 2003), 3.

29. Peter Whoriskey, "For decades, the government steered millions away from whole milk. Was that wrong?," *The Washington Post*, October 6, 2015. https://www.washingtonpost.com/news/wonk/wp/2015/10/06/for-decades-the-government-steered-millions-away-from-whole-milk-was-that-wrong/

30. Ibid.

31. Richard Kersley, "Fat: The New Health Paradigm," Credit Suisse Research Institute, September 2015. http://publications.credit-suisse.com/tasks/render/file/index.cfm?fileid=9163B920-CAEF-91FB-EE5769786A03D76E

32. William Niskanen Jr., *Bureaucracy and Representative Government*, (New Brunswick: Aldine Transaction, 2007), 3.

33. Ibid.

34. Sidney Milkis, *Theodore Roosevelt, the Progressive Party, and the Transformation of American Democracy*, (Lawrence, Kansas: University Press of Kansas, 2009), 38

35. Niskanen, *Bureaucracy and Representative Government*, 230.

36. Martin Sklar, *The Corporate Reconstruction of American Capitalism, 1890-1916: The Market, the Law, and Politics*, (New York: Cambridge University Press, 1988), 34.

37. Megan McArdle, "America's New Mandarins," The Daily Beast, February 21, 2013. http://www.thedailybeast.com/articles/2013/02/21/america-s-new-mandarins.html

38. Ibid.

39. Niall Ferguson, "How America Lost Its Way," *The Wall Street Journal*, June 7, 2013. http://www.wsj.com/articles/SB10001424127887324798904578527552326836118

40. Greg Jaffe and Jim Tankersley, "Capital gains: Spending on contracts and lobbying propels a wave of new wealth in D.C.," *The Washington Post*, November 18, 2013. https://www.washingtonpost.com/national/capital-gains-spending-on-contracts-and-lobbying-propels-a-wave-of-new-wealth-in-d-c/2013/11/17/6bd938aa-3c25-11e3-a94f-b58017bfee6c_story.html

41. Manyun Zou, "The DC Area Has the Highest Median Income in the US Again," Washingtonian.com, September 21, 2016. https://www.washingtonian.com/2016/09/21/the-dc-area-has-the-highest-median-income-in-the-us-again/

42. As measured by median income. Tom Van Riper, "America's Richest Counties, 2014," *Forbes*, April 1, 2014. http://www.forbes.com/sites/tomvanriper/2014/04/01/americas-richest-counties-2014/#19c695695120

43. Ellen Meyers, "Bake sale law? New guidelines put the squeeze on sugary fundraisers." *Christian Science Monitor*, August 5, 2014. http://www.csmonitor.com/Business/The-Bite/2014/0805/Bake-sale-law-New-guidelines-put-the-squeeze-on-sugary-fundraisers and Kim Peterson, "Will this federal law end school bake sales?," CBS Money Watch, August 5, 2013. http://www.cbsnews.com/news/will-this-federal-law-end-school-bake-sales/

44. Nicholas Confessore, "How School Lunch Became the Latest Political Battleground," *The New York Times Magazine*, October 7, 2014. http://www.nytimes.com/2014/10/12/magazine/how-school-lunch-became-the-latest-political-battleground.html?_r=0

45. "Flush Fact vs. Flush Fiction," United States Environmental Protection Agency: WaterSense, June 2008. http://www3.epa.gov/watersense/pubs/flush_fact_vs_fiction.html

46. Bernie Becker, "IRS mismanaged Tea Party groups, Senate report finds," *The Hill*, August, 5, 2015. http://thehill.com/policy/finance/250363-irs-mismanaged-tea-party-applications-senate-report

47. Keith Laing, "TSA to stop accepting some states' drivers licenses in 2018," *The Hill*, January 8, 2016. http://thehill.com/policy/transportation/265282-tsa-to-stop-accepting-unsecured-drivers-licenses-in-2018

48. "Ten Thousand Commandments 2015: A Fact Sheet," Competitive Enterprise Institute, May 12, 2015. https://cei.org/sites/default/files/Ten%20Thousand%20Commandments%20-%20Fact%20Sheet%20-%202015%20Edition%20%20-%2005-12-15.pdf

CHAPTER 8

1.   Larry Downes, "Take note Republicans and Democrats, this is what a pro-innovation platform looks like," *The Washington Post*, January 7, 2015. https://www.washingtonpost.com/news/innovations/wp/2015/01/07/take-note-republicans-and-democrats-this-is-what-a-pro-innovation-platform-looks-like/

2.   *Star Wars: Episode II: Attack of the Clones*, 20th Century Fox Film Corp., 2002.

3.   Senator Jim Inhofe, "EPA Official: EPAs 'philosophy' is to 'crucify' and 'make examples' of US energy producers," YouTube, April 25, 2012. https://www.youtube.com/watch?v=ze3GB_b7Nuo

4.   Barry Shlachter, "EPA drops action against Range Resources over Parker County water wells," *Star-Telegram*, March 30, 2012. http://www.star-telegram.com/living/family/moms/article3830897.html

5.   John Cochrane, "The Rule of Law in the Regulatory State," Hoover Institute, Stanford University, June 2015, 7.

6.   Ibid., 2.

7.   "Lord Acton Quote Archive," Acton Institute, 2017, accessed February 10, 2017. http://acton.org/research/lord-acton-quote-archive

8.   The full story is recounted in 1 Samuel 17: 1-58.

9.   Malcolm Gladwell, *David and Goliath: Underdogs, Misfits, and the Art of Battling Giants*, (New York: Back Bay Books, 2015).

10. Peter Block, *Community: The Structure of Belonging*, (Oakland, CA: Berrett-Koehler Publishers, 2009).

11. "Public Trust in Government: 1958-2014," Pew Research Center: U.S. Politics and Policy, November 13, 2014. http://www.people-press.org/2014/11/13/public-trust-in-government/

12. Alex Boyer, "What America Thinks: Politicians for Sale?," Rasmussen.com, April 18, 2016. http://www.rasmussenreports.com/public_content/videos/2016_04/what_america_thinks_politicians_for_sale

13. Justin McCarthy, "Americans Still Trust Local Government More Than State," Gallup.com, September 22, 2014. http://www.gallup.com/poll/176846/americans-trust-local-government-state.aspx

14. David Roberts, "This audacious plan would let Obama enact an economy-wide-cap-and-trade system – without Congress," Vox: Energy & Environment, January 21, 2016. http://www.vox.com/2016/1/21/10809684/epa-carbon-trading-section-115

15. Gary Lawson, "Burying the Constitution Under a Tarp," Boston University School of Law, No. 09-31. July 20, 2009, Accessed through SSRN.com. https://papers.ssrn.com/sol3/papers.cfm?abstract_id=1436462

16. John Cochrane, "The Rule of Law in the Regulatory State," *The Grumpy Economist*, June 2015, accessed February 10, 2017, 3. http://faculty. chicagobooth.edu/john.cochrane/research/papers/rule%20of%20law%20 and%20regulation%20essay.pdf

17. Gary Lawson, "Limited Government, Unlimited Administration: Is It Possible to Restore Constitutionalism," The Heritage Foundation, June 27, 2009, 13. file:///C:/Users/josia/Downloads/fp0023.pdf

18. Ricardo Fernholz and Christoffer Koch, "Why Are Big Banks Getting Bigger?," Claremont McKenna College and The Federal Reserve Bank of Dallas, Feb 18, 2016, 2. https://www.dallasfed.org/assets/documents/research/papers/2016/ wp1604.pdf

19. Charles Murray, *By the People*, (New York: Crown Forum, 2015), 117.

20. Ibid., 136.

21. Ibid.

22. Martin Luther King, Jr., "Letter from a Birmingham Jail," April 16, 1963, accessed through University of Pennsylvania African Studies Center February 10, 2017. https://www.africa.upenn.edu/Articles_Gen/Letter_Birmingham.html

23. Murray, By the People, 147.

24. "Summary Memorandum transmitting results from Heartland Monitor Survey XX," FTI Consulting, April 28, 2014. http://heartlandmonitor.com/wp-content/ uploads/2015/03/Heartland-XX-Key-Findings-Memo-04-28-14-5pm-CT.pdf

25. Richard Cornuelle, *Reclaiming the American Dream: the Role of Private Individuals and Voluntary Associations*, (Piscataway, NJ: Transaction Publishers, 1993), 61.

26. Margalit Fox, "Richard Cornuelle, Libertarian Author, Dies at 84," *The New York Times*, May 3, 2011. http://www.nytimes.com/2011/05/04/us/04cornuelle.html

27. Sylvia Wright, "Poverty's Free Enterpriser," *Life Magazine*, June 28, 1968, 36.

28. Cornuelle, *Reclaiming the American Dream*, 61.

29. Sylvia Wright, "Poverty's Free Enterpriser."

30. Robert Putnam, Lewis Feldstein, and Don Cohen, *Better Together: Restoring the American Community*, (New York: Simon & Schuster Paperbacks, 2004), 4.

31. Phillip Hamburger, *Is Administration Law Unlawful?*, (Chicago: University of Chicago Press, 2014), 509.

32. Larry Arnn, *The Founders' Key: The Divine and Natural Connection Between the Declaration and the Constitution and What We Risk by Losing It*, (New York: Thomas Nelson, 2012), 30.

33. Adam Thierer, *Permissionless Innovation: The Continuing Case for Comprehensive Technological Freedom*, (Arlington: Mercatus Center at George Mason University, 2016), 13.

34. 1982 MIT Handbook for Arpanet use, cited by Adam Thierer, *Permissionless Innovation: The Continuing Case for Comprehensive Technological Freedom*, (Arlington: Mercatus Center at George Mason University, 2016), 12.

35. Thierer, *Permissionless Innovation*, 14.

36. Ron Fournier, "The Outsiders: How Can Millennials Change Washington If They Hate It?," *The Atlantic*, August 26, 2013. http://www.theatlantic.com/politics/archive/2013/08/the-outsiders-how-can-millennials-change-washington-if-they-hate-it/278920/

CHAPTER 9

1. Craig Smith, "59 Amazing Uber Statistics (December 2016), DMR Stats Gadgets, February 11, 2017. http://expandedramblings.com/index.php/uber-statistics/2/

2. Rabiul Karim, "Uber job beats working for yellow cab," *New York Daily News*, July 22, 2015. http://www.nydailynews.com/new-york/guest-column-uber-job-beats-working-yellow-cab-article-1.2301278

3. "Taxi industry gave De Blasio over $550,000 for campaign," *New York Post*, May 17, 2014. http://nypost.com/2014/05/17/taxi-industry-gave-de-blasio-over-550000-for-campaign/

4. Fred Imbert, "De Blasio was wrong to go after Uber: Roger McNamee," CNBC, July 23, 2015. http://www.cnbc.com/2015/07/23/de-blasio-was-wrong-to-go-after-uber-roger-mcnamee.html

5. Brian Doherty "Austin, After Driving Out Uber and Lyft, Launches Sting Operations Against Those Who Dare to Serve the Public with Rides," Reason.com, June 21, 2016. http://reason.com/blog/2016/06/21/austin-after-driving-out-uber-and-lyft-l

6. Fitz Tepper, "Austin police are now impounding drivers in the peer-to-peer ridesharing group," TechCrunch.com, June 21, 2016. https://techcrunch.com/2016/06/21/austin-police-are-now-impounding-drivers-in-the-peer-to-peer-ridesharing-group/

7. Chris Anderson, *Makers: The New Industrial Revolution*, (New York: Crown Business, 2014), 62.

8. TJ McCue, "Wohlers Report 2016: 3D Printing Industry Surpassed $5.1 Billion," *Forbes*, April 25, 2016. http://www.forbes.com/sites/tjmccue/2016/04/25/wohlers-report-2016-3d-printer-industry-surpassed-5-1-billion/#43900b5a7cb1

9. Anderson, *Makers: The New Industrial Revolution*, 26.

10. Ibid., 78.

11. Michael Kanellos, "Andy Grove coins his own law," cnet.com, May 18, 2005. https://www.cnet.com/news/andy-grove-coins-his-own-law/

12. "Summary Memorandum transmitting results from Heartland Monitor Survey XX," FTI Consulting, April 28, 2014. http://heartlandmonitor.com/wp-content/uploads/2015/03/Heartland-XX-Key-Findings-Memo-04-28-14-5pm-CT.pdf

13. Ibid.

14. Sylvia Wright, "Poverty's Free Enterpriser," *Life Magazine*, June 28, 1968, 36.

15. Chris Anderson, *Free: The Future of a Radical Price*, (New York: Hyperion, 2009), 189.

16. Christopher Chabris and Daniel Simons, *The Invisible Gorilla*, (New York: Random House, 2009), 5.

17. Ibid., 6.

18. Ibid., 7.

19. "Sen. Al Franken tells canvassers: "Many of you have jobs. Many of you have families. Ignore them. Get on the doors," CNN, November 6, 2016. https://twitter.com/CNN/status/795266631878447104

20. "Census Bureau Reports There Are 89,004 Local Governments in the United States," United States Census Bureau, August 30, 2012. https://www.census.gov/newsroom/releases/archives/governments/cb12-161.html

21. "Small Business Administration: Frequently Asked Questions," Small Business Administration, September 2012. https://www.sba.gov/sites/default/files/FAQ_Sept_2012.pdf

22. "Quick Facts About Nonprofits," National Center for Charitable Statistics, April 2014. http://nccs.urban.org/data-statistics/quick-facts-about-nonprofits

23. "Fast Facts," National Center for Education Statistics, 2016, accessed February 16, 2017. https://nces.ed.gov/fastfacts/display.asp?id=84

24. Ibby Caputo and Jon Marcus, "The Controversial Reason Some Religious Colleges Forgo Federal Funding," *The Atlantic*, July 7, 2016. https://www.theatlantic.com/education/archive/2016/07/the-controversial-reason-some-religious-colleges-forgo-federal-funding/490253/

25. Kellie Woodhouse, "Impact of Pell Surge," Inside Higher Ed, June 12, 2015. https://www.insidehighered.com/news/2015/06/12/study-us-higher-education-receives-more-federal-state-governments

26. "20@$20," Wyoming Catholic College, accessed February 16, 2017. http://www.wyomingcatholiccollege.com/support-wcc/20at20/index.aspx

27. "HECA Announcements," Higher Education Compliance Alliance, accessed May 2016. http://www.higheredcompliance.org/

28. "Recalibrating Regulations of Colleges and Universities," Higher Education Task Force, March 7, 2015, 1. https://www.acenet.edu/news-room/Documents/Higher-Education-Regulations-Task-Force-Report.pdf

29. Josh Mitchell, "Millions of students may never repay their student loans," *The Wall Street Journal*, April 6, 2016. http://www.marketwatch.com/story/millions-of-students-may-never-repay-their-student-loans-2016-04-06

30. Kathleen Rudy, "2015 Associates Newsletter," Hillsdale College, October 21, 2015. https://www.hillsdale.edu/support/associates/2015-newsletter/

31. Suzanne Mettler, *Degrees of Inequality: How the Politics of Higher Education Sabotaged the American Dream*, (Philadelphia: Basic Books, 2014), 5.

32. Richard Cornuelle, *Reclaiming the American Dream: the Role of Private Individuals and Voluntary Associations*, (Piscataway, NJ: Transaction Publishers, 1993), 81-85.

33. Sylvia Wright, "Poverty's Free Enterpriser," *Life Magazine*, June 28, 1968, 36.

34. Jon Rauch, *Government's End: Why Washington Stopped Working*, (New York: Public Affairs, 1999), 260-275.

35. Martin Luther King, Jr., *Stride Toward Freedom: The Montgomery Story*, (Boston: Beacon Press, 2010), 53.

36. Stephen Covey, *The 7 Habits of Highly Effective People*, (New York: Simon and Schuster, 2013), 54.

37. David Hackett Fischer, *Liberty and Freedom: A Visual History of America's Founding Ideas*, (New York, Oxford University Press, 2004), 1-2.

38. Oscar Handlin and Mary Handlin, *Dimensions of Liberty*, (New York: Macmillan Pub Co, 1966), 5.

CHAPTER 10

1. Ricardo Fernholz and Christoffer Koch, "Why Are Big Banks Getting Bigger?," Claremont McKenna College and The Federal Reserve Bank of Dallas, Feb 18, 2016, 6. https://www.dallasfed.org/~/media/documents/research/papers/2016/wp1604.pdf

2. Mark Heschmeyer, "Silicon Valley Will Make Thousands of Bank Branches Disappear," *CoStar: News*, April 13, 2016. http://www.costar.com/News/Article/Silicon-Valley-Will-Make-Thousands-of-Bank-Branches-Disappear/181435

3. Ibid.

4. Ibid.

5. Alyson Shontell, "Jamie Dimon: Silicon Valley startups are coming to eat Wall Street's lunch," *Business Insider*, April 10, 2015. http://www.businessinsider.com/jamie-dimon-shareholder-letter-and-silicon-valley-2015-4

6. "The Millennial Disruption Index," Viacom Media Networks, Scratch, 2014, accessed August 3, 2016. http://www.millennialdisruptionindex.com/

7. Ibid.

8. Carleton English, "What JPMorgan's Jamie Dimon Thinks Banks Can Learn From Silicon Valley," *The Street*, May 27, 2015. https://www.thestreet.com/story/13165540/1/what-jpmorgans-jamie-dimon-thinks-banks-can-learn-from-silicon-valley.html

9. Simon Matthews, "The Uberization of Banking," *The Financial Brand*, June 3, 2015. http://thefinancialbrand.com/52148/uber-financial-services-banking-disruption/

10. "Disrupting Banking: The Fintech Startups That Are Unbundling Wells Fargo, Citi and Bank of America." CB Insights Blog, November 18, 2015. https://www.cbinsights.com/blog/disrupting-banking-fintech-startups/

11. "Providence College Professor's Study Finds Ride-Sharing Saves Lives, Reduces DUI," Providence College, June 7, 2016. http://www.providence.edu/media/press-releases/Pages/pc-study-ride-sharing-saves-lives.aspx

12. Michele Bertoncello and Dominik Wee, "Ten Ways Autonomous Driving Could Redefine the Automotive World," McKinsey, April 2015. http://www.mckinsey.com/practice-clients/automotive-assembly/ten-ways-autonomous-driving-could-redefine-the-automotive-world

13. "Technology Driving Innovation – 2025: Change in the Fast Lane," Goldman Sachs, December 2015. http://www.goldmansachs.com/our-thinking/pages/cars-2025-change-in-the-fast-lane.html

14. Dana Flavelle, "Could driverless technology make car ownership a thing of the past?," *The Star*, January 8, 2016. https://www.thestar.com/business/2016/01/08/is-this-your-new-car.html

15. Mark Harris, "Secretive Alphabet division funded by Google aims to fix public transit in US," *The Guardian*, June 27, 2016. https://www.theguardian.com/technology/2016/jun/27/google-flow-sidewalk-labs-columbus-ohio-parking-transit

16. Ibid.

17. $3.2 trillion on healthcare, $620 on education, $18 trillion GDP "National Health Expenditures 2015 Highlights," Centers for Medicare and Medicaid Services, July 2016, accessed February 16, 2017. https://www.cms.gov/Research-Statistics-Data-and-Systems/Statistics-Trends-and-Reports/NationalHealthExpendData/Downloads/Proj2015.pdf
"Fast Facts," National Center for Education Statistics, 2016, accessed February 16, 2017. https://nces.ed.gov/fastfacts/display.asp?id=84
"Gross domestic product 2015," World Bank, February 1, 2017. http://databank.worldbank.org/data/download/GDP.pdf

18. "Financial Services Spotlight: The Financial Services Industry in the United States," *Select USA*, 2016, accessed August 3, 2016. https://www.selectusa.gov/financial-services-industry-united-states

19. "NADA Data," Nada.org, July 2016, accessed February 17, 2017. https://www.nada.org/nadadata/

20. "Confidence in Institutions," *Gallup*, June 5, 2016. http://www.gallup.com/poll/1597/confidence-institutions.aspx

21. John Holt, *New Directions: Reading, Writing, and Critical Thinking*, (New York: Cambridge University Press, 2005), 57-58.

22. "Confidence in Institutions," *Gallup*, June 5, 2016. http://www.gallup.com/poll/1597/confidence-institutions.aspx

23. Jeffrey Jones, "In U.S., Private Schools Get Top Marks for Educating Children," *Gallup*, August 29, 2012. http://www.gallup.com/poll/156974/private-schools-top-marks-educating-children.aspx

24. *Listen to Us: Teacher Views and Voices*, Center on Education Policy, May 2016, 4, 6. http://www.cep-dc.org/cfcontent_file.cfm?Attachment=RentnerKoberFrizzell_Report_TeachViewVoice_5.5.16.pdf

25. Ibid., 4

26. Ibid., 17.

27. Ted Kolderie, "Ray Budde and the origins of the 'Charter Concept,'" Education|Evolving, June 2015. http://www.educationevolving.org/pdf/Ray-Budde-Origins-Of-Chartering.pdf

28. "Charter School Enrollment," National Center for Education Statistics, April 2016. https://nces.ed.gov/programs/coe/indicator_cgb.asp

29. "Ed Choice 101: Facts," American Federation for Children, accessed February 17, 2017. http://www.federationforchildren.org/ed-choice-101/facts/

30. "Death of Homeschooling Pioneer Dr. Raymond S. Moore," The Moore Foundation and Academy, July 13, 2007. http://www.moorefoundation.com/article/23/about-moore-home-schooling/moore-foundation/history-of-moore-academy/death-of-raymond-moore

31. J Michael Smith, "U.S. Department of Education: Homeschooling Continues to Grow!," Home School Legal Defense Association, September 3, 2013. https://www.hslda.org/docs/news/2013/201309030.asp

32. "Fast Facts," National Center for Education Statistics, accessed February 17, 2017. https://nces.ed.gov/fastfacts/display.asp?id=372

33. S. E. Carrell, T Maghakian, J. E. West, "A's from zzzz's? the causal effect of school start time on the academic achievement of adolescents," *American Economic Journal/Economic Policy*, 2011, No. 3, 62-81. http://econpapers.repec.org/article/aeaaejpol/v_3a3_3ay_3a2011_3ai_3a3_3ap_3a62-81.htm

34. "Where do governments spend money?," George Mason University: Mercatus Center, July 31, 2010. https://www.mercatus.org/publication/government-spending-101/where-do-governments-spend-money

35. Damon Root, "Ban Private Schools in the Name of the Collective Good?," Reason.com, May 8, 2015. http://reason.com/blog/2015/05/08/ban-private-schools-in-the-name-of-the-c

36. Gerard Robinson, "An Uncivil War," US News & World Report, October 14, 2015. http://www.usnews.com/opinion/knowledge-bank/2015/10/14/new-york-citys-uncivil-war-over-charter-schools

37. "Fast Facts," National Center for Education Statistics, 2016, accessed February 16, 2017. https://nces.ed.gov/fastfacts/display.asp?id=84

38. Dan Simon, "Is personalized learning the future of school?," CNN.com, October 27, 2016. http://www.cnn.com/2016/04/15/health/altschool-personalized-education/

39. Michael Porter and Elizabeth Teisberg, Redefining Health Care: Creating Value-Based Competition on Results, (Boston: Harvard Business Review Press, 2006), 1-2.

40. Ibid., 102.

41. Ibid., 98.

42. Jill Duffy, "10 Apps That Are Changing Healthcare," PCMag, February 11, 2015. http://www.pcmag.com/article2/0,2817,2476623,00.asp

43. Ibid.

44. "The Nobel Prize in Physiology or Medicine 1924," Nobelprize.org, 2014, accessed February 16, 2017. https://www.nobelprize.org/nobel_prizes/medicine/laureates/1924/

45. "Electrocardiogram (ECG or EKG)" Mayo Clinic, February 2, 2017. http://www.mayoclinic.org/tests-procedures/electrocardiogram/basics/definition/prc-20014152

46. "Electrocardiogram," WomensHealthAdvice.com, accessed February 16, 2017. http://www.womens-health-advice.com/heart-disease/electrocardiogram.html

47. "Kardia Mobile," AliveCor, accessed February 16, 2017. https://store.alivecor.com/

48. Eric Topol, "The Future of Medicine Is in Your Smartphone," *The Wall Street Journal*, January 9, 2015. http://www.wsj.com/articles/the-future-of-medicine-is-in-your-smartphone-1420828632

49. Vinod Khosla, "Technology will replace 80% of what doctors do," *Fortune*, December 4, 2012. http://fortune.com/2012/12/04/technology-will-replace-80-of-what-doctors-do/

50. Topol, "The Future of Medicine Is in Your Smartphone."

51. Ibid.

52. "A Policy Primer on Diagnostics," AdvaMedDx, June 2011, 12. https://dx.advamed.org/sites/dx.advamed.org/files/resource/advameddx-policy-primer-on-diagnostics-june-2011.pdf

53. "Hospital Utilization (in non-Federal short-stay hospitals)," Centers for Disease Control and Prevention, July 6, 2016. https://www.cdc.gov/nchs/fastats/hospital.htm

54. "NHE Fact Sheet," Centers for Medicare and Medicaid Services, December 2, 2016, accessed February 17, 2017. https://www.cms.gov/research-statistics-data-and-systems/statistics-trends-and-reports/nationalhealthexpenddata/nhe-fact-sheet.html

55. Erin McCann, "Telehealth takes off in rural areas," HealthcareITNews, February 4, 2014. http://www.healthcareitnews.com/news/telehealth-takes-nationwide

56. "Telehealth Policy Trends and Considerations," National Conference of State Legislatures, February 2, 2015. http://www.ncsl.org/research/health/telehealth-policy-trends-and-considerations.aspx

57. "Too Busy To Be Sick?," Doctor on Demand, 2017, accessed February 16, 2017. http://www.doctorondemand.com/

58. Duffy, "10 Apps That Are Changing Healthcare."

59. Dale Yamamoto, "Assessment of the Feasibility and Cost of Replacing In-Person Care with Acute Care Telehealth Services," Red Quill Consulting, Inc., December 2014, http://www.connectwithcare.org/wp-content/uploads/2014/12/Medicare-Acute-Care-Telehealth-Feasibility.pdf

60. Vinod Khosla, "Technology will replace 80% of what doctors do," *Fortune*, December 4, 2012. http://fortune.com/2012/12/04/technology-will-replace-80-of-what-doctors-do/

61. Anita Hamilton, "Could ePatient Networks Become the Superdoctors of the Future?," Fast Company, September 28, 2012. https://www.fastcoexist.com/1680617/could-epatient-networks-become-the-superdoctors-of-the-future

62. Khosla, "Technology will replace 80% of what doctors do."

63. "National Health Expenditures 2015 Highlights," Centers for Medicare and Medicaid Services, July 2016, accessed February 16, 2017. https://www.cms.gov/Research-Statistics-Data-and-Systems/Statistics-Trends-and-Reports/NationalHealthExpendData/Downloads/Proj2015.pdf

64. "Telehealth Policy Trends and Considerations," National Conference of State Legislatures, February 2, 2015. http://www.ncsl.org/research/health/telehealth-policy-trends-and-considerations.aspx

65. Ibid.

66. See Chapter 5 of this book, "Follow the Money."

67. Dave Chase, "Patient Engagement Is the Blockbuster Drug of the Century," *Forbes*, September 9, 2012. http://www.forbes.com/sites/davechase/2012/09/09/patient-engagement-is-the-blockbuster-drug-of-the-century/

CHAPTER 11

1. "Jamestown Rediscovery," Historic Jamestown, 2017, accessed February 17, 2017. http://historicjamestowne.org/history/history-of-jamestown/

2. "Jamestown's First Representative Assembly," National Parks Service, accessed February 17, 2017. https://www.nps.gov/jame/learn/historyculture/members-of-the-jamestown-first-representative-assembly.htm

3. Lisa Rein, "Mystery of Va.'s First Slaves is Unlocked 400 Years Later," *Washington Post*, September 3, 2006. http://www.washingtonpost.com/wp-dyn/content/article/2006/09/02/AR2006090201097.html

4. Ibid.

5. Ibid.

6. Charles Ventura, "Bill O'Reilly: Slaves who built White House were 'well-fed,'" *USA Today*, July 27, 2016. http://www.usatoday.com/story/news/politics/onpolitics/2016/07/27/bill-oreilly-michelle-obama-white-house-slaves-speech/87604632/

7. Peter Kolchin, *American Slavery: 1619-1877*, (New York: Hill and Wang, 2003), 22.

8. Michelle Alexander, *The New Jim Crow: Mass Incarceration in the Age of Colorblindness*, (New York: The New Press, 2012), 25.

9. Gunnar Myrdal and Sissela Bok, *An American Dilemma: The Negro Problem and Modern Democracy*, (Transaction Publishers, 1996), Introduction.

10. Lillian Smith, *Killers of the Dream*, (New York: Norton & Company, 1994), 27, 29.

11. H. Lee Cheek Jr. and John C. Calhoun, *John C. Calhoun: Selected Writings and Speeches*, (Washington D.C.: Regnery Publishing, 2003), 681.

12. Ibid., 31.

13. Ibid.

14. Gunnar Myrdal, *An American Dilemma: The Negro Problem and Modern Democracy*, (Transaction Publishers, 1996), 4.

15. Marc Landy and Sidney M. Milkis, *American Government: Enduring Principles, Critical Choices, 3rd Edition*, (New York: Cambridge University Press, 2014), 37.

16. Isaac Kramnick and Theodore Lowi, Frederick Douglass, "What to the Slave Is the Fourth of July?," American Political Thought, (New York: Norton, 2009), 598.

17. Marc Landy and Sidney M. Milkis, *American Government: Balancing Democracy and Rights*, (New York: Cambridge University Press, 2008), 44.

18. "Winter 1963: The Emancipation Proclamation Centennial," AlabamaHeritage. com, January 25, 2013. http://www.alabamaheritage.com/civil-rights-movement/ winter-1963-the-emancipation-proclamation-centennial

19. Ibid.

20. Martin Luther King Jr., *Why We Can't Wait*, (Boston: Signet, 2000), 15.

21. Douglas Blackmon, *Slavery by Another Name: The Re-Enslavement of Black Americans from the Civil War to World War II*, (New York: Anchor, 2009), 394.

22. Ibid., 402.

23. Ibid., 375.

24. Edward T. O'Donnell, *Turning Points in American History – Lecture 2*, The Great Courses, July 8, 2013.

25. Tim Hashaw, *The Birth of Black America: The First African Americans and the Pursuit of Freedom at Jamestown*, (New York: Basic Books, 2007), XVIII.

26. "First legislative assembly in America," History.com, 2010, accessed February 17, 2017. http://www.history.com/this-day-in-history/first-legislative-assembly-in-america

27. O'Donnell, *Turning Points in American History – Lecture 2*.

28. "An act about the casuall killing of slaves (1669)," Encyclopedia Virginia, July 25, 2014. http://www.encyclopediavirginia.org/_An_act_about_the_casuall_killing_of_slaves_1669

29. Abraham Lincoln, "House Divided," Springfield, IL, June 16, 1858. accessed through National Park Service, February 18, 2017. https://www.nps.gov/liho/learn/historyculture/housedivided.htm

30. Gunnar Myrdal, *An American Dilemma: The Negro Problem and Modern Democracy*, (Transaction Publishers, 1996), 7. Sourced from: Vernon Parrington, Main Currents in American Thought, Vol. I, "The Colonial Mind, 1620-1800," (1927), 179.

31. Martin Luther King Jr., *I Have A Dream*, Washington D.C., 1963. Accessed through National Archives, https://www.archives.gov/files/press/exhibits/dream-speech.pdf

32. John McWilliams, "Unsung Partner Against Crime," Pennsylvania Magazine of History and Biography, April 1989, 207-236.

33. Johann Hari, *Chasing the Scream: The First and Last Days of the War on Drugs*, (Bloomsbury, 2016), 15.

34. Mike Gray, *Drug Crazy: How We Got into This Mess and How We Can Get Out*, (New York: Routledge, 2000), 90.

35. Hari, *Chasing the Scream: The First and Last Days of the War on Drugs*, 15.

36. Ibid., 18.

37. Ibid., 19.

38. Johann Hari, "The Hunting of Billie Holiday," *Politico Magazine*, January 17, 2015.

39. "Lynchings, by Year and Race, 1882-1968," The Charles Chesnutt Digital Archive, 2001, accessed February 18, 2017. http://www.chesnuttarchive.org/classroom/lynching_table_year.html

40. Dorian Lynskey, *33 Revolutions Per Minute*, (Faber & Faber, 2011), 4-8.

41. Hari, *Chasing the Scream: The First and Last Days of the War on Drugs*, 10.

42. "5- Great Jazz Vocals," Jazz24, 2013, accessed February 18, 2017. http://www.jazz24.org/50-great-jazz-vocals/

43. "Top 365 Songs of the Twentieth Century," Recording Industry Association of America, 2017, accessed February 18, 2017. http://www.theassociation.net/txt-music5.html

44. Terry Teachout, "Can Jazz Be Saved?," *The Wall Street Journal*, August 9, 2009. https://www.wsj.com/articles/SB10001424052970204619004574320303103850572

45. David Margolick, *Strange Fruit: The Biography of a Song*, (New York: HarperCollins, 2001), 61-62.

46. Hari, *Chasing the Scream: The First and Last Days of the War on Drugs*, 10.

47. Ibid., 29.

48. Ibid.

49. Ibid., 26.

50. Ibid., 10.

51. Ibid., 24.

52. Ibid., 31.

53. Alexander, *The New Jim Crow: Mass Incarceration in the Age of Colorblindness*, 5.

54. "The War on Marijuana in Black and White: Billions of Dollars Wasted on Racially Biased Arrests," American Civil Liberties Union, June 2013, 12. https://www.aclu.org/sites/default/files/field_document/1114413-mj-report-rfs-rel1.pdf

55. "Race Relations Worsen," Monmouth University Polling Institute, July 19, 2016. https://www.monmouth.edu/polling-institute/reports/MonmouthPoll_US_071916/

56. "On Views of Race and Inequality, Blacks and Whites Are Worlds Apart," Pew Research Center, June 27, 2016. http://www.pewsocialtrends.org/2016/06/27/on-views-of-race-and-inequality-blacks-and-whites-are-worlds-apart/

57. Martin Luther King, Jr., "Letter from a Birmingham Jail," April 16, 1963, accessed through University of Pennsylvania African Studies Center February 10, 2017. https://www.africa.upenn.edu/Articles_Gen/Letter_Birmingham.html

58. "82% Hold Favorable View of Martin Luther King, Jr." Rasmussen Reports, January 17, 2011. http://www.rasmussenreports.com/public_content/lifestyle/holidays/january_2011/82_hold_favorable_view_of_martin_luther_king_jr

59. Megan Thee-Brenan, "More Americans Say Race Relations Are Bad, and a Survey Explores Why," The New York Times, June 27, 2016. http://www.nytimes.com/2016/06/28/us/more-americans-say-race-relations-are-bad-and-a-survey-explores-why.html

60. Shiva Maniam, "Many voters, especially blacks, expect race relations to worsen following Trump's election," Pew Research Center, November 21, 2016. http://www.pewresearch.org/fact-tank/2016/11/21/race-relations-following-trumps-election/

61. "On Views of Race and Inequality, Blacks and Whites Are Worlds Apart."

62. Heather K. Gerken, "A New Progressive Federalism," *Democracy: A Journal of Ideas*, Spring 2012, No. 24. http://democracyjournal.org/magazine/24/a-new-progressive-federalism/

63. Michael Holt, *By One Vote: The Disputed Presidential Election of 1876*, (Lawrence, KS: University of Kansas, 2008), 2.

64. "Black Leaders During Reconstruction," History.com, 2010, accessed February 18, 2017. http://www.history.com/topics/american-civil-war/black-leaders-during-reconstruction

65. "Ku Klux Klan," History.com, 2009, accessed February 17, 2017. http://www.history.com/topics/ku-klux-klan

66. Holt, *By One Vote: The Disputed Presidential Election of 1876*, 181.

67. Ibid.

68. Lloyd Robinson, *The Stolen Election: Hayes Versus Tilden—1876*, (New York: Forge Books, 2001), 187.

69. Ibid., 202.

70. "Ku Klux Klan," History.com, 2009, accessed February 17, 2017. http://www.history.com/topics/ku-klux-klan

71. "Liberty Enlightening the World," National Park Service, accessed February 17, 2017. https://www.nps.gov/stli/index.htm

72. Mark Lane, *Citizen Lane: Defending Our Rights in the Courts, the Capital, and the Streets*, (Chicago: Chicago Review Press, 2012), 139.

73. Derek Charles Catsam, *Freedom's Main Line: The Journey of Reconciliation and the Freedom Rides*, (Lexington, KY: University Press of Kentucky, 2011), 223.

74. Martin Luther King, Jr., *Stride Toward Freedom: The Montgomery Story*, (Boston: Beacon Press, 2010), 144.

75. Sheldon Appleton, "Martin Luther King in Life . . . And Memory," *The Public Perspective*, February/March 1995. https://ropercenter.cornell.edu/public-perspective/ppscan/62/62011.pdf

76. "82% Hold Favorable View of Martin Luther King, Jr.," Rasmussen Reports.

77. Lydia Saad, "On King Holiday, a Split Review of Civil Rights Progress," Gallup.com, January 21, 2008. http://www.gallup.com/poll/103828/civil-rights-progress-seen-more.aspx

78. "Public Believes Communists Involved in Demonstrations," Gallup Poll, November 19, 1965, accessed through American Institute of Public Opinion.

79. Linda Lyons, "Gallup Brain: The Darkest Hours of Racial Unrest," Gallup.com, June 3, 2003. http://www.gallup.com/poll/8539/gallup-brain-darkest-hours-racial-unrest.aspx

80. Andrew Kohut, "50 Years Ago: Mixed Views About Civil Rights but Support for Selma Demonstrators," Pew Research Center, March 5, 2015. http://www.pewresearch.org/fact-tank/2015/03/05/50-years-ago-mixed-views- about-civil-rights-but-support-for-selma-demonstrators/

81. Ibid.

82. Sonya Rastogi, Tallese Johnson, Elizabeth Hoeffel, and Malcolm Drewery, "The Black Population: 2010," 2010 Census Briefs, September 2011. https://www.census.gov/prod/cen2010/briefs/c2010br-06.pdf
"Profile of General Population and Housing Characteristics: 2010: Atlanta Georgia," 2010 Census, United States Census Bureau, 2010. https://factfinder.census.gov/faces/tableservices/jsf/pages/productview.xhtml?src=CF
"Profile of General Population and Housing Characteristics: 2010: Cleveland, Ohio," 2010 Census, United States Census Bureau, 2010. https://factfinder.census.gov/faces/tableservices/jsf/pages/productview.xhtml?src=CF
"Profile of General Population and Housing Characteristics: 2010: Richmond City, Virginia" 2010 Census, United States Census Bureau, 2010. https://factfinder.census.gov/faces/tableservices/jsf/pages/productview.xhtml?src=CF

83. Gerken, "A New Progressive Federalism."

84. Katie Benner, "Wachovia apologizes for slavery ties," CNN Money, June 2, 2005. http://money.cnn.com/2005/06/02/news/fortune500/wachovia_slavery/

85. Blackmon, *Slavery by Another Name*, 392.

86. Ibid., 391.

87. Benner, "Wachovia apologizes for slavery ties."

88. "Massachusetts Constitution and the Abolition of Slavery," Massachusetts Court System, Mass.gov, 2017. http://www.mass.gov/courts/court-info/sjc/edu-res-center/abolition/abolition1-gen.html

89. Kate Clifford Larson, *Bound for the Promised Land: Harriet Tubman: Portrait of an American Hero*, (New York: Random House, 2004), XVII.

90. Ibid.

91. James Banks, *March Toward freedom: A History of Black Americans*, (Belmont, CA: Fearon Publishers, 1974), 43.

92. Nicolas Lemann, *The Promised Land: The Great Black Migration and How It Changed America*, (New York: Vintage Books, 1992), 6.

93. Richard Wormser, "Jim Crow Stories: The Harlem Renaissance (1917-1935)," PBS.org, 2002, accessed February 20, 2017. http://www.pbs.org/wnet/jimcrow/stories_events_harlem.html

94. Charles Blow, "Harry and Sidney: Soul Brothers," *The New York Times*, February 20, 2017. https://www.nytimes.com/2017/02/20/opinion/harry-and-sidney-soul-brothers.html

95. Donald McRae, "Perspective; A Special Bond Between Champions," *The New York Times*, May 25, 2003. http://www.nytimes.com/2003/05/25/sports/perspective-a-special-bond-between-champions.html

96. Andrew Frank, *American Revolution: People and Perspectives*, (Santa Barbara, CA: BAC-CLIO, 2007), XII.

CHAPTER 12

1. Abraham Lincoln, "Speech at New Haven," March 6, 1860, accessed through TheHistoryPlace.com, February 19, 2017. http://www.historyplace.com/lincoln/haven.htm

2. Brenda Krueger Huffman, "Condoleezza Rice Reaffirmed 'American Exceptionalism,' During Her Republican Convention Speech Last Night," *Business Insider: Politics*, January 22, 2013. http://www.businessinsider.com/condoleezza-rice-rnc-speech-reaffirmed-american-exceptionalism-2012-8

3. "James Truslow Adams papers, 1918-1949," Columbia University Libraries Archival Collections, accessed February 19, 2017. http://www.columbia.edu/cu/lweb/archival/collections/ldpd_4078384/

4.   James Truslow Adams and Howard Schneiderman, *The Epic of America*, (Piscataway, NJ: Transaction Publishers, 2012), xiii.

5.   Paul Andrews, "Mary Gates Dies – Cancers Claims Longtime Seattle Civic Leader and Mother of Microsoft Founder Bill Gates," *The Seattle Times*, June 10, 1994. http://community.seattletimes.nwsource.com/archive/?date=19940610&slug= 1914904

6.   Ibid.

7.   "Bill Gates," *Forbes*, February 21, 2017. http://www.forbes.com/profile/bill-gates/

8.   Paul Andrews, "Mary Gates Dies – Cancers Claims Longtime Seattle Civic Leader and Mother of Microsoft Founder Bill Gates," *The Seattle Times*, June 10, 1994. http://community.seattletimes.nwsource.com/ archive/?date=19940610&slug=1914904

9.   Caroline Graham, "This is not the way I'd imagined Bill Gates … A rare and remarkable interview with the world's second richest man," *Daily Mail*, June 9, 2011. http://www.dailymail.co.uk/home/moslive/article-2001697/Microsofts-Bill-Gates-A-rare-remarkable-interview-worlds-second-richest-man. html#ixzz4ZADMvsrb

10. "Who We Are: Foundation Facts," Bill and Melinda Gates Foundation, 2017, accessed February 19, 2017. http://www.gatesfoundation.org/Who-We-Are/ General-Information/Foundation-Factsheet

11. "Frequently Asked Questions," The Giving Pledge, accessed February 19, 2017. https://givingpledge.org/faq.aspx#faq1

12. Jackie Wattles, "5 billionaires giving their fortunes away," CNN Money, June 2, 2015. http://money.cnn.com/2015/06/01/news/companies/giving-pledge-billionaires/

13. "Frequently Asked Questions," The Giving Pledge, accessed February 19, 2017. https://givingpledge.org/faq.aspx#faq1

14. "Who We Are: History," Bill and Melinda Gates Foundation, 2017, accessed February 19, 2017. http://www.gatesfoundation.org/Who-We-Are/General-Information/Foundation-Factsheet

15. Mark Rank, Thomas Hirschl, and Kirk Foster, *Chasing the American Dream: Understanding What Shapes Our Fortunes*, (New York: Oxford University Press, 2014), 2.

16. "2012 Values Survey," Pew Research Center, April 4-15, 2012. http://www.people-press.org/files/legacy-questionnaires/Values%20topline%20for%20release.pdf

17. Arthur Brooks, "Five myths about free enterprise," *The Washington Post*, July 13, 2012. https://www.washingtonpost.com/opinions/five-myths-about-free-enterprise/2012/07/13/gJQAYMwGiW_story.html?utm_term=.bd2c9e8d8a22

18. Arthur Brooks, "America's new culture war: Free enterprise vs. government control," *Washington Post*, May 12, 2010. http://www.washingtonpost.com/wp-dyn/content/article/2010/05/21/AR2010052101854_pf.html

19. "Real Gross Domestic Product Per Capita," Federal Reserve Bank of St. Louis: Economic Research, accessed Jan 27, 2017. https://fred.stlouisfed.org/series/A939RX0Q048SBEA

20. Arthur Brooks, *The Conservative Heart*, (New York: Harper Collins, 2015), 39.

21. Allyssa Birth, "Doctor Tops List of Prestigious Occupations," the harris poll, March 29, 2016. http://www.theharrispoll.com/business/Doctor-Tops-List-Prestigious-Occupations.html

22. Ibid.

23. David Warsh, *Knowledge and the Wealth of Nations*, (New York: Norton, 2007), 276.

24. "Robert Barro Bio-CV, RBarro.com, 2011, accessed February 19, 2017. http://rbarro.com/bio-cv/
"About Paul Romer," PaulRomer.com, accessed February 19, 2017. https://paulromer.net/about-paul-romer/

25. Joseph Stiglitz, "The Price of Inequality," Project Syndicate, June 5, 2012. https://www.project-syndicate.org/commentary/the-price-of-inequality?barrier=true

26. "Allstate/National Journal Heartland Monitor XXV Key Findings," FTI Consulting, January 11, 2016. http://heartlandmonitor.com/wp-content/uploads/2016/01/FTI-Allstate-NJ-Heartland-Poll-XXV-Findings-Memo-Jan-11-at-4pm-ET.pdf

27. Ibid.

28. Mollie Orshansky, "Counting the Poor: Another Look at the Poverty Profile," *Social Security Bulletin*, January 1965. https://www.ssa.gov/policy/docs/ssb/v28n1/v28n1p3.pdf

29. Mark Rank, *One Nation, Underprivileged: Why American Poverty Affects Us All*, (New York: Oxford University Press, 2005), 28.

30. "Census Bureau Survey Shows Poverty is Primarily a Temporary Condition," United States Census Bureau, March 16, 2011. https://www.census.gov/newsroom/releases/archives/poverty/cb11-49.html

31. Robert Rector, "How Do America's Poor Really Live? Examining the Census Poverty Report," *Daily Signal*, September 16, 2015. http://dailysignal.com/2015/09/16/are-there-really-40-million-poor-americans-looking-at-the-census-bureaus-definition-of-poverty

32. Bernadette Proctor, Jessica Semega, and Melissa Kollar, *Income and Poverty in the United States: 2015*, Census.gov, September 2016, 3. http://www.census.gov/content/dam/Census/library/publications/2016/demo/p60-256.pdf

33. Mark Rank, Thomas Hirschl, and Kirk Foster, *Chasing the American Dream: Understanding What Shapes Our Fortunes*, (New York: Oxford University Press, 2014), 4.

34. Bernadette Proctor, Jessica Semega, and Melissa Kollar, *Income and Poverty in the United States: 2015.*

35.   David Lauter, "How do Americans view poverty? Many blue-collar whites, key to Trump, criticize poor people as lazy and content to stay on welfare," *LA Times*, August 14, 2016. http://www.latimes.com/projects/la-na-pol-poverty-poll/

36.   Ibid.

37.   Luke 4:16-21

38.   "Do All the Good You Can; In All the Ways You Can," QuoteInvestigator.com, September 24, 2016. http://quoteinvestigator.com/2016/09/24/all-good/

39.   Abraham Joshua Heschel, "Toward a Just Society," Moral Grandeur and Spiritual Audacity: Essays," (New York: Farrar Straus & Giroux, 1996), 225.

40.   Kristen Scharold, "Tim Keller: What We Owe the Poor," *Christianity Today*, December 6, 2010. http://www.christianitytoday.com/ct/2010/december/10.69.html

41.   "Kiva: About Us," Kiva.org, 2017, accessed February 19, 2017. https://www.kiva.org/about

42.   Ibid.

43.   Ibid.

44.   John Coleman, "Pope Francis on the Dignity of Labor," *America: The Jesuit Review*, November 20, 2013. http://www.americamagazine.org/content/all-things/pope-francis-dignity-labor

45.   Sylvia Wright, "Poverty's Free Enterpriser," *Life Magazine*, June 28, 1968, 36.

46.   Amy Glasmeier, "Living Wage Calculator," Massachusetts Institute of Technology, 2017, accessed February 19, 2017. http://livingwage.mit.edu/

47.   Bernadette Proctor, Jessica Semega, and Melissa Kollar, "Interrelationships of 3-Year Average State Poverty Rates: 2013-2015," Income and Poverty in the Untied States: 2015, Census.gov, September 2016. http://www.census.gov/library/publications/2016/demo/p60-256.html
        "Cost of Living Data Series: 2016 Annual Average," Missouri Economic Research and Information Center, accessed February 21, 2017. https://www.missourieconomy.org/indicators/cost_of_living/

48.   Lyndon Johnson, "91-Annual Message to the Congress on the State of the Union," January 8, 1964. http://www.presidency.ucsb.edu/ws/?pid=26787

49.   Peter Cove, "Work: The only answer to poverty," *Daily News*, February 11, 2013. http://www.nydailynews.com/opinion/work-answer-poverty-article-1.1259031

50.   Peter Cove, "America Works of New York, Inc." United States House Committee on Ways and Means, April 30, 2015. https://waysandmeans.house.gov/wp-content/uploads/2015/06/Peter-Cove-Testimony-043015-HR3.pdf

51.   Ibid.

52.   "Allstate/National Journal Heartland Monitor XXV Key Findings," FTI Consulting, January 11, 2016. http://heartlandmonitor.com/wp-content/uploads/2016/01/FTI-Allstate-NJ-Heartland-Poll-XXV-Findings-Memo-Jan-11-at-4pm-ET.pdf

CHAPTER 13

1. Jennifer Lawless, *Becoming a Candidate*, (New York: Cambridge University Press, 2011), 40-45.

2. Email to author, January 12, 2017

3. Clifford Grammich, Kirk Hadaway, Richard Houseal, Dale E. Jones, Alexei Krindatch, Richie Stanley, and Richard H. Taylor, "U.S. Religion Census 2010: Summary Findings," Association of Statisticians of American Religious Bodies, May 1, 2012, 10. http://www.rcms2010.org/press_release/ACP%2020120501.pdf

4. "Who We Are," Lions Club International, 2017, accessed February 20, 2017. http://www.lionsclubs.org/EN/who-we-are/index.php

5. Lee Rainie, Kristen Purcell, and Aaron Smith, "Section 1: the state of groups and voluntary organizations in America," Pew Research Center, January 18, 2011. http://www.pewinternet.org/2011/01/18/section-1-the-state-of-groups-and-voluntary-organizations-in-america/

6. Robert Putnam, Lewis Feldstein, and Don Cohen, *Better Together: Restoring the American Community*, (New York: Simon & Schuster Paperbacks, 2004), 270.

7. Robert Putnam, *Bowling Alone: The Collapse and Revival of American Community*, (New York: Simon and Schuster, 2001) 24.

8. "Social Capital Glossary," Harvard Kennedy School: The Saguaro Seminar – Civic Engagement in America, 2012, accessed February 20, 2017. https://www.hks.harvard.edu/saguaro/glossary

9. Putnam, Feldstein, and Cohen, *Better Together: Restoring the American Community*, 3.

10. Ibid.

11. Jonathan Rauch, "Gay Rights, Nondiscrimination, and Religious Liberty: Can We Avoid a Train Wreck?," University of Illinois Baum Lecture, October 18, 2016. https://www.youtube.com/watch?v=3YezwtRX9XU

12. Rauch is citing quote from Virginia House Delegate Todd Gilbert, reported on here: Mollie Jackson, "How Southern states are now challenging gay marriage," *The Christian Science Monitor*, February 20, 2016. http://www.csmonitor.com/USA/Society/2016/0220/How-Southern-states-are-now-challenging-gay-marriage

13. Rauch, "Gay Rights, Nondiscrimination, and Religious Liberty: Can We Avoid a Train Wreck?"

14. Amy Goodman, with Jim Dabakis and Troy Williams, "As Anti-LGBT Laws Sweep U.S., How Did GOP-Led Utah Pass a Landmark Nondiscrimination Bill?," Democracy Now!, April 19, 2016. https://www.democracynow.org/2016/4/19/as_anti_lgbt_laws_sweep_us

15. Alan Cooperman, Gregory Smith, Jessica Martinez, "Where the Public Stands on Religious Liberty vs. Nondiscrimination," Pew Research Center, September 28, 2016, 28. http://www.pewforum.org/2016/09/28/5-vast-majority-of-americans-know-someone-who-is-gay-fewer-know-someone-who-is-transgender/

16.   Rauch, "Gay Rights, Nondiscrimination, and Religious Liberty: Can We Avoid a Train Wreck?"

17.   Ibid.

18.   Ibid.

19.   Ibid.

20.   Eric Metaxas, "Jackie Robinson a man of faith: Column," *USA Today*, April 11, 2013. http://www.usatoday.com/story/opinion/2013/04/11/jackie-robinson-a-man-of-faith-column/2075367/

21.   William Rubinstein, "Jackie Robinson and the Integration of Major League Baseball," *History Today*, Volume 52, Issue 9, September 2003. http://www.historytoday.com/william-rubinstein/jackie-robinson-and-integration-major-league-baseball

22.   Eric Metaxas, *Seven Men: And the Secret of Their Greatness*, (Nashville: Thomas Nelson, 2015), 124.

23.   Metaxas, "Jackie Robinson a man of faith."

24.   "MLB Awards – MVP," ESPN, 2017, accessed February 20, 2017. http://www.espn.com/mlb/history/awards/_/id/16

25.   Ira Berkow, "Two Men Who Did the Right Thing," *The New York Times*, November 2, 2005. http://www.nytimes.com/2005/11/02/sports/baseball/two-men-who-did-the-right-thing.html?_r=0

26.   Richard Wormser, "Jim Crow Stories: Jackie Robinson Integrates Major League Baseball (1947)," Jim Crow Stories, PBS.org, 2002, accessed February 20, 2017. http://www.pbs.org/wnet/jimcrow/stories_events_jackie.html

27.   Ibid.

28.   David Brown, "Baseball's impact on Martin Luther King Jr.," Yahoo! Sports, January 21, 2013. http://sports.yahoo.com/blogs/mlb-big-league-stew/baseball-impact-martin-luther-king-jr-155634569—mlb.html

29.   Rauch, "Gay Rights, Nondiscrimination, and Religious Liberty: Can We Avoid a Train Wreck?"

30.   Gillian Brown, *The Consent of the Governed: The Lockean Legacy in Early American Culture*, (New York: Harvard University Press, 2001), 3.

31.   Ibid.

32.   Gordon Wood, *The Idea of America: Reflections on the Birth of the United States*, (New York: Penguin Books, 2012), 28.

33.   George Washington, "From George Washington to Bryan Fairfax," July 20, 1774. Accessed through FoundersArchives.gov on February 20, 2017. https://founders.archives.gov/GEWN-02-10-02-0081

34.   Thomas Paine, *Common Sense*, (Philadelphia: W. & T. Bradford, 1776). Accessed through Project Gutenberg, https://www.gutenberg.org/files/147/147-h/147-h.htm

CHAPTER 14

1. Catherine Drinker Bowen, *Miracle At Philadelphia: The Story of the Constitutional Convention – September 1787*, (Back Bay Books, 1986), XI.

2. Daniel Hannan, *Inventing Freedom: How the English-Speaking Peoples Made the Modern World*, (New York: Broadside Books, 2014), 50.

3. Kevin Phillips, *The Cousins' Wars: Religion, Politics, Civil Warfare, and the Triumph of Anglo-America*, (New York: Basic Books, 1999), XVIII.

4. Hannan, *Inventing Freedom: How the English-Speaking Peoples Made the Modern World*, 50.

5. "Crown v. John Peter Zenger," Historical Society of New York Courts, accessed February 20, 2017. http://www.nycourts.gov/history/legal-history-new-york/legal-history-eras-01/history-new-york-legal-eras-crown-zenger.html

6. Ibid.

7. Ibid.

8. Bowen, *Miracle At Philadelphia: The Story of the Constitutional Convention – September 1787*, XI.

9. Larry Arnn, *The Founders' Key: The Divine and Natural Connection Between the Declaration and the Constitution and What We Risk by Losing It*, (New York: Thomas Nelson, 2012), 84.

10. Eric Posner and Adrian Vermeule, *The Executive Unbound: After the Madisonian Republic*, (New York: Oxford University Press, 2013), 4.

11. Ibid., 15.

12. Ibid., 10.

13. Ibid., 185.

14. Ibid., 187.

15. Ibid., 14.

16. Ibid., 209.

17. Ibid., 180.

18. Bowen, *Miracle At Philadelphia: The Story of the Constitutional Convention – September 1787*, 44.

19. James Madison, edited by Max Farrand, *The Records of the Federal Convention of 1787, Volume I*, (New Haven: Yale University Press, 1966), 288-290.

20. "Interstate Commerce Act (1887)," OurDocuments.Gov, February 20, 2017. https://ourdocuments.gov/doc.php?flash=false&doc=49

21. Woodrow Wilson, "The Study of Administration," *Political Science Quarterly*, Vol 2, No. 2, June 1887. http://www.psqonline.org/article.cfm?id=91

22. Ibid.

23.   David McCullough, *The Wright Brothers*, (New York: Simon and Schuster, 2016), 93.

24.   Ibid.

25.   Ibid., 35.

26.   Ibid., 108.

27.   Ibid., 259.

28.   Ibid.

29.   Fred Howard, *Wilbur and Orville*, (New York: Knopf, 1987), 401.

30.   McCullough, *The Wright Brothers*, 259.

31.   Craig Shirley, *December 1941: 31 Days that Changed America and Saved the World*, (Nashville: Thomas Nelson, 2013), XV.

32.   "Employment Act of 1946" 79th Congress, 2nd Session, Chapters 32-33, February 20, 1946. http://www.legisworks.org/congress/79/publaw-304.pdf

33.   "Economic Report of the President," (Washington D.C.: United States Government Printing Office, 1962), 37.

34.   Robert Nisbet, *The Quest for Community: A Study in the Ethics of Order and Freedom*, (Wilmington, DE: Intercollegiate Studies Institute, 2010), 269.

35.   Richard Cornuelle, *Reclaiming the American Dream: the Role of Private Individuals and Voluntary Associations*, (Piscataway, NJ: Transaction Publishers, 1993), 81.

36.   Nicco Mele, *The End of Big: How the Internet Makes David the New Goliath* (New York: St. Martin's Press, 2013), 5.

37.   Ibid., 2.

38.   Martin Luther King, Jr., *Where Do We Go From Here: Chaos or Community?*, (Boston: Beacon Press, 2010), XVIII.

ABOUT THE AUTHOR

SCOTT RASMUSSEN is one of the world's leading public opinion pollsters and political analysts. As publisher of ScottRasmussen. com, his polls monitor political environment, underlying public values, and breaking news.

Scott also serves as the Editor-At-Large for Ballotpedia, the Encyclopedia of American Politics. For Ballotpedia, he writes "Scott Rasmussen's Number of the Day," exploring newsworthy and interesting topics at the intersection of politics, culture, and technology.

Early in his career, Scott was a co-founder of ESPN. He is also a *New York Times* bestselling author, public speaker, and syndicated columnist.

Scott graduated with a degree in history from DePauw University and earned his MBA at Wake Forest University.

CPSIA information can be obtained
at www.ICGtesting.com
Printed in the USA
BVHW081001261118
534009BV00003B/118/P